THE CRITICS HAIL
YOUR FIRST INVESTMENT
THIS BOOK.

"A vital book for market novices or even for those who are simply curious about how Wall Street works."

—San Francisco Examiner

"At last there is a book—a two-plus-two-makes-four kind of a book—for incipient investors."

—The New York Times

"Would recommend this book without reservation to all potential investors."

—American Banker

"Concise explanation of what it means to invest, how stocks are bought and sold."

—Christian Science Monitor

"Probably the first book that could hold the interest of trader or novice."

—Des Moines Register

Sixth Revised Edition

How to Buy Stocks

by Louis Engel in collaboration with Peter Wyckoff

RLI: $\dfrac{\text{VLM 8 (VLR 7–10)}}{\text{IL 8–adult}}$

HOW TO BUY STOCKS

*A Bantam Book / published by arrangement with
Little, Brown and Company*

PRINTING HISTORY

Original Little, Brown edition / April 1953
15 printings through June 1956
Little, Brown revised edition / May 1957
Little, Brown third revised edition / January 1962
Little, Brown fourth revised edition / February 1967
Little, Brown fifth revised edition / September 1971
Little, Brown sixth revised edition / October 1976

Bantam edition / February 1955
7 printings through September 1956
Bantam revised edition / June 1957
8 printings through May 1962
Bantam third revised edition / January 1963
7 printings through September 1966
Bantam fourth revised edition / July 1967
9 printings through April 1970
Bantam fifth revised edition / February 1972
10 printings through April 1976
Bantam sixth revised edition / July 1977
1st printing
2nd printing
3rd printing

The author is grateful to the Center for Research in Security Prices for permission to reprint the tables on pages 296–299. From "Rates of Return on Investment in Common Stock: Preliminary Year-by-Year Record, January 30, 1926–March 31, 1976," *Proceedings of the Seminar on the Analysis of Security Prices,* May 1975.

ISBN 0-553-10932-4

Published simultaneously in the United States and Canada

PRINTED IN THE UNITED STATES OF AMERICA

Acknowledgments

Such is the process of learning that it is never possible for anyone to say exactly how he acquired any given body of knowledge. And that circumstance I now find somewhat consoling, because in a very real sense this book is not my book, but it is the product of hundreds of different people who over the years have taught me what I have simply written down here.

Obviously, I cannot acknowledge my indebtedness to all these people and so I must necessarily limit my thanks to those who helped me directly in the preparation and checking of the material in this book through all its six versions, from 1952 to 1976. Some are no longer associated with the institutions whose names are used to identify them here. Some are no longer even alive. But all of them are people to whom I owe a debt beyond repayment.

These include Alger B. Chapman, Jr., Cecil Mac-Coy, Willard K. Vanderbeck, Stanley West, F. W. Reiniger, Richard I. Callanan, Aileen Lyons, Thomas T. Murphy and George Christopolous, all of the New York Stock Exchange; John W. Sheehan of the American Stock Exchange; James H. Lorie and Lawrence Fisher of the University of Chicago; John McKenzie, Russell Morrison, George Olsen and Donald A. Moser of Standard & Poor's Corporation; Max Fromkin of Fromkin & Fromkin; J. Scott Rattray and Huntly W. F. McKay of the Toronto Stock Exchange; Joseph H. Cooper of the National Association of Securities Dealers; and a score of individuals actively engaged in the securities business—Kenneth R. Williams, Robert L. Stott, Victor B. Cook, Edward A. Pierce, Milija Rubezanin, James E. Thomson, Donald T. Regan, Howard T. Sprow, Peter F. McCourt, James Albee, Cecil C. Burgin, John J. Cahill, Rudolph J. Chval, James D. Corbett, Dwight H. Emanuelson, John F.

Ferguson, John A. Fitzgerald, Richard P. Gillette, Calvin Gogolin, Allan D. Gulliver, Gilbert Hammer, Stephen B. Kagan, Arthur L. Kerrigan, George T. Lee, George J. Leness, Josiah O. Low, Gillette K. Martin, Michael W. McCarthy, Anthony G. Meyer, Harvey L. Miller, John H. Moller, Samuel Mothner, Joseph C. Quinn, Walter A. Scholl, Julius H. Sedlmayr, Thomas B. Shearman, George L. Shinn, John W. Adams, Jr., David Western, Jay Robinson-Duff, Wallace Sellers, John Anderson, Thomas J. Christie, Robert E. Cleary, Francis J. Ripepi, Robert Rittereiser, Martin Portnoy, Nancy K. Hartley, Thomas E. Engel, and—most importantly—Robert L. Tebeau and Frederick P. Groll.

Last but certainly not least, let me list Muriel D. Nutzel, Ann Scourby, Loretta A. Gigante, Elizabeth J. Gibson, Loretta D. Hanley, Zita Millet, Agnes Rother, Janet K. Low, Lorraine M. Hanley, and Gloria Duck.

To Nina and Molly for their forbearance and patient understanding

It bought the Sure-Fire Wire Company to allow for
an additional issue of common stock and ordered to
have the Sure-Fire shares distributed ... ...
Fold for every three shares of Surplus common
owned.

Contents

Foreword

IN the past ten years, Wall Street has gone through a revolution, a revolution of unprecedented proportions that no one would have thought possible only a dozen years ago.

The very cornerstone of the New York Stock Exchange has been blasted away by the federal government. Since its founding in 1792, the exchange had operated on a fixed-commission system; all brokers charged the same. But not any longer! Now, by law, all rates are subject to negotiation, and brokers are competing fiercely for the investor's business—not your business necessarily, but certainly that of the big customer like the banks and insurance companies. They're the ones who are getting the big commission discounts.

Hundreds of old, established brokerage firms, including some who were once giants in the business, have folded or been absorbed by competitors as a result of the market collapses in 1969–1970 and 1973–1974. And the end of the funeral parade is not in sight. Competitive commission rates mean that the big, efficient firms will get bigger, and the small, less efficient houses will go to the wall. But the customer is protected, for the federal government now insures him against loss resulting from the failure of any securities firm.

The old New York Stock Exchange ticker has gone by the boards. Intent on establishing one central securities market, the Securities and Exchange Commission has forced on the securities industry the new consolidated tape which reports all transactions in all listed stocks, no matter where they take place—on the New York Stock Exchange, a regional exchange, or the over-the-counter market.

The Securities and Exchange Commission has

tightened its overall regulation of the securities business in dozens of different ways to protect the investor against price manipulation, "insider" trading, and dishonest dealings of a dozen varieties—all to make sure that every investor gets a fair shake in Wall Street—and they monitor suspicious movements in the market with an eagle eye.

That "second-class citizen," the securities dealer who was not a member of the New York Stock Exchange, has been enfranchised by the Securities and Exchange Commission. As a result, he may now compete on even terms for much of the business that the members had previously reserved to themselves. But he has paid a price for his new status, for the S.E.C. now subjects the over-the-counter market to much the same regulation as that imposed on the exchanges.

Automation has come to the securities business. Computers, scanning systems, and all kinds of electronic gear now speed up the reporting of stock transactions, the issuance of margin calls, and the preparation of customer's statements. They also churn out data in a matter of seconds about securities—and the companies behind them—that it would have taken an analyst weeks to compile only a few years ago. And there are some who say the computer will someday take over the whole business of securities trading, thus consigning the broker to the limbo of the auk and the dodo bird.

Finally, to the delight of speculators, the Chicago Board Options Exchange introduced "the hottest game in town"—options trading—in 1973. Now, even the little man can put up just a few hundred dollars and try his luck at winning thousands.

Yes, Wall Street has indeed gone through a revolution. But it has survived. Survived despite the enactment of two stringent federal laws—the Securities Acts Amendment of 1964 and the Securities Reform Act of 1975—and despite the disaster wrought by three of the worst market slumps since the 1929 crash. In 1966, the market dropped 25% from February to October; in 1969–1970 the drop was 36%; and beginning in January 1973 prices tumbled 45% to their low in December 1974. And yet, the market always comes back to climb into new high ground.

Hence, despite the revolution and havoc of the past ten years in Wall Street, I see no reason to change the Foreword as I wrote it on August 11, 1952, for the first edition. So here it is:

THIS book is based on a very simple premise: that the stock market is going up.

Tomorrow? Next month? Next year?

Maybe yes, maybe no. Maybe the market will be a lot lower then than it is today.

But over any long period of time—10 years, 20 years, 50 years—this book assumes that the market is bound to go up.

Why?

Because it always has.

Because the market is a measure of the vigor of American business, and unless something drastic happens to America, business is going to go on growing.

Because prices of food and clothing and almost everything else in this country—including stocks—have steadily gone up as the buying power of the dollar has gone down. That's a trend that isn't likely to be reversed.

And so these are the reasons why the author is sold on the value of investing, of buying stocks for the long pull—and not for a quick profit tomorrow.

There's nothing hidden about this prejudice. You'll see it when you read the book. And you will find other prejudices, other opinions, despite an earnest effort to focus this book strictly on facts—the facts about investing that have been obscured all too long by double talk, by financial jargon, and by unnecessary mystery.

Of course it can be said that there are no facts when you get beyond the simple business of adding one and one. That's true. So let's say that here are the facts as the author sees them—and as plainly as he can state them.

He has only one hope: that they will add up to good common sense in your own mind.

On the day that Foreword was written, August 11, 1952, the Dow Jones industrial average—then as now the most widely accepted measure of stock market performance—closed at 280.29.

On August 2, 1957, when the Foreword to the second edition was written the average stood at 505.10.

On June 18, 1962, when the third edition was ready for press, it stood at 574.21.

On October 27, 1966, the fourth edition records the average at 809.57.

On April 15, 1971, when the Foreword was written for the fifth time, the Dow Jones stood at 938.17.

Today, June 30, 1976, as this sixth edition goes to press—thanks in large measure to my colleague and friend, Peter Wyckoff—the Dow industrial average closed at 1002.78. It has recovered 425.18 points, or 73.6%, from its low of 577.60 on December 6, 1974, but it still stands 48.92 points below its previous high of 1,051.70, which it reached on January 11, 1973.

And long before a Foreword for a seventh edition is written, I have every confidence that that ceiling will be pierced. Certainly, the performance of the market reflected here—an increase in the Dow Jones industrial average of 258% over a period of little more than twenty years—gives validity to such confidence.

Louis Engel

How to Buy Stocks

tion of bond issued by big, well-established industrial corporation today, and in the case of Rhodes Refineries those good bonds are not dangerous. In fact they have not been ruined by an exactly similar method of stock manipulation as still vex unregulated industrial management. He forecasts that defensive warfare

A Note on How to Read This Book

MANY people are afraid to buy stocks because they think investing is a complicated business.

If it were really complicated, more than twenty-five million Americans wouldn't own stocks, as they do today.

Actually, investing only *sounds* complicated, and that is because it uses a lot of unfamiliar words. The words themselves stand for very simple things.

Winston Churchill once said, "Old words are best, and old words when short are best of all." This book tries to use old, short words instead of Wall Street jargon. It seeks to explain the technical words of the securities business by explaining the things they stand for. In other words, each term is explained in *context* as the story of investing unfolds. You won't find a glossary or any long list of definitions anywhere in this book.

In telling the investment story, the book begins with the common words in the business—stock, share, capital—and just to be sure that the reader realizes he has encountered a technical term, possibly new to him, the word is italicized the first time it is used. And to be further sure there is no misunderstanding or confusion, no technical term is used until the reader comes logically upon it in the development of the whole thesis.

If the reader has by any chance forgotten the meaning of a particular word, all he has to do is refer to the index and look back in the book to that page on which the word is first used.

Here, then, is the story of investing told in terms that the author believes everyone can understand—himself included.

CHAPTER 1

What Investment Means to You

THIS is a book about how to make your money earn more money for you by investing it.

It is not a book about how to make a million in the stock market. If there were any certain way to do that, all the brokers in the world, the men who are supposed to know more than most people about the market, would be millionaires. Needless to say, they're not.

This is a book about investing. Specifically, it's a book about investing in stocks and bonds, which is one way of putting your extra money to work so that in the long run it will earn a good return for you—either in the form of a regular income from dividends or in the form of a profit resulting from growth in value or a combination of both.

Most people, if they have anything left at all after paying their bills, will think first of putting that extra money into a savings bank or into life insurance. Nobody could possibly quarrel with such a prudent course, because these forms of saving or investment are essential if a man is going to protect himself properly against the always unpredictable emergencies of life.

But today millions of people have come to regard *securities*—stocks and bonds in all their varied forms—as another equally good form of investment.

Of course, there's a risk in buying stocks and bonds —and for most people it's a far bigger risk than it needs to be, because they've never taken the time to study securities or find out how to invest in them wisely.

But it should never be forgotten that there's some risk in any form of investment. There's a risk in just

3

having money. Actually, it's a double-barreled risk. The one risk—the risk that you might lose some of your money regardless of what you do with it—is always evident. The other risk is never so apparent. And that's the risk that the money you save today may not buy as much at some future time if prices of food and clothing and almost everything else continue to go up, as indeed they have, more or less steadily, since this country began. The man who simply hoards his extra dollars—puts them in a vault or buries them in the ground—may avoid that first evident risk, the risk of losing any of them, but he can never sidestep the unseen risk, the risk of *inflation*.

So every decision you make about what to do with your extra money should take into consideration those two kinds of risk—the evident and the unseen.

Naturally, too, you must also consider the return you hope to realize on your money. In most forms of investment the greater the return you try to get, the greater the risk, the *evident* risk, you must be prepared to take.

If you put your money in a savings account, it's almost impossible to lose money because your savings are insured up to $40,000 by the Federal Deposit Insurance Corporation. But most times you have to be willing to accept a return of only 4% or 5% a year—rarely as much as 6%—and you have to realize that a savings account provides no protection against the *unseen* risk of inflation. Your money, or capital, won't grow except by the redeposit of the interest you get, and then only slowly.

Life insurance is also virtually 100% safe, thanks to state and federal laws. But there's more sense in buying a standard life insurance policy to protect your family than there is in buying it as an investment. Over a long period of years, the usual life insurance policy may yield a return somewhat better than that of a savings account, but it too fails to protect you against the *unseen* risk. The money you may get on such a policy when you retire is not likely to buy as much as you could have bought with all the money you paid out on premiums over the years.

What else might you do with your money? Well, you might put it into a savings and loan association which makes a business of lending money on home mortgages. Thanks again to government supervision, that kind of investment on your part will be relatively safe as far as the *evident* risk is concerned, but it will probably pay you only about 1% more interest than you would get on a savings account, and it will not protect you against the *unseen* risk of inflation.

You can invest in real estate. And as a general rule real estate prices are likely to rise if the prices of other things do. So there, you say, you can find protection against that *unseen* risk. Yes, there you can— provided you buy the right piece of property at the right time and at the right figure, and provided you're just as lucky when you sell it. Provided, too, that all the taxes you pay while you own the property don't eat up your potential profit, and provided you cope with all the unpredictable actions of local zoning and assessment boards. Here the *evident* risks are so great, even for those who work full time at buying, developing, managing and selling properties, that real estate must be classified not as an investment but as a speculation for the average man with only a little extra money.

Finally, you can invest in stocks and bonds. That's what banks do with at least part of the money you deposit with them, in order to earn the interest they pay you and to earn a profit for themselves. The same thing is true of insurance companies. Both kinds of institutions have always invested heavily in bonds, but today they are buying more and more stocks to the limits permitted by the various state laws. Furthermore, commercial banks and trust companies, which are responsible for funds left with them to invest for various beneficiaries, are putting a greater proportion of those funds into stocks.

Why?

Because over the years, the record shows that the average stock has paid a better return and provided a better balance of protection against the evident and unseen risks than any other form of investment.

The stockholders of America are the people who

own much of America's business—virtually all its more important business. As that business has grown, stock-owners have prospered. As it continues to grow, they will continue to prosper.

Not all of them have prospered all the time. Of course not. But most of them have most of the time. Some have made millions, and some have gone broke, just as some companies have succeeded and some have failed. But over the years, the average investor has generally earned from 3% to 7% in annual payments on his money. Most important of all, he has seen his stockholdings go up in value as prices generally have risen. He has been able most times to sell his stocks at a profit, especially if he has held them a long time, and he has thus protected his money against the unseen risk of inflation.

These are the reasons why millions of people are buying stocks today who never gave them a thought until a few years ago. And uniformly they're finding that it pays to know something about the fundamentals of the business. So . . .

CHAPTER 2

What You Should Know about Common Stocks

THERE'S nothing commonplace about *common stock*. It's the number one security in our system, basic to all corporate business and to our whole free enterprise system. If you own a *share* of stock in a company, you own part of that company. You and the other shareholders own the company in common.

How does common stock come into being?

Assume for the moment that you've invented a fine new collapsible metal fishing rod. You've got your patents, and you're convinced there is a splendid market for your pocket fishing pole.

You're all ready to begin production, except for that one essential: *capital*. You haven't got the money to rent a small factory, buy the necessary machinery, and hire labor and salesmen. You could get your business under way for $20,000, but you haven't got $20,000. The bank won't lend it to you simply on the strength of your patents, and you can't find an "angel" with that kind of cash to put in your business.

So you decide to form a company and sell shares in the venture. You file the necessary incorporation papers as required by your state law, and the Pocket Pole Company, Incorporated, comes into being.

In setting up that company, you might find twenty men, each of whom was willing to put up an even $1,000 of *venture capital*. In that case you'd have to issue and sell only twenty shares of stock at $1,000 apiece. Then every man who bought such a share would own 1/20 of the company.

But one man might be willing to put $2,000 into your Pocket Pole Company, while another man could only afford to invest $200. So instead of issuing twenty

7

shares of stock at $1,000 each, you decide it's better to put a lower price on every share of stock and sell more shares. Such a plan would be more attractive to the people who might be interested in buying the stock, because if they ever had to sell it, they would probably find it easier to dispose of lower-priced shares. After all, more people can spare $10 or $100 than can afford to invest in $1,000 units.

So you finally decide to issue 2,000 shares at $10 apiece. Taken collectively, those shares would represent the common stock issue of the Pocket Pole Company, and the $10 price you set would represent its *par value*.

You sell the 2,000 shares at $10 apiece, and by this means you raise the $20,000 capital you need. The Pocket Pole Company is in business. Actually, of course, you might well think of Pocket Pole as *your* business, and when the company was set up, you might bargain with the other stockholders so that you could acquire a stock interest in the company at little or no cost to yourself, but for purposes of simplicity it can be assumed here that you simply buy your stock like any other stockholder.

Every man who owns a share of Pocket Pole stock is a stockholder in the company. He is a share owner, a part owner. How big a part of the company he owns depends on how many shares he buys in relation to the 2,000 which are sold, or *outstanding*. If he buys one share, he owns 1/2000 of the company. If he buys twenty shares he owns 1/100, or 1%, of the company. As evidence of his ownership, a *stock certificate* is issued to each stockholder showing the number of shares he owns.

When the stock is all sold, let's assume the company finds that it has 50 stockholders on its books. Now it would be difficult to operate Pocket Pole if all 50 of them had to be consulted about every major decision —whether to buy this lathe or that one, whether to price the product at $40 or $50.

So the stockholders elect a *board of directors* to oversee the operations of the company. How is the board picked? By the stockholders on the basis of the number of shares of stock each man owns. If there are five men to be elected to the board, each for a set term, the man who owns one share of stock will, as a matter of general practice, be allowed one vote for each of the five vacancies, and the man who owns ten shares will have ten votes for each vacancy.

This five-man board of directors elects its own *chairman,* and, once organized, it is responsible for managing the affairs of the Pocket Pole Company. Since in most instances the board members can't give their full time to the job of running the company, they pick a president to be the actual operating head, and they also name the other major officers. Such officers may or may not be members of the board, but they are responsible to the full board, and periodically— perhaps once a month or once a quarter—the officers report to the board on the progress of the company and their conduct of its affairs.

Then once a year the Pocket Pole Company board of directors will conduct a meeting open to all the stockholders at which the management makes its *annual report* to the owners. Futhermore, the board supplies all stockholders, those present and those absent, with a copy of the report.

If any stockholder is dissatisfied with the way things are going, he can speak his mind at the meeting. He may even make a motion that the board adopt some policy or procedure that he thinks is an improvement on present practice, and if the motion is in order, it will be submitted to the stockholders for a vote. In most instances, such issues are decided by a simply majority vote with cach stockholder being allowed as many votes as he has shares.

If an action that requires a vote of the shareowners is scheduled to come before a meeting, such as the election of new directors, each stockholder is notified, and if he cannot attend the *annual meeting* and vote, he is usually asked to sign a paper that authorizes one or more of the officers or directors to act as his *proxy,* or representative, and vote for him; that's why these papers are called *proxies.* Sometimes when new directors are to be elected, a dissident group of stockholders will propose a rival slate in opposition to those picked by the management. In such a fight, each side will try to get signed proxies from the stockholders favoring its slate. This is called a proxy fight.

In addition to the regular meetings of the board or the annual meeting of the stockholders, special meetings of either group may be called to deal with special problems.

Why should anybody invest his money in the Pocket Pole Company? Because he thinks it has a good product and one that is likely to make money. If it does, he as a part owner stands to make money. That can happen in two ways: first, through the payment of *dividends,* and second, through an increase in the value of Pocket Pole stock.

Let's look at the dividend picture first. Suppose in the first year after paying all bills and taxes the company has *earnings,* or profits, of $2,000, or 10% on its $20,000 *capitalization,* the money that it raised by selling 2,000 shares of common stock. That would be a handsome profit for a new company, but not impossible.

It would then be up to the board of directors to decide what to do with that profit. It could pay it all out to the stockholders in dividends, or it could vote to keep every penny of it in the company treasury and use it to buy more machinery to make more pocket poles and earn more profit the following year. Since all stockholders like dividends and all boards of directors know that, Pocket Pole's board might very properly decide on a middle course. It might vote to pay out $1,000 in dividends and plow the other $1,000 back into the business as *retained earnings*.

Now if the board has $1,000 for dividends and 2,000 shares of stock outstanding, the divdend per share is going to be 50¢. That's what the man with one share of stock gets, while the man with ten shares gets $5, and the man with 100 shares gets $50. For all of them that would represent a 5% return on their investment, regardless of the number of shares they own.

But there's also another intangible return that they would get on their money. Presumably that $1,000 which the board decided to retain and plow back into the business will serve to increase the value of every man's share in the company—his *equity* in the company, as it's called in financial lingo.

If an original share of stock in Pocket Pole was fairly valued at $10, each of the 2,000 shares might now be considered worth $10.50, since the company has an extra $1,000 in addition to the original capital of $20,000.

Already that par value figure of $10 has been made slightly fictitious, and as the years roll by, it will bear no real relation to the value of the stock, if the company continues to earn good money and if the directors continue, year after year, to put a portion of those earnings back into the company. In comparatively few years, the total *assets* of the company—everything it owns: its plant, machinery, and products—might well be doubled without a corresponding increase in its *liabilities*—the sum total of what the company owes. In that case, the *book value* of each share of stock—assets, less liabilities, divided by the number of shares outstanding—would also be increased.

Par value is a term so generally misunderstood and so completely without significance that many companies today either do not set any value on their stock, in which case it is known as *no-par stock,* or they fix the value at $1 or $5, a figure so low that it could not possibly be misinterpreted as an index of its real value.

Even book value is a term with little real meaning today, although it had a real significance in the last century when *watered stock* was all too often sold to an unsuspecting public. That graphic expression, watered stock, is supposed to have had its origin in the practice of feeding cattle large quantities of salt on their way to market and then giving them a big drink of water just before they went on the weighing scales.

As applied to securities, the phrase describes that kind of company stock which was issued with an inflated value. For instance, an unscrupulous operator might pay only half a million dollars for some company, then issue a million dollars' worth of stock in it. He might sell all that stock to others and pocket a half million profit. Or after he sold half the stock and got his cost back, he might keep the remaining shares and thus own a half-interest in the company at no cost to himself. Such stock issues are now virtually non-existent, thanks to improved business ethics and government regulation.

Most stockholders have come to realize that book value doesn't mean very much. What counts is the earning power of a company and its growth prospects, not the total value of its plants and machinery. The stock of many a big company sells frequently at a price considerably more than its book value—sometimes double or triple the book value. In contrast, other stocks, like those of the railroads, which have gigantic investments in equipment, sell for much less than book value. Book value is frequently thought of as representing what the owner of a share of stock could expect to get if the company were *liquidated*—if it went out of business and sold off all its property. This is often a misconception, because when a company is in liquidation it can rarely get full value for the property it must dispose of.

So how do you know what a share of stock is worth —Pocket Pole stock or any other?

There's only one answer to that. Bluntly, it's only worth what somebody else is willing to pay for it when you want to sell it.

If the product isn't popular and sales suffer, if the cost of wages and raw materials is too high, if the management is inefficient, Pocket Pole or any other company can fail. And if it goes into bankruptcy, your stock can be valueless.

That's the black side of the picture. That's what can happen if the risk you assumed in buying the stock proves to be a bad one.

But if Pocket Pole proves to be a successful company, if it has a consistent record of good earnings, if part of those earnings is paid out regularly in dividends and another part of them wisely used to expand the company—then your stock is likely to be worth more than the $10 you paid for it. Perhaps a good deal more.

And that is the second way in which the stockholder expects to make money on his investment. First, through dividends. Second, through an increase in the value of his stock—or, rather, an increase in the price which somebody else will pay for it. This is known as *price appreciation.*

The price of a stock, like the price of almost everything else in this world, is determined by supply and demand—what one man is willing to pay for a stock and what another one is willing to sell it for, what one man bids and another man asks. That's why stocks always have a *bid* and an *asked* price. And don't forget that price is not necessarily a reliable guide to good investing. Some people think that a low-priced stock is a good buy because it is cheap, and they shy away from a high-priced stock because they think it is expensive. That just isn't so. The stock of one company may sell at a low price simply because it has a large number of shares outstanding—because the whole pie has been cut up into lots and lots of little pieces—while the stock of another equally good company may sell at a high price because it hasn't been cut up into so many pieces and there are relatively fewer shares outstanding. The price of a stock takes on meaning only as you consider it in relation to earnings and dividends per share.

Here, in brief, is the story of common stock—what it is, how it comes into being, what it means to own it.

American Telephone & Telegraph, General Motors, and General Electric may have millions of shares of stock outstanding, and they may even count their shareholders in the millions, but in these giant corporations, each share of stock plays precisely the same kind of role as a share of stock in our Pocket Pole Company, and each stockholder has the same rights, privileges, and responsibilities.

There is only one significant difference between buying a share of Pocket Pole and investing in a share of American Telephone & Telegraph, General Motors, or General Electric. These big companies have been in business for many years. You know something about them and the reputations they enjoy. You know how good their products or services are. You can examine their financial history, see for yourself how the prices of their stocks have moved over the years and what kind of record they have made as far as earnings and dividends are concerned. And on the basis of such information you can form a more reliable judgment about whether the stocks of these companies are overpriced or underpriced.

In contrast, the man who buys stock in our Pocket Pole Company has nothing to go on other than his own estimate of how good a product the company has and how big its sales are likely to be. There are no bench marks to guide him, no past records on which to base an appraisal of the future.

As a matter of literal truth, the Pocket Pole stockholder cannot properly be called an investor. Most times when a man buys stock in a brand-new company, he isn't investing in it; he's speculating in it. An *investor* is a man who is willing to take a moderate risk with his money for the sake of earning a moderate return, which in the case of common stocks might mean annual dividends averaging 4% or 5% and a growth factor of about the same amount, representing the increase in the value of his holdings over the years. A *speculator* is a man who takes a big risk in the hope of making a big profit as a result of an increase in the price of a stock. An investor usually has his eye on long-term values to be realized over a period of years; a speculator usually hopes to make a profit in a relatively short period of time.

American business needs both kinds of risk takers. Without the speculator, new business wouldn't be born, nor would many an old business be tided over a rough spot. Without the investor, a company would not have the capital to carry on, much less grow and expand.

CHAPTER 3

How and Why New Stock Is Sold

LET'S assume that the years are good to our Pocket Pole Company. It continues to grow. The original collapsible fishing pole has proved a best-seller, and the company now has a full line of models. Good earnings year after year have enabled the management to put the stock on a regular annual dividend basis. It now pays $1 a year per share—25¢ a quarter—and in several good years the directors even declared *extra dividends,* one of 25¢ and two of 50¢ a share.

Now the company feels that the time has come when it should expand. It could sell twice as many pocket poles, make twice as much profit, if only it had a bigger factory. So the board of directors decides to expand the plant. That means it will need more machinery, more manpower, and, above all things, more money—a lot more money than it has in the company treasury. Problem: how to get about $40,000.

A bank might advance the money. Maybe two or three banks would each put up part of the loan. But some of the directors don't like the idea of being in hock to the banks. They worry not only about paying interest on the loan every year but also about paying the money back in installments. That kind of steady drain on the company treasury for years ahead could eat into earnings and result in few if any dividends. Furthermore, banks don't usually like to make such long-term loans, and even if they were willing to, they might—to protect their loans—insist on having their representatives sit on the board of directors—and that is a prospect some of the directors don't relish.

Isn't there some other way to raise the money?

Yes, there is.

Maybe the present stockholders would like to put more money into the company. Maybe there are other people who would like to invest in a nice thriving little business like Pocket Pole. There's an idea.

And so the board of directors proposes to the stockholders that they authorize the company to issue 3,000 additional shares of stock—2,000 shares to be sold at once, and the remaining 1,000 to be held against the day when the company may want to raise more money by selling more stock. Each of the new shares of stock will carry with it the same rights and privileges as an original share.

This proposal is approved by a substantial majority of the stockholders, but not without some disagreement. One stockholder objected to the plan. He thought the company should have two classes of common stock—a *Class A stock* which would consist of the original issue, enjoying full rights and privileges, and a new *Class B stock* on which the same dividends would be paid but which would not carry any voting privileges. In other words, he wanted control of the company kept in the hands of the original stockholders.

The board chairman replied to this suggestion by pointing out that such *classified-stock* setups, A stock and B stock, are no longer popular with investors. True, some companies still have two issues of common stock outstanding, but few companies have followed such a practice in recent years.

Furthermore, the chairman explained, the old stockholders would probably still retain about the same measure of control, since they could be expected to buy most of the new issue anyway. This appeared likely, because it would be offered to them first and on especially favorable terms. This is the usual procedure for companies that have a *new issue* of stock to sell.

In this instance, the board recommended that old stockholders be permitted to buy the new stock at $20 a share—a figure about $2 less than the price at which the original stock was then being bought or sold—while others who might buy any of the new issue that was left over would have to pay whatever the going price might be at the time.

After the stockholders approved the plan, each was given *rights* which entitled them to buy new shares in the company at a discount from the market price and this right was clearly set forth on a certificate mailed to each shareholder. Everyone who owned one of the original 2,000 shares was permitted to buy one of the new 2,000 shares at $20. And the owner of ten old shares could buy ten new ones if he chose to exercise his rights. But they had to be exercised within two weeks—for rights are relatively short-lived. If the right were good for a long time, perhaps for years or even perpetually, it would be called not a right but a *warrant*—a certificate which gives the holder the right to buy a specific number of shares of a company's stock at a stipulated price within a certain time limit, or perpetually.

Some Pocket Pole shareholders, unable or unwilling to purchase additional stock, sold their rights. Often the market in such rights is a brisk one, even when they entitle the holder to buy only a part of a share—a tenth, a fifth, or a quarter of a share of new stock for each old share that he owns.

In the case of Pocket Pole each right was worth $1. Here is the way the value would have been arrived at: If you owned one share of Pocket Pole worth $22 and you exercised your right to buy an additional share at $20, you would then own two shares at an average of $21 apiece, or just $1 less than the going price per share. Hence the right could be figured to have a value of just $1. Actually, some stockholders might sell their rights for a fraction of that, while others might get more than $1 apiece, if the price of Pocket Pole advanced while the rights were still on the market. And, of course, some careless stockholders would ignore their rights, forgetting either to sell or to exercise them, in which case the rights would become worthless after the expiration date.

The standard formula for figuring the value of rights works this way: First take the prevailing market price of the stock (in this case $22) and subtract the subscription price (here $20); divide this difference ($2) by the number of old shares necessary to buy one new share (1) *plus* an additional one (1 plus 1 is 2, and $2 divided by 2 is $1).

When the rights expired, Pocket Pole discovered that all of them had been exercised except for 50 shares of the new issue, and these were readily sold at a price of $22. The company had raised $40,100 of new capital and had 4,000 shares of common stock outstanding.

Pocket Pole's plan for expanding the plant was put into effect, but because of delays in getting the machinery needed, it was two years before the new factory was in full operation. That situation raised for the board the awkward problem of how to continue paying dividends to the stockholders. In the first year of the transition period, the board felt obligated to continue paying the customary $1 dividend; but that put a serious dent in the company treasury. The second year the directors decided it would be foolhardy to do that again. They concluded that the only prudent thing they could do was to *pass the dividend* and keep the full year's earnings in the treasury until the new plant was operating efficiently.

But if the company paid no dividend, what would the stockholders say? Omission of the dividend would certainly mean that the price of the stock would go down, for it would be interpreted as a sign of trouble by those who might be interested in buying the stock.

The board found an answer to that problem in the 1,000 shares of new stock which had been authorized but not issued. With the approval of the stockholders, it took those 1,000 shares and distributed them without any charge among the owners of the 4,000 outstanding shares on the basis of one-quarter of a share of free stock for every single share which a stockholder owned.

Actually, the *stock dividend* did nothing to improve the lot of any individual stockholder. He was not one penny richer, nor did he actually own any greater proportion of the company. The man who had one share before the stock dividend owned 1/4000 of the company. Now with 1¼ shares out of the 5,000 outstanding, he still owned exactly 1/4000.

And yet in terms of future prospects that extra quarter of a share had real potential value. When the company got rolling again, that extra quarter share could represent a real profit and extra dividends, too.

That, happily, is exactly what happened. Pocket Pole prospered. The next year it earned $2 a share, and the directors felt they could prudently restore the old $1 dividend on each share, and to the man who held 1¼ shares that meant a return of $1.25.

CHAPTER 4

What You Should Know about Preferred Stocks

WITH its new plant and its new machinery, the Pocket Pole Company forged rapidly ahead. Earnings doubled. Then they doubled again. And most of those earnings, by decision of the directors, were reinvested in the business to expand production and improve operations. Dividends were modest. But the company was growing. Now its assets totaled almost $200,000.

Then another problem—and another opportunity—presented itself. The Rapid Reel Company, a well-known competitor owned and operated by a single family, could be acquired for $75,000. It was, the Pocket Pole directors agreed, a good buy at that price, but where could they get the $75,000?

Negotiations with the president of Rapid Reel indicated that he was anxious to retire from business, that he planned to invest whatever he got from the sale of the company so that it would yield him and his family a safe, reasonable income. Further, it was evident that he had a high regard for the management of Pocket Pole and was favorably impressed with the company's prospects. Here was the basis of a deal.

So the directors of Pocket Pole proposed that they take over Rapid Reel as a going concern and merge it into their own. How would they pay for it? By issuing *preferred* stock in the Pocket Pole Company—an issue of 750 shares with a par value of $100 per share—and giving it to the owners of Rapid Reel in exchange for their company.

Like most preferred stock, this issue would assure to the owners a first claim on the assets of Pocket Pole, after all debts had been taken care of, should it ever be necessary to liquidate the company. Further, it was provided that the stock would carry a specific dividend payable every year on every share before any dividends could be paid to common-stock holders. To make the deal as attractive as possible for the owners of Rapid Reel, the company was willing to pay a good dividend—$6 on every share, or 6%.

Sometimes such a preferred dividend is not paid in a given year because the company did not earn enough that year to cover it. But the most common type of preferred stock is *cumulative preferred,* and that is the kind Pocket Pole issued to the owners of Rapid Reel. Pocket Pole's cumulative preferred stock provided that if Pocket Pole could not pay the $6 dividend in any year, the amount due for that year would accrue to the preferred-stock holders and would be paid the following year or whenever the company had sufficient earnings to pay it. If the company could not make the payments on the preferred for a period of years, they would continue to accrue during all that time and would have to be paid in full before the common-stock holders got as much as a dime in dividend payments.

On the other hand, it was agreed that this would not be an issue of *participating preferred.* This meant that the holders of the preferred would not participate, beyond the stipulated dividend payment, in any of the extra profits the company might earn in good years. Even if earnings were so good that dividends on the common stock were doubled or trebled, the holders of the preferred would still get just their $6 a share and no more. Furthermore, they would have no participation in company affairs and no voting rights except on matters that might adversely affect the rights guaranteed them as preferred-stock holders. They were also guaranteed the right to elect two directors to the board if the company should ever pass, or fail to pay, the preferred dividend for eight consecutive quarters.

Although the terms of this issue might be regarded as fairly typical, there is no such thing as a standard preferred stock. About the only common denominator of all such issues is the guarantee that the owner will be accorded a preferential treatment, ahead of the common-stock holder, in the payment of dividends and in the distribution of any assets that might remain if the company was liquidated. That's why it is called preferred stock, and that's why its price usually doesn't fluctuate, either up or down, as much as the price of the company common stock.

From that point on, specifications vary widely. Most preferreds have a $100 par value, but some are no-par stocks. Dividends range from 4% up to 7% in normal times and even higher—as much as 10%—when interest rates on borrowed money are high as in 1973–1974. Most preferreds are *nonparticipating,* but there are many exceptions.

Many preferreds are issued, as in the case of Pocket Pole, to acquire another company, but most of them are issued simply to acquire more capital for expansion or improvements at a time when the company's circumstances are such that its stockholders and the public at large might not be willing to invest in more of its common stock.

Cumulative preferreds are by all odds the most common, but there are some *noncumulative* issues on the market—principally those of railroads. Occasionally, on cumulative preferreds, *accrued dividends* pile up in bad years to a point where it becomes impossible for a company to pay them. In such a situation, it may attempt to negotiate a settlement with the preferred holders on the basis of a partial payment. However, some companies have paid off more than $100 a share in accumulated back dividends due on their preferred stock which cost the owner originally just $100 a share.

Another kind of preferred stock that has become increasingly popular in recent years is the *convertible preferred.* Such a stock carries a provision permitting the owner to convert it into a specified number of shares of common stock. Suppose, for instance, that a company sold a new issue of convertible preferred at a time when its common stock was quoted at $17 or $18 a share; in such a situation, the conversion clause might provide that every share of the new $100 preferred could be exchanged for five shares of the company's common stock at any time in the next five years. Obviously, there would be no advantage to the preferred-stock holders in making such a swap unless the common stock advanced in price to more than $20 a share.

The price of a convertible is apt to fluctuate more than the price of other preferreds because a convertible is always tied to the common stock of a company. This has its good and bad points. If the company is successful and the price of its common stock rises, the holder of a convertible preferred will find that his stock has had a corresponding increase in value, since it can be exchanged for the common. On the other hand, if the common declines, the convertible preferred is apt to suffer too, because one of the features which was counted on to make it attractive has suddenly lost something of its value, and the other features of the issue, such as its dividend rate, may not prove as attractive or substantial as those of orthodox preferreds. Convertibles are always especially popular when stock prices are rising generally.

Most preferreds carry a provision which permits the company to *call* in the issue and pay it off at full value, plus a premium of perhaps 5%. A company will usually exercise this right to call in its preferred stock if it thinks it can replace the outstanding issue with one that carries a lower dividend rate.

From the point of view of the owners of Rapid Reel, the plan which Pocket Pole proposed looked attractive. So they accepted it—after the common-stock holders of Pocket Pole had approved the plan and authorized issuance of 750 shares of 5% cumulative preferred stock with $100 par value in exchange for the Rapid Reel Company.

With this acquisition, Pocket Pole was on its way to becoming big business. And in the next ten years, with booming sales, it strode forward along that path with seven-league boots.

It bought the little Nylon Line Company for cash.

It acquired the Fishing Supplies Corporation by another issue of preferred stock, which it called *second-preferred,* because it had to recognize the prior claim to assets and earnings that had been granted the owners of Rapid Reel. To make this issue more attractive to the owners of Fishing Supplies, a conversion privilege was included in it; in other words, it was a convertible preferred.

It bought the Sure-Fire Rifle Company by authorizing an additional issue of common stock and arranging to trade the Sure-Fire stockowners one share of Pocket Pole for every three shares of Sure-Fire that they owned.

Finally, it acquired control of Camping Supplies, Incorporated, on a similar *stock-swapping* basis.

Now, with a full, well-rounded line of all kinds of fishing, hunting, and camping supplies, backed by an aggressive advertising and merchandising campaign, the company experimented with its own retail outlets. In a few years, these grew into a small chain of 30 sporting-goods stores, known as the Rod & Reel Centers.

Sales multiplied, and so did earnings—up to $10 and $12 a share. Dividends were boosted correspondingly, and with the adoption of a regular $6 annual dividend, Pocket Pole stock was frequently quoted at $120 a share and higher. Stockholders complained that it was too high-priced, that it couldn't be sold easily if they wanted to dispose of their holdings.

So the company decided to *split* the stock on a ten-for-one basis and simultaneously to change its corporate name to Rod & Reel, Incorporated—a much more appropriate name, since most fishermen consider the fishing "pole" passé. Hence it issued new certificates for ten shares of Rod & Reel common stock for every single share of the old Pocket Pole stock. Theoretically, each of the new shares should have been worth about $12, but since stock splits frequently excite unusual investor interest, it wasn't long before the new shares were being bought and sold at prices a dollar or two higher, even though there had been substantially no change in the outlook for the company.

Along its road to success, Rod & Reel encountered only one misadventure. Eyeing its growth, its sales and earnings record, and its general financial strength, the Double-X Sporting Goods Company proposed to Rod & Reel that they *merge* their two businesses. After many joint meetings and careful examination of the pluses and minuses in the proposal, the directors of Rod & Reel decided that the interests of their stockholders would best be served if the company continued to row its own boat, and so it declined the offer to merge.

But Double-X wasn't prepared to take no for an answer; it wanted Rod & Reel and its successful retail outlets. And so Double-X made a *tender* offer to each Rod & Reel stockholder, agreeing to buy his stock on a set date at a set price almost 10% above its prevailing market price, provided enough other stockholders surrendered their shares so that Double-X could obtain control of Rod & Reel. If Rod & Reel stockholders signed the form agreeing to sell, they would have to tender their stock to Double-X on demand at the set price and on the given date.

Rod & Reel fought the tender offer and urged its stockholders not to sign up. In the end Rod & Reel won out. So few stockholders were willing to sell, even at the higher price, that Double-X realized it could not gain control of Rod & Reel, and so it was forced to withdraw its tender offer.

This is the story of Rod & Reel, Incorporated, formerly Pocket Pole Company, Incorporated. It is a success story, as it was meant to be, to show the various kinds of stock operations that may mark a company's growth. But for that matter, it is no more of a success story than the real-life stories of General Motors or International Business Machines, Xerox or Polaroid, or any of hundreds of other companies in which the original investors (or speculators) have seen the value of their stockholdings multiplied 10, 20, even 100 times over.

CHAPTER 5

What You Should Know about Bonds and Investment Banking

Do you have a lot of money to invest—say, $20,000, $50,000 or more? Or is there some reason why you should be particularly conservative in your investments?

If so, then you ought to know about *corporate bonds,* the kind of bond issued by companies like Rod & Reel, Inc., and bought principally by *institutional investors*—banks, insurance companies, pension funds, colleges and universities, and charitable foundations.

If you don't have substantial sums to invest or some good reason for being especially conservative, chances are that there are better investments for you than corporate bonds, except in unusual periods such as 1973–1974, when many individuals found bonds more attractive than stocks because of the stock market slump.

But who can tell when you might get a lot of money? And anyway, every intelligent investor should know something about bonds just so he'll have a grasp of the whole securities business.

The easiest way to understand bonds is to consider the plight of Rod & Reel's treasurer at a time when the company needed $1 million of new capital—a much greater sum than any it had ever had to raise before.

It needed that money because over the years it had grown rather haphazardly, acquiring a manufacturing plant here and another one there, a warehouse here and some retail stores there.

Now the whole operation had to be pulled together, made to function efficiently. An independent firm of engineers had figured just what economies Rod & Reel could effect by centralizing most of its manufacturing operations in one big new plant and modernizing its equipment. In the long run, the $1 million would unquestionably prove to be money well spent.

But how to get the money?

As company treasurer, you might first discuss the matter with the officers of your regular bank. They are perfectly willing to supply you from month to month with the credit you need for raw materials, but a million-dollar loan to construct a new plant—well, that is not for them. What you need in the present situation, they suggest, is help from a very special kind of banker, an *investment banker*.

Investment bankers specialize in raising the kind of money that business needs for long-term use, usually in amounts considerably greater than the million Rod & Reel wanted.

Most times when a company wants money, it would like to get it without any strings attached—without obligating itself to pay any set return on the money. In short, it wants *equity capital,* the kind of money it can get only by selling common stock.

If the company's condition is sound, if its prospects are good, and if the stock market is then very active and healthy, an investment banker may agree to *underwrite* such an issue. That means he will buy all the new stock himself from the company, and then resell it at a set price per share to individual buyers. As a general rule, this is the only time in the entire life of a stock issue that its price will be fixed—at the time when it is originally issued, either to start a new company or raise new capital. Once the stock is in public hands, its price will be determined solely by how much the buyer will pay and how much the seller wants for the stock he owns—the law of supply and demand.

For the risk that the investment banker assumes, the risk that he may not be able to resell the entire issue that he has bought, he expects to make a profit on each share of the issue.

On small issues, involving only $1 million or $2 million, he may be able and willing to carry the whole risk himself, but on most issues he shares the risk with other investment bankers who join with him in forming an *underwriting group* or *syndicate* under his management.

When it comes time to sell the issue to the public the underwriters usually invite other security dealers to join with them in a *selling group*.

The costs of underwriting and selling an issue of stock depend primarily on how salable the underwriting group thinks the issue will be when it is put on the market. Those costs might run anywhere from 3% to 10% of the final selling price, and they are wholly paid by the seller. The buyers get such stock at the announced price, free of all commission cost or other charges. On some issues, such as cheap mining or oil stocks offered at a dollar or two a share, charges might even run as high as 20%, for these *penny stocks* can usually be sold only by costly merchandising effort. A third to a half of the total commission on any new issue might go to those who underwrite it, with the *manager* of the group getting an extra fee for his services, and the balance to those who sell it, but if the issue looks as though it might be "sticky," or hard to sell, the selling commission is likely to be increased and the underwriting commission reduced correspondingly.

Whenever a company wants to raise capital by selling a new securities issue, it may well shop around to see which investment banker will offer the best terms and handle the new issue at the lowest total cost. Once an underwriter is selected, the relationship between the company and the underwriter is apt to develop naturally into a close one, and if the company needs to raise additional capital at some future time, it will usually expect to get help again from the same underwriter. When an underwriting is arranged in this fashion, it is described as a *negotiated* deal as distinct from a deal that is arrived at through *competitive bidding* by various investment bankers interested in obtaining the business.

For years, public utilities were required by law to obtain competitive bids on all new securities issues, but this regulation has been somewhat relaxed; under certain circumstances utilities may now obtain permission to negotiate public offerings. Thus, in 1975, the American Electric Power Company, a registered public utility holding company, successfully negotiated the sale of $164 million of common stock through a large group of underwriters. The biggest single securities offering in history was American Telephone & Telegraph's $1,540,000,000 bond issue arranged with Morgan Stanley & Company in 1970.

Competitive bids are also required on railroad securities, and certain types of issues up to approximately $15 million in size are sold in this fashion. But the Interstate Commerce Commission, which exercises control in this field, has often exempted them from competitive bidding requirements on certain larger issues, or specific types of securities.

While most companies might prefer to raise new capital by selling stock, this is not the kind of securities issue which an investment banker is likely to sanction most times, especially in the case of a comparatively small company like Rod & Reel. He is far more apt to suggest an issue of bonds rather than an issue of stock. In normal years, the aggregate value of new bond issues may be five or ten times greater than the value of new stock issues. As a matter of fact, in the modern era, business has raised little more than 5% of the money it has needed through the sale of stock. Most of the balance it has raised by selling bonds, and that is why the bond market is many times bigger than the stock market.

Bonds always represent borrowed money which the company that issues them is obligated to repay. That's why they are called *obligations*. They are a kind of promissory note. When a company sells bonds, it borrows the money from the buyers, and the bonds stand as a formal evidence of that debt. Each bond is an agreement on the part of the company to repay the face value of the bond—usually $1,000—at a specified time and in most cases to pay a set annual rate of *interest* from the day it is issued to the day it is redeemed.

The man who buys stock in a company actually buys a part of that company. The man who buys a company's bonds simply lends his money to the company.

The stockholder expects to collect dividends on his stock and thus share in the company's profits. The bondholder expects only to earn a fixed return on his investment in the form of interest payments.

There's one other important difference between stocks and bonds. If a company is successful, the stockholder can hope to make a substantial profit because the price of his stock should go up. The bondholder enjoys no such extravagant hope. Market price appreciation for a company's bonds is usually limited, regardless of how successful the company may be. But price changes sparked by interest rate fluctuations have often been quite dramatic.

On the other hand, if the bondholder can't expect to gain as much on his capital, neither does he run the risk of losing as much. His investment is much better protected, thanks to the fact that bonds do represent debt, and if a company is dissolved, the debt it owes its bondholders, like any other debt it owes for labor and materials, must be paid before the stockholders, either common or preferred, can get a nickel out of what's left of the company. The claims of bondholders come first, then the preferred-stock holders—and last, the common-stock holders.

It is because the element of risk in bonds is so comparatively slight that they are such a popular form of investment with institutional investors. This is the market the investment banker has his eye on when he underwrites a bond issue. Very often, an issuer may succeed in selling an entire bond issue to just one or two large institutional customers—a bank, an insurance company, or a pension fund—and not try to market the issue publicly. This is known as a *private placement.*

Because the institutional market for bonds is such a good market, the underwriting and selling commissions are usually much lower on an issue of bonds than on an issue of stock. Otherwise, the two kinds of securities are issued and sold in much the same way.

From the point of view of any company treasurer, a bond issue has obvious disadvantages as compared with a stock issue. The interest that must be paid on bonds represents a fixed charge that has to be met in bad times as well as good times, and the bonds must be paid off when they come due. The stockholder has to be paid only if the company makes money—and even that is not a binding obligation.

If the company is successful, it doesn't mind having to pay 5% or 6% interest—sometimes even double that, as in 1974 when interest rates hit their all-time high—on money borrowed from bondholders if it can make a substantially greater profit on the extra capital that it raises by the bond issue. Again, bond interest payments are an expense item deducted from a company's earnings before it pays its federal income *tax* on those earnings. In contrast, dividends are paid out of what is left after a company has paid the tax on its earnings. Thus, it actually costs a company less to pay a given amount of money to bondholders than it does to pay the same amount of money to stockholders.

From the investor's point of view, the best bonds are those that have behind them the strongest assurance that they will be repaid—in full and with the specified interest.

Here the situation is not much different from what it would be if you as an individual sought to get a loan from a bank. If the banker knew you and knew that you would be able to repay the money, he might lend it to you without asking you to put up any collateral, such as your life insurance policies or other property, to guarantee the loan. But if it was a sizable loan, he might even insist that you give him a mortgage on your home.

It's much the same way with companies when they issue bonds. They would prefer to get the money without posting their property as a guarantee that the contract set in the bond will be fulfilled. That, as a matter of fact, is precisely the way the Rod & Reel treasurer felt when the investment banker told him the company would have to *float* a bond issue, not a stock issue.

As long as it had to be bonds, the treasurer proposed that his company issue $1 million of debentures. A *debenture* is a bond that is backed only by the general credit of the corporation. No specific real estate or property stands as security behind it. It is, in effect, a giant-size I.O.U. Debentures are the most common type of bond issued by big, well-established industrial companies today. But in the case of Rod & Reel, the investment banker was not disposed to feel that such an issue would be in order, because the company, though successful, was still relatively small and not too well known. He was afraid the debentures wouldn't sell.

The treasurer then asked if a debenture might not be made more attractive by including a convertible provision in it. There are many *convertible bonds* on the market and their terms vary widely, but like convertible preferreds, all of them offer the owner the privilege of converting his bond into a specified number of shares of common stock.

Such a provision may add a certain speculative appeal to the bond—the chance to make an extra profit if the common stock rises—but the typical bond buyer may look askance at such a "sweetener." He knows better than most security buyers that you don't get something for nothing in a security, any more than you do in any other kind of merchandise. A convertible bond may offer the possibility of price appreciation, but its guarantee of safety is not as substantial; such issues are considered to be subordinate to other bonds.

In Rod & Reel's case, the investment banker did not feel that a convertible was feasible, and in the light of his attitude, the treasurer did not even raise the question of whether the company could issue some kind of *income* or *adjustment bond*.

These bonds are a kind of hybrid security, something like a noncumulative preferred stock, since they provide that the interest is to be paid on the bond only as it is earned. If earnings are sufficient to pay only a part of the interest on such bonds, the company must make whatever payment it can to the nearest ½ of 1%; thus on a 5% bond a company might pay only 2½% or 3% or 3½%, depending on its earnings. Hence, most income bonds have a very low quality rating.

There is still another kind of bond, the *collateral-trust* bond, which, like the income bond, used to be more popular than it is today, but Rod & Reel's circumstances were such that this type of security was obviously not suited to them. When a company issues a collateral-trust bond, it deposits securities with a trustee as a guarantee that the bonds will be redeemed and interest paid on them. Usually the securities on deposit are worth at least 25% more than the total value of the bond issue, and they are frequently the securities of subsidiary companies.

As the discussions progressed, it became apparent that the investment banker felt there was only one kind of industrial bond that Rod & Reel could offer, and that was a *first-mortgage bond*—the kind of bond which is secured by a mortgage on all of a company's property, not only on its existing property but sometimes even on all property which it might later acquire.

Industrial bonds of this type are considered to be among the highest-grade security investments, because they offer the investor an undisputed first claim on company earnings and the greatest possible safety. That first mortgage takes absolute precedence over the claims of all other owners of a company's securities, including the holders of debentures, adjustment bonds, or secondary-mortgage bonds that may be issued after a first mortgage has been made.

Having resigned himself to the fact that Rod & Reel would have to mortgage its property, including the new plant which it expected to build, in order to float a $1 million bond issue, the treasurer next took up with the banker the question of what rate of interest the company might have to pay. Here the banker was in no position to supply an answer, because the rate a company has to pay always depends primarily on its credit standing and its earning capacity. And these were the crucial factors on which the banker could not commit himself without a thorough, painstaking investigation of all aspects of the company—the same kind of survey which every investment banker must make, with the help of outside accountants, engineers, and other specialists, before underwriting any new issue of securities for a company.

Bond interest rates vary not only with the health of the company but also with the bond's quality and with general business conditions. Whenever a new bond issue is floated, Moody's Investors Service and Standard & Poor's Corporation, America's two outstanding organizations in the field of securities research and statistics, assign it a quality rating. Most times the two companies agree on the ratings but they don't quite agree on the form of the designation. Thus, Moody's grades bonds (downward in quality) as Aaa, Aa, A, Baa, Ba, etc., while Standard & Poor's prefers capital letters, using AAA, AA, etc., and also assigns plus and minus ratings to most major quality groups.

In 1920, Aaa or AAA bonds paid over 6%, while in 1945 they were paying only 2½%. In the early sixties, Aaa bonds were paying 4½% to 5%—a range that bond dealers consider fairly typical over a long period of years—but by the end of the decade, the return on such bonds had soared to highs of 7%, even 8% and better; in 1974, Aaa rated long-term bonds were offered at a record 10%.

When money is "tight," as it was in 1974, banks increase the rates they charge on mortgages and loans, and they pay higher interest rates on deposits. At such a time bond interest rates usually go up, too. If this happens at a time when stock dividends, expressed as a percentage of the price, have been going down, a situation develops where the investor can get a better return from bonds than he can from stocks, and he is frequently tempted to shift to the "safer" investment.

But it is a mistake to think that bond prices never fluctuate. Thus when new bonds are issued with interest rates of 8% or 9%, the prices of outstanding bonds, offered originally at 4% or 5%, are bound to decline. No one is going to pay face value for an old bond with an interest rate of 4%, if he can buy a new bond of equal quality with an interest rate of 8%. The only way the old 4% bond could compete with the new 8% bond on even terms would be for the 4% bond to sell in the market at just half the price. So when interest rates rise, strong pressure is exerted on the market for older bonds with low interest rates.

The interest rate of a bond is frequently referred to as the *coupon* rate, because traditionally bonds have appended to them a number of detachable coupons, one for each six months of the bond's life. The owner clips each coupon as it comes due and presents it to the company's paying agent for payment. Coupons were used at first because bonds were not registered on the company's books in the owner's name, as stock certificates are. Instead, they were the property of the bearer —whoever had them at a given time—and hence were called *bearer bonds*.

Today, there has been a departure from this practice. Nearly all companies now issue bonds that are registered in each owner's name, just like stocks. On some *registered bonds,* coupon's are still used for the payment of interest, but on others the bondholder gets a check automatically from the company, and this practice has become increasingly popular. In time, the phrase "coupon-clipper" to denote a wealthy individual may vanish from the language.

Just as crucial as the interest rate of any company issuing bonds is the question of *maturity*—how long a life the bonds will have, how soon the company will have to redeem them, or pay them off. In general, the stronger the company, the longer the maturities. For a company like Rod & Reel, ten years might be considered the maximum time limit. Furthermore, the company would probably be required to establish a *sinking fund* and put enough into it every year to provide for an annual repayment of a portion of the issue, just as one pays off part of the principal on a mortgage each year. In view of its building and reorganization plans, Rod & Reel would probably be allowed a breathing spell of two or three years before it had to start putting money into the sinking fund.

Like preferreds, most bonds have call provisions which permit a company to redeem them before maturity if it has the money.

There is a wide variation in how long bond issues

run, but a period of 20 or 30 years is about as common as any. Curiously, the railroads have issued bonds with the longest life on record, and they also have some with about as short a life as any. Many old rail bonds run for 100 years, and some have no maturity date; they were issued in perpetuity—a frank recognition of the fact that no one expects the rails ever to pay all their debts.

At the other end of the scale are *equipment trust* obligations, which mature in only one to fifteen years. These serial maturity bonds enable a railroad to buy freight cars, passenger cars, locomotives and other such equipment virtually on the installment plan; some have carried interest rates under 1½%. On this kind of bond, the equipment itself stands as the guarantee of repayment.

The maturity of a bond can affect the return you realize on it. You can buy a bond with a 6% coupon rate, but it may *yield* you something less—or something more—than 6%, depending on how much you pay for the bond and what its maturity is. If you pay exactly $1,000 for a bond and get $60 interest on it every year, you do realize a 6% yield. But if you pay $1,050 for the bond, the $60 annual interest payment obviously represents less than a 6% return on the money you've invested. Furthermore, if you hold the bond until it matures, you will get only $1,000 for it on redemption, a loss of $50. If the bond has a twenty-year maturity, that $50 loss would represent, in effect, a reduction of $2.50 a year in your interest payment. Furthermore, over the full twenty years you would have lost the amount of interest that you might have earned on that $50.

The net of it all is that if you pay $1,050 for a 6% twenty-year bond, you will realize a *yield to maturity* of just 5.58%, but only if all coupons when paid are reinvested (interest on interest) at the yield they would provide if held to maturity. Of course, if you buy the bond at a discount instead of a premium—for $950 instead of $1,050, for example—you will earn more than 6% on it.

It was the yield to maturity that made many old bonds issued at 4% or 5% in earlier years especially attractive in 1973–1974. In mid-1974, for instance, it was possible to buy a top-quality bond, such as American Telephone & Telegraph's 4% bonds due in 1985 at around 66. As the price of the old bond was forced down, its yield was increased so that it was able to compete in the marketplace with the new bonds issued at 9% or 10%. The A.T.&T. bond—scheduled to be paid off in 11 years at a full par—would have to gain 34 points before 1985, when it would be redeemable at full value, and that built-in gain gave the bond a yield to maturity of about 9.4%.

When a company like Rod & Reel has a stock or bond issue to raise new capital, such an issue represents new *financing*. But very often preferred stocks or bonds are issued as part of a *refinancing* operation. Thus, when a company refinances, it may seek to substitute some new bond issue for an outstanding one that it issued many years ago—a process known as *refunding*.

Why should such substitution be made? Because it can be to a company's advantage. As business and investment conditions change, it is frequently worthwhile to call an outstanding issue of bonds or preferred stock on which the company may be paying a high rate of interest. Such an issue can be paid off out of funds raised by the sale of a new issue carrying a lower rate.

When a company has a substantial amount of bonds or preferred stock outstanding in relation to the amount of its common stock, the common stock is said to have high *leverage*. This phrase is used because the price of such a stock is likely to be disproportionately influenced by any increase or decrease in the company's earnings. Here's why: Suppose a company is obligated to pay $500,000 in bond interest and preferred dividends every year; if the company has earnings of $1 million before paying such fixed charges, it has only $500,000 left for the common-stock holders. But if the company has earnings of $3 million, it will have $2,500,000 available for the benefit of the common-stock holders in the form either of dividends or of re-invested capital which would serve to increase the value of the company and its stock. In this situation, a three-fold increase in the company's earnings would have meant a five-fold increase in the amount of earnings available to the common-stock holders, because the holders of the bonds and preferred stock would still have received only the prescribed $500,000.

Of course, if the company's earnings decreased from $1 million to $500,000, there would be no earnings available to the common-stock holders. Because fluctuations in earnings can have such magnified effects on earnings available to the common-stock holders, high-leveraged stocks are likely to fluctuate more drastically in price than the stocks of companies that have relatively small amounts of outstanding bonds or preferred stocks.

CHAPTER 6

How New Issues Are Regulated

WHENEVER a company like Rod & Reel wants to raise capital by floating a new issue of stocks or bonds, it must comply with the federal law that governs the sale of any such issue offered to the public.

In the boom days of the twenties, many a new stock was sold with few facts and lots of glittering promises. In 1933, Congress changed all that. It enacted a new law, widely known as the *Truth in Securities Act,* and then in 1934, with the passage of the *Securities Exchange Act,* it set up the *Securities and Exchange Commission* to administer both laws.

The S.E.C. requires *full disclosure* of all the pertinent facts about any company before it makes a *public offering* of new stocks or bonds. The company must file a lengthy *registration statement* with the S.E.C. in which it sets forth the data about its financial condition—its assets and its liabilities, what it owns and what it owes. It must also furnish the profit and loss record for the past several years. It must describe all outstanding issues of its securities and their terms, list all its officers and directors, together with their salaries, bonuses, and stock interests, and reveal the identity of anyone who holds more than 10% of any of its securities issues, or who is paid more than $20,000 a year. Finally, it must provide a description of its operations.

If the data appear to be complete and honest, the S.E.C. gives a green light to the new issue. But this does not mean that it passes any judgment whatsoever on the quality of the securities, how good or bad they may be for any investor.

The Securities and Exchange Commission also sees that the information which is filed with it is made available to any possible buyer of the new issue. A company is required to put all the essential facts into a printed *prospectus,* and every security dealer who offers the new stock or bond for sale must give a copy of that prospectus to everyone who buys the new issue and also to anyone who might request a copy. These prospectus regulations are generally binding on all publicly owned companies for forty days after the new issue is offered for sale. If a company is offering its securities to the public for the first time, these prospectus regulations are binding for ninety days.

Prior to setting the price on a new issue, a preliminary draft of the prospectus is usually printed up. Such drafts, not yet reviewed by the S.E.C., are known as *red herrings,* because in the early days of its regulatory work, the S.E.C. often found them to be little more than outright sales promotion, designed not so much to divulge information as to distract the reader from facts about the new issue that the S.E.C. might regard critically. A red herring is usually distributed only to members of the underwriting and selling groups, but because some copies may reach the public, a red herring must carry on its face a warning printed in red ink to the effect that the prospectus has not yet been reviewed by the S.E.C.

The prospectus is usually about 20 to 30 pages long, sometimes even more, but some well-established companies, notably utilities, that can meet certain high standards of financial responsibility have for years been permitted by the Securities and Exchange Commission to use a *short-form prospectus* on bond issues, and in 1970 the S.E.C. relaxed its rules and extended the short-form privilege to stock issues of companies that had a strong financial position and a record of consistent earnings over a period of years.

During the period when a new issue is under prospectus regulation, no broker or dealer can provide the public with any information or opinion about that new issue or any outstanding issue related to it. He is strictly limited to what the prospectus says. If he wants to he can publish the prospectus or a detailed summary of it as an advertisement, but apart from that the only other kind of advertising he can use for the issue is the so-called *tombstone* announcement, in which no information is provided beyond the name of the issue, its price, its size, and the names of the underwriters and dealers who have it for sale. And above even this austere announcement the underwriters usually insert a precautionary note to the effect that the advertisement is not to be interpreted as an offer to buy or sell the security, since the offer is made only through the prospectus.

Sometimes you may see a tombstone ad announcing a new issue and simultaneously stating that the issue has already been completely sold. You may well wonder why such an ad appears. The answer is simple. Underwriting houses are proud of their financing activities, and when they have arranged to sell all of a given issue —usually to big investors—even before it is scheduled for public offering, they go ahead and publish the new-issue advertisement as a matter of prestige.

Even if a company satisfies all the requirements of the Securities and Exchange Commission on a new issue, its troubles may not necessarily end there. Most of the states also have laws governing the registration and sale of new securities. While the requirements of these so-called *blue sky laws* are much like those of the S.E.C., they are sufficiently varied to cause a company a lot of trouble and a good deal of extra expense in filing the necessary forms to comply with the various state laws.

All told, preparing a new issue for sale can be a very expensive undertaking. The bill for preparing the necessary forms and printing a prospectus may run to $15,000 or $20,000, and it can run as high as $100,-000. This is the case when a large company brings out a new stock issue and has to offer rights to all its stockholders, for each of them must be supplied with a prospectus. Fees for lawyers and accountants can add a lot more to this bill.

However, the federal law, as well as most state laws, provides an "out" for little companies like Rod & Reel. For instance, if the new issue has a value of not more than $500,000, the company need file only a short registration form with the S.E.C. This is known as a *Regulation A* filing, and companies using it can satisfy the requirements of the law by distributing an *offering circular*, as it is called. On issues of less than $50,000, it isn't even necessary to prepare a circular. Again, if the new issue can be classified as a private placement— usually one that will be purchased by no more than 35 persons—rather than as a public offering, it doesn't even have to be registered with the S.E.C.

In the case of a small company like Rod & Reel, the investment banker would try to qualify any new issue as a private placement by lining up one or two institutional buyers, perhaps an insurance company or a charitable foundation, before the deal was finally set. If he succeeds in doing so, he would insist that the issue be of topflight quality, for such customers are only interested in high-grade securities. In Rod & Reel's case this would mean a first-mortgage bond.

While the Securities and Exchange Commission's "full disclosure" rules have undoubtedly done much to protect the investor, it is frequently argued that they are more exacting than they have to be, and this may deter some companies from trying to raise new money for expansion. Again, the prohibition on disseminating *any* information about a company while its new issue is under prospectus regulation can deprive investors who own existing securities of essential information about the company during the period of the prospectus blackout. The intent of the rule—to prohibit promotion of the new issue—is good, but the application sometimes works hardships on investors.

Furthermore, it has been argued that the individual investor doesn't really benefit as he should from the protection that the prospectus regulations provide. Most individuals who buy a new issue—and their number is few compared with those who buy securities already on the market—rarely examine the prospectus, or understand it if they do. As a matter of fact, if the buyer knows that the Securities and Exchange Commission cleared the issue, he is apt to believe that the commission has endorsed it—and anything that is good enough for the S.E.C. is good enough for him.

Nothing, of course, could be further from the truth. Full disclosure can protect against fraud. It can't guarantee a profit or protect against loss. *Caveat emptor* —"Let the buyer beware"—is still the rule of the market, and it applies with particular force to new, unseasoned issues. This is especially true, for example, with respect to the low-priced oil and uranium shares which were unloaded on the public a few years ago. Many of these stocks were not worth the paper they were printed on, but the S.E.C. often lacked the necessary power to deal with the promoters behind them. Needless to say, many new issues of these worthless penny stocks avail themselves of the "small-issue" or Regulation A exemption to that they won't have to "tell all" in a full prospectus.

CHAPTER 7

What You Should Know about
Government and Municipal Bonds

THE *government bond* poses an interesting paradox. Here is the one security about which more people know something than they do about any other. And yet here is the one security which is *fully* understood by probably fewer people than any other.

An estimated 85 million Americans learned what it meant to lend their money on a bond, with the promise of repayment and the assurance of interest, during World War II when they bought the famous Series E bonds, and there are still other millions whose education in investments has been initiated by buying these savings bonds since the war.

But only the big institutional buyers of government bonds, plus a comparative handful of dealers who regularly buy and sell hundreds of millions of these securities for a profit measured in fractions of 1%, really understand the government bond market and know how it can be affected by subtle shifts in the credit and money policies of our own government or another government half the world away.

There are dozens and dozens of different government issues, carrying different coupon rates, different maturities, different call provisions.

Some are issued for very short periods of time. These are *Treasury bills* with maturities as short as 91 days, and *notes* that may run up to seven years. On the short-term issues, interest rates have ranged from 2% or 3%, a level that was once considered fairly standard, to the high of 9.91% (August 1974) for the 91-day Treasury bill. During World War II, the government pegged interest rates on bills at an all-time low of ⅜ of 1%, but the practice was terminated in March 1951 by an agreement between the Treasury and the Federal Reserve Board.

Long-term issues of *Treasury bonds,* usually called *Treasuries,* have maturities in excess of five years and range up to 25 years. The longest outstanding bond in 1975 had a 25-year maturity; the longest outstanding note had a maturity of about 6½ years.

By law, the Treasury may not issue bonds with an interest rate of more than 4¼%, which makes it difficult for the government to issue new bonds at such a time when interest rates on other forms of investment are substantially higher. In periods of tight money, Treasuries usually sell in the open market at a discount, and the investor who buys a bond at less than par may well realize a yield in excess of 4¼% if he holds to maturity.

Thus, when interest rates are high, as they were in 1973–1974, a bond yielding only 4¼% would be so unattractive to investors that its price might drop 25%, and a $1,000 bond would be worth only $750. If you bought the bond at that price, you would still be collecting $42.50 a year in interest, and that return on a $750 investment would mean that you would be earning an effective rate of 5.66%.

Actually, during that 1973–1974 period, government bonds were selling at prices that yielded 6½% to 7½%. One issue of government bonds actually yielded an effective rate of return equal to 8.75%, and one issue of government notes yielded a high of 10.20%.

No matter how cheaply you buy a government bond, you can count on getting the full face value of the bond, the full $1,000, from the government if you hold it till its maturity date, and all that time you would be collecting a higher effective rate of interest, based on the low purchasing price.

While Treasuries may sell at a discount in the open market when competitive interest rates are high, it is equally true that they are apt to sell at a premium—a price above par—and return a lower maturity yield when interest rates are generally low.

Treasury bonds, representing the great bulk of the federal debt, are always freely traded in the market at prices which change only slightly from day to day, rarely as much as a quarter or a half point. As a matter of fact, price spreads in this market are usually so close that the minimum price fluctuation on government bonds is only 1/32 of a point—occasionally even 1/64 —as compared with ⅛ of a point on stocks.

Regularly traded by the same dealers and on much the same basis as the government bonds are those bonds issued by various government agencies, such as the Federal Home Loan Banks and the Federal Land Banks.

And there are other government bonds which are not traded in any market, bonds that can be bought only from the government and sold back to the government at set prices, bonds that never suffer any fluctuations in market price. These are the *savings bonds* —*Series E* and *Series H*—and they can be bought at virtually any bank. No commission is charged; they are handled free as a patriotic service.

When savings bonds were first introduced during World War II, the maximum yield that you could get was 2.9%. You paid $75 for an E bond, and then ten years later you could cash it in for $100, thus realizing an average annual return of 2.9%. If you cashed it in earlier, you got less on your investment.

As interest rates increased in later years, the government was forced to liberalize the return on its savings bonds, and it accomplished this objective by shortening the maturity. Step by step, the length of time you had to hold an E bond before cashing it in at face value was cut from ten years down to five years and ten months in 1969, and with this shortened maturity, the yield was boosted from 2.9% to 5%. A year later the Treasury added a bonus of ½ of 1% to encourage sales, and by 1975, through the combination of shortened maturities and increased interest, an E bond was yielding 6% for a five-year maturity.

All along the line, the Treasury also made similar changes in its Series H bonds. Unlike E bonds, which are sold at a discount ($75 for a $100 bond, for instance), H bonds are sold at their full face value, and the government sends the buyer an interest payment every half year, smaller payments in the early years, larger payments as the bonds approach maturity. Thus, in 1975 H bonds yielded 4.2% for the first six months and 5.8% for the next 4½ years, with a 6½% yield during the last five years. Whereas E bonds come in denominations as small as $25, the smallest H bond is $500.

Despite all the differences between various issues, government bonds have one common characteristic: they are regarded as the safest investments in the world.

What security lies behind them? The pledged word of the government of the United States. Just that. Nothing else. As long as that word is believed and accepted —as it must be by all Americans, since we *are* the government in the last analysis—government bonds, if held to maturity, offer the best protection you can find against the risk of losing any of your capital.

But because their prices do not rise in an inflation, they offer poor protection against the risk that your dollars will lose something of their purchasing power if prices generally go up. Thus, if you had paid $75 for an E bond in June 1964 and held it, that bond would have been worth $123 to you in June 1975, but the goods that you could buy with that amount of money would have cost you only $72.28 in June 1964. You would actually have lost $2.72 in buying power on the deal, thanks to the tremendous increase in the cost of living.

Like the federal government, states, cities, and other units of local government, such as school districts and housing authorities, need capital—to build schools, roads, hospitals, and sewers and to carry on the many other public projects which are their responsibility. So they too issue bonds, and these are called *municipal bonds*.

Unlike the federal government, which underwrites its own bonds, these local units of government go to the investment bankers for their money, just as a corporation does, and the banker underwrites municipal bond issues in very much the way that corporate bonds are underwritten and sold.

The growth of municipal bond issues since the end of World War II has been little short of fantastic. In the early 1940s when new municipal bonds were being issued at the rate of only about $1 billion a year, the total value of all outstanding issues was just short of $20 billion. By the end of 1974, thanks to our expanding economy and public demand for all kinds of new municipal facilities, that figure had grown to nearly $190 billion, almost a ten-fold increase.

With tens of thousands of municipal bond issues on the market, the investor is confronted with a wide range of maturities, quality ratings, and yields. For many years, interest rates on municipal bonds ranged in the neighborhood of 3% to 4%, occasionally as high as 5%, but when interest rates surged to all-time highs in 1973–1974, municipals sold at prices that yielded returns of 7%, 8%, even 9%.

And what made those rates especially attractive was that the interest collected on a municipal bond is totally exempt from federal income tax. Thus an investor in a 50% tax bracket who got a return of 7% in dividends on common stock or in interest on bonds would only be able to retain half the income, but if he got 7% on a municipal bond he would be able to keep all of it, free of federal income tax.

Not only that, but in many states if he bought a municipal bond issued by some city or town or other taxing authority within the state, the interest he collected on that bond would also be exempt from state taxes. That might mean another 5% or 6% of tax-free income. In short, an individual with an income in the $100,000 range might realize more aggregate "take home" income from municipal bonds than he would get from an investment that yielded him a taxable return of nearly 20%, assuming he could find such an animal.

Is it any wonder that municipal bonds have proved increasingly attractive to investors in the upper income brackets? So much so, in fact, that Congress has been repeatedly tempted to revoke that exemption from the federal income tax which municipal bonds enjoy, but on such occasions cities, towns, and other local taxing authorities have complained so loudly that Congress has always backed down. But that may not always be the case.

No one but an expert can hope to know all about the different characteristics, the different qualities, of municipal bonds, but in the main they offer the investor a good degree of safety, plus the assurance that he can always sell his bond in the open market if he doesn't want to hold it to maturity. Consequently, municipal bond prices are usually more stable than those of stocks, although in the 1973–1974 slump prices did fall about 25%, and it was this drop, of course, that resulted in the spectacular increase in yields, up to a level of 9%

As far as the ultimate payoff on maturity is concerned, municipal bonds can be considered "safe" because the word of any unit of government, like the word of the federal government, can generally be believed and accepted.

There are five generally recognized kinds of municipal bonds. *General obligation bonds,* which constitute by far the largest category of municipals, are generally considered to be the blue chips of the business, because with rare exceptions they are backed by the full faith, credit, and taxing power of the state or municipality that issues them. Both the principal and interest on such bonds are virtually guaranteed by the ability of the state or city to tap tax revenues as necessary to pay off its obligations. In contrast, *special tax bonds* are payable only from the proceeds of a particular tax or some other particular source of revenue and do not carry a "full faith and credit" guarantee.

One type of bond which may appear to be a general obligation bond but actually isn't, because it is not backed by the full faith and credit of the issuing agency, ran into a great deal of trouble in 1975. These bonds are generally known as *unsecured bonds* and the issuing agency simply acknowledges its *"moral obligation"* to guarantee repayment. New York State issued such bonds to raise money to finance urban renewal projects built by its *Urban Development Corp.,* but when New York banks in 1975 refused to buy more of these bonds, the U.D.C. was forced into bankruptcy, and the state had to reorganize its method of financing such institutions. Other similar unsecured bonds have been issued by various agencies in many states, and these too were threatened by the same sort of cold shoulder from the banks, always the principal buyers of such issues.

Revenue bonds are issued to finance specific projects —toll roads, bridges, power projects, hospitals, various utilities, and the like—and the principal and interest on such bonds are payable solely from the revenues collected on such projects. In some cases a state will back a toll road project with its own credit, but this is not usual. Turnpike bonds are also known as *dollar bonds* because they are quoted on a price basis rather than in terms of their yields, as most municipals are quoted. Again, unlike most municipals, dollar bonds usually mature on a single date rather than over a period of time.

Housing Authority bonds are issued to finance low-rent housing projects and are backed by the Federal Housing Assistance Agency, and this guarantee gives them a top-quality rating, since the full faith and credit of the United States stands behind them.

Industrial revenue bonds are issued to finance the building of industrial plants and thus attract industry to a community and expand the local tax base. The bonds are secured by the lease payments which the issuing authority collects from the corporate tenants. Their popularity was such that $1.6 billion of these bonds were issued in 1968, but toward the end of the year Congress raised the question of whether such developments were entitled to tax exemptions and imposed legislative restrictions of such stringency that new issues were sharply curtailed.

There are no restrictions, however, on certain types of industrial revenue bonds, such as those issued to build airports, pollution control facilities, or hospitals. Hospital bonds have been especially popular in the past few years, because of a growing reliance on Blue Cross, Blue Shield, and other programs which probably pay about 90% of all hospital bills.

Most municipal bonds are bearer bonds, and they

The Advantage of Owning Tax-Free Municipal Bonds

Comparative after-tax yields from taxable vs. tax-exempt securities based on federal tax rates as of January 1975. At the various income levels shown in the column at the left, you can realize as great a return from municipal bonds with yields shown on the top line as you can from taxable dividends or interest shown in the corresponding box below.

If you are married,* and your taxable income is	3%	3½%	4%	4½%	5%	5½%	6%	6½%	7%	7½%	8%
$ 28,000–32,000	4.92	5.74	6.56	7.38	8.20	9.02	9.84	10.66	11.48	12.30	13.11
32,000–36,000	5.17	6.03	6.90	7.76	8.62	9.48	10.34	11.21	12.07	12.93	13.79
36,000–40,000	5.45	6.36	7.27	8.18	9.09	10.00	10.91	11.82	12.73	13.64	14.55
40,000–44,000	5.77	6.73	7.69	8.65	9.62	10.58	11.54	12.50	13.46	14.42	15.38
44,000–52,000	6.00	7.00	8.00	9.00	10.00	11.00	12.00	13.00	14.00	15.00	16.00
52,000–64,000	6.38	7.45	8.51	9.57	10.64	11.70	12.77	13.83	14.89	15.96	17.02
64,000–76,000	6.67	7.78	8.89	10.00	11.11	12.22	13.33	14.44	15.56	16.67	17.78
76,000–88,000	7.14	8.33	9.52	10.71	11.90	13.10	14.29	15.58	16.67	17.86	19.05
88,000–100,000	7.50	8.75	10.00	11.25	12.50	13.75	15.00	16.25	17.50	18.75	20.00
100,000–120,000	7.89	9.21	10.53	11.84	13.16	14.47	15.79	17.11	18.42	19.74	21.05
120,000–140,000	8.33	9.72	11.11	12.50	13.89	15.28	16.67	18.06	19.44	20.83	22.22
140,000–160,000	8.82	10.29	11.76	13.24	14.71	16.18	17.65	19.12	20.59	22.06	23.53
160,000–180,000	9.38	10.94	12.50	14.06	15.63	17.19	18.75	20.31	21.88	23.44	25.00
180,000–200,000	9.68	11.29	12.90	14.52	16.13	17.74	19.35	20.97	22.58	24.19	25.81
Over 200,000	10.00	11.67	13.33	15.00	16.67	18.33	20.00	21.67	23.33	25.00	26.67

*Single persons can find out how they would fare in owning tax-exempt securities by looking at the income level double their present income.

mature serially—that is, a certain number of bonds in each issue mature in each year over a period ranging up to 50 years. Quality ratings are provided on municipal bonds (Aaa, Aa, A, Baa, etc.) just as they are on corporate bonds.

Municipal bonds are bought principally by banks, fire and casualty insurance companies, and estates, but the wealthy individual constitutes a steadily widening market because of that all-important tax exemption feature.

The table on page 51 shows just what return an individual at various income levels would have to earn on stocks or other taxable investments in order to retain after federal income taxes as much as he could realize from tax-exempt municipal bonds with coupons ranging from 3% to 8%. These figures are based on tax rates as they existed in 1975.

CHAPTER 8

How Stocks Are Bought and Sold

THE stocks of the biggest and best-known corporations in America are bought and sold on the New York Stock Exchange. In World War II days, the average daily trading volume was less than a million shares, but with increased interest in share ownership, trading volume has expanded almost steadily so that even in a market slump as in 1973–1974, the daily volume averaged 15 million shares, and when the bull market really took hold at the beginning of 1976, the turnover rose to 30 million shares or more a day. The all-time trading record was broken on February 19 with 39.2 million shares and again the next day with 44.5 million, and prospects were that even that record wouldn't last long.

A 20-million-share day is likely to represent about a billion dollars worth of stock, and that much money has a lot of glamour about it. It builds its own folklore. As a consequence, the New York Stock Exchange is one of the most publicized institutions in the world, the very symbol of American capitalism.

But somehow that publicity has got in the way of public understanding, so much so that the stock exchange could almost be described as the business nobody knows—the business nobody knows but everybody talks about.

A lot of people think the stock exchange sells stock. It doesn't. It doesn't own any, doesn't sell any, doesn't buy any. If stocks sold on the exchange lose or gain $100 million in the aggregate on a given day, the exchange itself neither loses nor gains a plugged nickel. It is simply a marketplace where thousands of people buy and sell stocks every day through their agents, the brokers.

Nor does the stock exchange have anything to do with fixing the price at which any of those stocks is bought and sold. The prices are arrived at in a two-way auction system: the buyer competes with other buyers for the lowest price, and the seller competes with other sellers for the highest price. Hence, the stock exchange can boast that it's the freest free market in the world, the one in which there is the least impediment to the free interplay of supply and demand.

When the buyer with the highest bid and the seller with the lowest offering price conclude a transaction, each can know that he got the best price he could at that moment. As buyer or seller, you may not be wholly satisfied, but you can't blame the stock exchange any more than you can blame the weatherman if it's too hot or too cold for you.

Stock prices can and do fluctuate sharply—they dropped 36% in 1969–1970 and 45% in 1973–1974—but these price movements simply reflect the optimism or pessimism of shareowners about business prospects at that time.

Perhaps you've heard that the stock market is "rigged," that big operators drive prices up or hammer them down to suit themselves and make a profit at the little fellow's expense. Yes, that did happen—as recently as the 1920s. Big market operators resorted to all kinds of questionable devices to *manipulate* stock prices to their own advantage.

But today there are laws, stringent laws, to prevent price manipulation, and they are vigorously enforced by the Securities and Exchange Commission. The abuses of the twenties, which were blamed in part for the great market crash of 1929–1932, when prices fell 89%, brought the Securities and Exchange Commission into being in 1934, and thirty years later, after an exhaustive study of the securities business, the commission got from Congress a substantial grant of additional power to help it in its work of policing the markets. This was the Securities Acts Amendment of 1964.

The Securities Reform Act of 1975 not only augmented that power by revising certain old regulations and introducing new ones, but it also gave the S.E.C.

additional funds to increase its staff, thus enabling it to supervise the markets more closely and to enforce its rules and regulations more rigorously.

Actually, the commission leaves much of the regulatory work in the hands of the exchange which, in turn, clamps down on its member firms. The N.Y.S.E. rules are generally designed to prevent unfair trading practices and protect the individual investor. They were tightened when the exchange was reorganized in the thirties, and they were tightened again in many areas as a result of the enactment of the 1964 amendment. But these reforms were as nothing compared to that imposed on Wall Street by the Reform Act of 1975. Repercussions to that reform will be felt right down the line for a long time to come—from top management right down to the *"runners,"* or messengers, who make daily deliveries and pickups all over the financial district.

Today, there is probably no business in the world that operates under more stringent regulation or with a stricter self-imposed code of ethics than the New York Stock Exchange.

For instance, the exchange has a computerized *stockwatching* service which keeps under constant surveillance the price and volume movements of all stocks traded on the exchange. The computer is programmed to flag automatically any unusual movements in a stock, and these are followed up by investigators. Sometimes a rumor can make a stock "act up." Is there anything to it? If not, the exchange takes immediate steps to scotch the rumor; sometimes it asks the company itself to clarify the facts in the situation and announce them to the public. And if the computer ever turns up evidence of illegal manipulation, the exchange turns those facts over to the S.E.C. for action.

When the original securities law was first enacted in 1934, Congress even undertook to protect the buyer of securities (and the seller too) against himself—against his own greed and rashness. Before 1934, you could buy securities with only a small down payment, or *margin*. Typically it was 20%. Often it was less. And an occasional customer even "bought" securities 100% on credit—without putting up a dime. That's how a few people made a fortune on a shoestring, but it's also how more of them brought disaster on themselves and thousands of others in the 1929 crash.

Nowadays, the *Federal Reserve Board* decides what the minimum down payment shall be, and its decision is binding on everybody. The board changes the figure from time to time, depending on how much restraint it thinks it should apply to the market. Since 1934, it has ranged from as low as 40% of the purchase price up to 100%, and when the 100% rule prevailed, that meant there was no credit at all; the buyer had to pay in full for his stocks.

This power alone—the power of the Reserve Board to say what the minimum margin shall be—guarantees that there will never be another market crash quite like 1929. Stock prices are bound to go down from time to time, and down sharply. Indeed, in 1937–1938, despite the regulatory powers of the federal government, they dropped about 50% in just twelve months; and there have been many drops of 25% or more since then. But it can still be said that the market can never crash as spectacularly as it did in 1929.

That can't happen again, because under the Reserve Board's margin regulation, prices can never be as over-inflated as they were when people bought hundreds of millions of dollars worth of stocks by putting up only a small fraction of that amount in cash.

One noteworthy result of all the regulations that have been imposed on the market has been a change in the character of the market itself. It has become more of an investor's market, less of a speculator's market. Of course, speculators still buy and sell stocks in the hope of making a profit, and this function is not only legitimate but useful and desirable in the main, because it helps provide a continuous and liquid market. It helps stabilize prices, thus permitting the investor to buy and sell more readily and at fairer prices.

Nevertheless, more of the people who buy stocks to-day are doing so for the sake of earning a good return on their money over the long pull. They are not *"in-and-outers,"* people trading for a small profit on every market move. Generally, they hold their stocks for years and years. They're investors—people who want to be part owners of those biggest and best-known corporations.

All told, on the New York Stock Exchange, the stocks of 1,559 of these companies were *listed* as of January 31, 1976, which means that they have been accepted for trading there. Collectively, these listed companies employ about 20% of all workers, but they account for almost 40% of sales and over 70% of all corporate profits.

To qualify for listing on the exchange a company has to pay an initial listing fee of $25,000, plus a small per share charge. It also must pay an annual fee for as long as its stock is listed, which ranges from $10,000 to $50,000 depending upon the number of listed shares. More important, it must meet certain requirements, which have become more exacting over the years. In 1975, these were the principal qualifications a company had to meet if it wished to have its securities traded on the New York Stock Exchange:

(1) A minimum of 2,000 shareholders of 100 shares or more.

(2) A minimum of 1 million common shares outstanding, which must be owned by the public, not by the company itself.

(3) A market value for its publicly owned shares of at least $16 million.

(4) Annual earnings of at least $2.5 million before taxes in the most recent year and at least $2 million in each of the two preceding years.

(5) Net tangible assets of at least $16 million.

Most of the listed companies exceed these regulations by a wide margin. The biggest of the companies, American Telephone & Telegraph, had 2,926,000 shareholders at the end of 1974. General Motors ranked second with 1,326,000. American Telephone also held top ranking in the number of shares listed with 559.8 million, and in the market value of listed shares with nearly $25 billion.

Not all companies prosper, of course, and that's why

the exchange has a set of minimum standards that a company must meet in order to keep its stock listed there. It might be *delisted* unless it has at least 1,200 shareholders, each of whom must own a minimum of 100 shares; unless publicly owned shares total at least 600,000 with a market value of $5 million; or unless the aggregate market value of all its common stock is at least $8 million and net earnings for the past three years have averaged $600,000 minimum. About 40 common stocks on average have been delisted every year over the past fifteen years for various reasons, but many of these delistings resulted from mergers with other listed companies, particularly in the late 1960s.

But these mathematical standards are not the only basis for delisting. In recent years, companies have been delisted for management's refusal to give voting rights to holders of its common stock or because of consistent failure to produce timely and meaningful financial reports. Indeed, the exchange may suspend or delist at any time a security in which it considers that continued dealings are not advisable, even though that security meets listing standards.

All listed companies must agree to publish *quarterly reports* on their financial condition, as certified by independent accountants. In the old days, only annual reports were required, and some companies were admitted on these terms. Nevertheless, almost all listed companies now report quarterly.

A company must agree not to issue any additional shares without exchange approval, and it must have a *registrar* in New York City to see that no more shares of stock are issued than a company has authority to sell. It must also have a *transfer agent* who keeps an exact record of all stockholders, their names, addresses, and number of shares owned.

The companies whose stocks and bonds are traded on the exchange have nothing to say about its operation. The brokers run their own show, although the paid chairman of the exchange must be a man who has no connection with the securities business and the 21-man board of directors, which includes the chairman, must contain ten public members who have no identification with the securities business. The chairman is chosen annually by the board of directors.

Although the exchange became incorporated in 1971, primarily to relieve its officers and directors of individual liability in the event of lawsuits against the exchange, it remains essentially what it has always been —a purely voluntary association of individual members, whose number totals 1,366. It is the "private club" aspect of the exchange which disturbs the S.E.C. deeply, and in recent years, as the exchange has become increasingly aware of its social responsibilities, it has begun to operate more like a publicly owned business and less like a club.

The business of trading in stocks in New York goes back to the early eighteenth century, when merchants and auctioneers used to congregate at the foot of Wall Street to buy and sell not only stocks but wheat, tobacco, and other commodities, including slaves.

In 1792, two dozen merchants who used to meet daily under a buttonwood tree on Wall Street and trade various stocks agreed from then on to deal only with each other and to charge their customers a fixed commission. Thus began the New York Stock Exchange.

How do you become a member of this association today? If you are approved by the exchange's board of directors, you buy a *seat*. Since nobody but a mailman is on his feet more continuously than a broker, that is one of the classic misnomers of our language. It had its origin in the leisurely days of 1793 when the new association took up quarters in the Tontine Coffee House and the members could be seated while they transacted business.

What does a seat cost? That depends on how good business is on the exchange. In 1929, three different seats were sold at $625,000 each. Later the number of seats was increased 25%, so no one of them afterwards was worth quite as much, but it is hard to believe they could ever fall again to the low they hit in 1942, when one was sold for $17,000, which is less than the amount regularly given as a gift to the family of a member on his death out of the exchange's *gra-*

tuity fund, supported by all the members. In 1968, a seat was sold for $515,000, and, considering the 25% increase in the number of seats, this figure represented an even higher price than in 1929. So discouraging were the succeeding market slumps of 1969 and 1973–1974, however, that in 1975 a stock exchange seat brought only $55,000.

A number of the seats—about eighty in 1975, as contrasted with more than a hundred some years ago —are owned by men who aren't really brokers at all. They are *registered floor traders,* men who buy and sell stocks wholly for themselves. Because they pay no commissions, by virtue of their membership in the exchange, they are able to make money by moving in and out of the market, trying to make a quarter of a point here, an eighth of a point there—usually in the most active stocks.

In its extensive study of the market, which supplied the groundwork for the 1964 act, the Securities and Exchange Commission took the position that floor traders performed no useful economic function and that they should be phased out of existence. This the exchange has strongly resisted. Nevertheless, it did come up with a set of new rules to govern traders' activities. These provide that 75% of a trader's transactions must be of a "stabilizing" nature. To qualify as "stabilizing," a purchase can be made only when the price on the preceding sale was down, and a sale can be made only when the price on the preceding sale was up. Other rules are designed to make sure that the traders, who now account for less than 1% of total volume, enjoy no advantage over the public.

Many brokers on the floor earn their living by executing buy or sell orders for the public and, especially, for large institutions, either directly or indirectly. In 1975, there were 500 *member firms* represented on the exchange, of which half were partnerships and half were corporations, and they owned some 1,300 seats. In 1975, these brokerage firms operated 3,198 offices throughout the United States and 243 offices abroad. In still other cities they are represented by thousands of *correspondents.* Usually these correspondents are local security dealers or banks that have wire connections to some member firm.

At least a million miles of private telephone and teletype wires keep all the offices of these brokerage firms, the so-called *wire houses,* in almost instantaneous touch with the exchange, and as a result the man who may have his office next door to the exchange has no advantage over the man who lives 3,000 miles away.

CHAPTER 9

What It Costs to Buy Stocks

FROM the time the New York Stock Exchange was founded in 1792 until May 1, 1975, any broker in the business could have told you to the penny just how much commission you would have to pay on the purchase or sale of 100 shares or 1,000 shares of any listed stock. It was all very simple because those two dozen founding fathers of the New York Stock Exchange had agreed from the outset to charge the same commission on any security transaction, and they had further agreed to deal only with each other—no outsiders admitted. For more than 192 years, the succeeding members of the New York Stock Exchange maintained that same tight little monopoly.

Then came May 1, 1975. That was the day the Securities and Exchange Commission put an end to all fixed commissions on the stock exchange. In one blow, the S.E.C. on "Mayday" blasted away the very cornerstone of the exchange.

So how much will it cost you to buy stocks today in this new era of competitive commissions?

There are several different answers to that.

The first is—a lot less than you probably think, especially if you are thinking in terms of the 6% to 10% commission you might pay on a real estate transaction, or the even higher commissions paid to automobile or life insurance salesmen. The fact is that no goods or services of comparable value change hands at as low a commission cost as do stocks. And that has always been true whether commissions were fixed or unfixed. It's still true.

The second and more realistic answer is to tell you that the amount of commission you pay is going to vary with the total dollar value of your transaction. If your transaction is a modest one—say, an investment of $2,000 or $3,000—the commission is apt to be somewhere near 2½%. But if your investment involves $10,000 or $20,000, the commission may be only around 1½%. And if you're a really big operator with a transaction involving $100,000 or more, you might well bargain yourself into a commission cost that is only a fraction of 1%.

Despite the outlawing of fixed commissions, don't be surprised if you find three or four firms all quoting you pretty much the same commission on a modest transaction involving only a few thousand dollars. But that won't be the case if you are talking big money—anything above $10,000 or $15,000. Then it's going to pay you to shop around for the best commission deal you can get. Another thing to remember is that you will probably get a better commission deal if you agree to pay for stock in advance and if you are willing to give the broker an extra day to execute your order.

Regardless of the size of your transaction, you might feel that it would be helpful if you knew just what the commission would have been on the same transaction back in the days when commissions were fixed, back before May 1, 1975. That's understandable, but the blunt fact of the matter is that the last commission schedule of the New York Stock Exchange was so complicated that to set it down here would only confuse you the more. If you really want to know what the commission would have been then on a given number of shares bought or sold at a given price, you had better ask your broker. If he still has an old schedule around and time for all the mathematical calculations involved, he should be able to come up with a precise answer. Here is the story of how the once sacrosanct schedule of fixed commissions on the New York Stock Exchange disintegrated in just a few short years.

Complications in the old commission schedule arose because when the market fell in 1973–1974 and volume dried up, the brokers sought one increase after another from the Securities and Exchange Commission. For example, before those increases, the basic commission on a 100-share order involving more than $2,000 but less than $2,500 was 1.3% plus $12, and on orders of $2,500 or more it was 0.9% plus $22, and no commission on such an order could exceed $65. Then the brokers got the S.E.C. to give them their first increase—an additional 10% on all orders up to and including $5,000 and 15% on orders of more than $5,000. Then another increase of 8% was permitted on orders exceeding $5,000. With all these increases taken into consideration, the maximum commission was moved up from $65 to $80.73 for any 100-share order, or *round lot,* as such an order is called.

Since the commission on 100 shares of a stock selling just above $50 a share—say, 50⅛—figures out to just a few dollars more than that maximum commission of $80.73, it is obvious that the higher the price of the stock you bought, the lower your commission as a percentage of the total sales price. For instance, anyone who bought or sold a round lot of IBM at $220 a share under the fixed commission system got a real break because that $80.73 maximum commission amounted to only 0.37% of the total value of the order.

Not long before Mayday a different and even more complicated schedule of commissions was applied to orders of 200, 300, or 400 shares—any multiple of a round lot of the same stock. Nevertheless, under this schedule the commission you were charged could not exceed the regular 100-share commission on that stock times the number of such round lots you bought or sold.

Finally, there was a third schedule of fixed commissions that applied only to orders involving fewer than 100 shares of a single stock. These commissions were actually $2 lower than the commissions charged on round lots of equal dollar value, but this saving was more apparent than real because anyone who bought less than 100 shares of a stock had to pay an extra ⅛ of a point or 12½¢ a share above the last execution price of a round lot of that stock, and he lost ⅛ of a point if he sold less than 100 shares.

All three schedules provided that the commission was to be "negotiated"—usually at a higher rate—on any order of $2,000 or less. Consequently, the investor who bought or sold less than a round lot or who traded in low-priced stocks, had to watch his step pretty carefully if he wanted to have the advantage of the fixed schedule. Because of that $2,000 minimum, he would find himself forced into negotiating the commission— probably a higher commission percentagewise—if he bought or sold fewer than 101 shares of a $20 stock, 67 shares of a $30 stock, 41 shares of a $50 stock, 29 shares of a $70 stock and 21 shares of a $100 stock.

Yes, the last fixed commission schedule was pretty complicated. But if you want a few guideposts to help you when you are shopping around nowadays to see which broker will give you the best commission deal, here they are:

(1) Under fixed commissions, the maximum commission on any round lot was $80.73. The old schedule might have yielded a higher commission on stocks selling above $50, but $80.73 was the most you could have been charged per 100 shares regardless of the price of the stock.

(2) On a round lot of a stock selling at $50 or less a share, here are representative commissions you would have had to pay at different price levels.

On a $50 stock	$71.50	1.43
On a $45 stock	68.75	1.53
On a $40 stock	63.80	1.60
On a $35 stock	58.85	1.68
On a $30 stock	53.90	1.80
On a $25 stock	48.95	1.96
On a $22 stock	44.66	2.03
Stocks selling at		
$20 or below		negotiable

(3) On any order involving multiple round lots—200, 300, 400 shares—your commission would have been the round lot commission, as above, times the multiple—2, 3, 4, etc.

(4) On orders of less than 100 shares, the commission charge would have been $2.00 less than those in the table above where equal amounts of dollars were involved, but you would have to pay 12½¢ more per share if you bought and you would receive 12½¢ less per share if you sold. And remember, too, that you

had to buy at least $2,000 worth of stock or resign yourself to paying a negotiated commission somewhat above the fixed rate—maybe as much as 3% or 4%, and if you only wanted to buy ten shares of a $10 stock, you might conceivably have paid the maximum of 6%.

So these are some of the guideposts to keep in mind when a broker tells you what his commission rates are nowadays.

But there's something else to keep in mind too, and that's the possibility that the broker might exact a service charge over and above the commission for executing your order.

Service charges come in a variety of different packages. Some brokers may charge you for keeping your stocks for you, thus saving you the cost of renting a safe deposit box, and they might even add a further charge for collecting dividends on your stocks and crediting them to your account.

Of course, if you were a good customer, if you bought and sold stocks frequently, the brokers might be willing to waive such service charges on your account just to keep you happy. But remember, no firm wants to hold 100 shares of stock for you year after year, credit dividends to your account, and send you regular statements unless the firm gets something for it. Such service costs the broker money, and he likes to see a little action in your account to generate commissions that will offset the firm's out-of-pocket costs.

Service charges may also be exacted to cover the cost of statistical reports on individual companies that he furnishes you—reports that the broker may buy from one of the large securities research firms or that his own research department may produce.

And if you hold stocks in a number of different companies and want advice from his research department on what to hold, what to sell, and what to buy as replacements—with reasons why in all cases—you may well be charged for that kind of service.

So when you go shopping for a broker, don't just

ask about his commission rates; ask about his service charges too.

There are some brokers who make no service charge of any kind. They figure they ought to be able to give the average customer whatever he wants just for the sake of the commissions they earn on his business.

The Securities and Exchange Commission, however, looks with some disfavor on this one-charge-for-everything concept. It is a strong advocate of what it calls *unbundling*—hanging specific price tags on all the services that a broker may render, over and above the commission that he earns just for executing orders. The S.E.C. argues that if a broker provides various services for customers, he has to pay for those services, and the cost of each should be clearly marked, not just wrapped up together in the total commission cost. Brokers who follow a "no-service-charge" policy reply that the S.E.C. has no right to tell them how to run their business. They contend that it's their business if they want to absorb the cost of supplying special services to their customers, all for a single commission. If they can cover those costs and still keep their rates competitive with other brokers, they figure they will be able to attract more customers.

One thing you should always remember is that some brokers will have an interest in your business if you only want to buy 10 or 20 shares and some brokers won't—and their commission schedules are geared that way. Some brokers may be willing, even anxious, to execute a small order for you, even if they lose money on it from a cost accounting point of view, because they are willing to gamble that somewhere down the line you will become a more substantial customer, maybe even a big trader. But many brokers, probably most of them, aren't willing to take that gamble. They are interested in the big-ticket customer—and you can be sure their commission schedules will be skewed to discourage you from bringing them your 10-share order.

One final word about brokerage service: You can get as much or as little as you want and are willing to pay for, so it pays to find your kind of broker. If you are an investor who makes up his own mind about what he wants to buy or sell—a person who doesn't want any advice or help from his broker—you might as well take your order to one of the firms that Wall Street calls *"pipe rack" stores*—firms that specialize in easy-to-fill orders, or "no brainers," as they are called. Chances are that their commission charges will be somewhat lower because they don't pretend to offer any service other than the execution of orders.

On the other hand, you may want or need a good deal of help—maybe even a little psychological support. If you're that kind of person, then the brokerage firm that runs what Wall Street calls *"boutique shops"* will happily give you everything you want—at a price.

So while you're shopping around for a broker, collecting commission rate schedules, give an eye to the kind of service provided to a customer and find out what that is going to cost you. One thing you needn't bother looking for is a cut price. When a broker sets a commission schedule he expects all his salesmen to stick by it, and if you think a special exception should be made in your case, you're probably going to have to argue your case with somebody pretty far up the line —and it's not likely to be an argument you are going to win very easily.

When you are out looking for a broker, you may find yourself wondering what happened that brought this revolution to Wall Street. For almost 200 years you had to pay the same commission charge no matter what member firm you dealt with—and now brokers are really competing with each other. What accounts for the change?

The explanation is really very simple. Even the monolithic, monopolistic New York Stock Exchange could not withstand the pressures of the marketplace—the inexorable operation of the law of supply and demand. This is what actually brought the stock exchange to its knees. The S.E.C. simply administered the *coup de grace*.

It all began back in the fifties when big-money institutions—banks, insurance companies, foundations, trusts—began to realize that common stocks were pretty good investments in inflationary times. And when a big institution goes into the market, it's apt to make quite a splash because it buys and sells stocks in big blocks—10,000, 25,000, and maybe even 50,000 shares at a time. But back in the fifties and sixties the lowest commission rate charged by the New York Stock Exchange was the commission on 100 shares, a round lot. If somebody wanted to buy 5,000 shares of stock, he had to pay 50 times the fixed round-lot commission. And if he wanted 10,000 shares, he had to pay 100 times the round-lot commission.

That didn't make much sense to the institutions. They felt they deserved a commission break on their big-volume business—something better than the fixed round-lot commission rate. True, the New York Stock Exchange did provide various means by which big buyers and sellers could circumvent the exchange's iron-clad commission rules, but these devices were at best cumbersome and cost the institutions more than they thought they should have to pay.

So the big institutions began looking for a better way, a way to trade blocks of stock more easily and at a lower cost to themselves. And they found it—outside the New York Stock Exchange. They found that there were big securities dealers—firms like Weeden & Co. that were not members of the exchange, hence not bound by its commission rules—who were quite willing and able to buy, or *position,* a block of stocks, thousands of shares at a crack, and then assume the risk of reselling it, hopefully at a profit to themselves over a period of time.

Such nonmember firms didn't even bother with commissions. They simply bought the stock at a *net price,* a price that was a little lower than the price prevailing on the exchange but high enough to guarantee the seller a better net return than if he had sold the stock on the exchange and paid the commission cost.

Thus the *third market* was born—"third" because the two big exchanges, the New York Stock Exchange and the *American Stock Exchange,* had long ago usurped the right to be known as the first and second markets for securities in the United States.

Alarmed by the sensational growth of the third market—and the loss of institutional business transacted on the exchange—member firms in 1966 went to the S.E.C. and asked for the right to relax the shackles that the exchange had forged for itself.

First, they asked for an amendment to *Rule 394,* the rule that compelled members to execute all orders for listed stocks on the floor of the exchange and effectively prevented any trading with nonmembers or splitting of commissions with them. This rule, of course, was nothing but the twentieth-century successor to the agreement which the founding fathers had reached under the buttonwood tree in 1792 that they would buy and sell securities only with each other. Obligingly, the S.E.C. permitted a modification of Rule 394 to permit a member to buy or sell off the floor of the exchange—in short, to participate in the third market—if he could demonstrate that such a deal with a nonmember would result in a more advantageous trade to his customer.

That amendment helped, but still the shackles of the fixed commission system chafed. In 1969, rates were reduced on orders of 1,000 shares or more, but that wasn't enough to satisfy the institutions by a long shot. Soon member firms began agitating for total abandonment of fixed commissions on all big-ticket orders, and the S.E.C. tentatively suggested that commissions on all orders exceeding $100,000 might be made subject to negotiation between the member firm and the buyer or seller.

That suggestion shocked many of the more staid members of the exchange who were used to doing business with a select clientele that definitely did not include hard-bargaining institutions. But then came the real bombshell. Robert W. Haack, then president of the New York Stock Exchange, advanced the revolutionary idea that no commissions should be fixed on orders *of any size* executed on the exchange, that the law of supply and demand, the rule of free competition, should supplant the monopolistic schedule of fixed commissions.

This was heresy, indeed—and from a paid hand at that! And when *Merrill Lynch, Pierce, Fenner & Smith, Inc.,* the world's largest brokerage firm, and *Salomon Brothers,* a member firm that played a dominant role in handling institutional business, endorsed the no-fixed-commission proposal, the fears of many smaller firms about how they might fare in an era of free competition were scarcely allayed.

Caught between the big firms that wanted a larger slice of the institutional business and the smaller firms that feared they might go under without the protection of a fixed-commission system, the S.E.C. finally stuck a timid toe in the water. In April 1971, the commission ruled there should be no more fixed rates on orders involving $500,000 or more, that commissions on all such orders should be subject to negotiation or bargaining between customer and broker. Soon member firms began to get more and more of the big-ticket business, and institutional transactions which had accounted for only about 20% of exchange volume in the early sixties soon doubled, and they were destined to account for 60% of exchange transactions in a decade—some days even as much as 75%. However, as long as the third market also continued to prosper, the big-ticket brokers weren't happy. So within a year, they were back knocking on the S.E.C.'s door asking for the right to negotiate commissions on all transactions of more than $300,000.

It was then, just when the commission was putting its case together to ask Congress for many basic reforms in the law governing the securities business, that the decision was made to go all out and order the abandonment of fixed commissions on all exchanges, effective May 1, 1975—a position strongly supported by the Antitrust Division of the Department of Justice.

Ten years earlier, a Chicago investor had brought suit against the New York Stock Exchange, contending that its fixed commission system violated the *antitrust laws,* but the United States Supreme Court held finally that the exchange was exempt from the antitrust laws because the S.E.C. had the power to regulate its commission rates. Despite this defeat in the *Kaplan case,* the Antitrust Division, which bluntly told the S.E.C. that it considered all "private rate fixing illegal," persisted in its campaign against the exchange. Ironically, the United States Supreme Court, still turning a deaf ear to the Antitrust Division, ruled in June 1975 (*Gordon vs. New York Stock Exchange*), as it had before, that the exchange was immune to the antitrust laws because of the S.E.C.'s authority to fix commission rates. But by the that time, the whole question was purely academic, for Mayday had come and gone and the fixed commission schedule had become a dead letter—by order of the S.E.C. and with the obvious blessing of Congress.

In the end, the New York Stock Exchange, responding as it did to the pressure of outside competition for institutional business, had no one but itself to blame —or credit—for the result.

With the fixed-commission cornerstone blasted away, the question arose whether the New York Stock Exchange could continue to stand. Or maybe the question was how long it could stand. As long as Rule 394 remained on the books, exchange members were obligated to try to execute an order there before concluding a deal with a nonmember in the third market. But the S.E.C. had the power of life and death over Rule 394. How would it use that power?

There was no clear or immediate answer. On the one hand, it was obvious that the commission was dedicated to the concept of a *central securities market* in which exchange members and other *market-makers* would compete with one another in offering the best prices for securities. On the other hand, it was equally obvious that the S.E.C. could not sign the death warrant of an institution so vital to the stability of stock trading throughout the country and throughout the world as the New York Stock Exchange.

The S.E.C. adopted the first alternative when it introduced a second set of rules in May 1976 that increased the competition among brokers on the trading floor. By forcing them to bargain among themselves over the commission they charged each other for executing orders to buy or sell, the S.E.C. hoped to eventually reduce the cost of handling all transactions, regardless of the market where they take place.

In the long run it could be that the answer to the question of the exchange's future might not be supplied by the Securities and Exchange Commission—or even the Congress of the United States—but again by the inexorable laws of the marketplace, the interplay of free competition.

Only a few days after Mayday, Weeden & Co., probably the biggest factor in the development of the third market, announced that it had formed a subsidiary, Dexter Securities Corporation, which would buy a seat on the New York Stock Exchange, thus enabling Weeden & Co. to work both sides of the street, dealing alike with members and nonmembers.

Actually, that idea was not a new one. Five months before Mayday, Dreyfus Corporation, an institution that buys and sells many millions of N.Y.S.E. stocks, had applied for membership on the exchange, and although the application was turned down because exchange rules forbade any such institution to own a seat on the exchange, the handwriting on the wall was writ for all to see.

Day by day, year by year, pressure was sure to mount, and the exchange could not fend off forever the big institutions that sought the right to buy and sell securities without paying tribute to an intermediary—in short, without paying a commission. Within days after May 1, 1975, some member firms of the exchange—and many nonmembers—were cutting their rates on big volume orders right down to the no-profit bone, seeking to appease the institutional customer and trying to postpone the day when they would demand seats on the exchange for themselves.

As for the average investor, he was not faring nearly as well as the big customer. Few if any of the member firms were courting his favor, and virtually no one was offering him bargain commission rates. So Mr. Average Man sat on the sidelines for many months, but even he couldn't resist the attraction of the big bull market that seemed under way in earnest at the beginning of 1976. What if he did have to pay a few more dollars in commissions? He didn't want to miss out on a chance to make big money in the market. What if he was discriminated against as far as commission rates were concerned? Wasn't that always the lot of the little man?

And in this brave new world of free competition, what was the future of the brokerage business? Probably not much different from that of the broker's customers. The big and efficient firms seemed likely to grow bigger and more prosperous, whether they did business on the New York Stock Exchange or in the new national marketplace just a-borning. As for the smaller firm, the future was not rosy. Without the protection of the fixed-rate schedule, such a firm seemed likely to be swallowed up by its big competitor or fall by the wayside. In 1975, nine firms closed their doors and eleven others were swallowed up by bigger, stronger firms. And there were those in Wall Street who freely predicted that only a comparative handful of brokerage firms would be doing business a decade hence—perhaps a hundred, maybe only a half or a quarter that many.

Meanwhile, among the big brokerage firms with their worldwide networks of offices, few were content to sit back and simply count the commission dollars rolling in. They too had reason to worry. Nobody was guaranteeing them the fruits of a future monopoly in the stock-trading business, not as long as those big institutions were intent on getting rid of all middlemen and handling their own securities transactions. To protect themselves, many firms were diversifying their business as rapidly as possible, moving into new fields.

Even before Mayday, Merrill Lynch & Co., by then the parent company of Merrill Lynch, Pierce, Fenner & Smith, had ventured into the insurance field, real estate, merchant banking abroad, and investment counseling. Other big competitors were following Merrill's lead. The figures shown in their annual reports clearly marked the trend. In 1974, at Merrill Lynch, commissions from listed securities accounted for only 30.6% of total income, but ten years earlier commissions had been 50.6% of revenues—a drop of 20% in ten years. At E. F. Hutton, commission revenues as a percentage of income dropped from 62% to 44% between 1970 and 1974, and at Paine, Webber, Jackson & Curtis the decline in the same period was from 55% to 49%.

Clearly, the order of the day in Wall Street was to diversify, and as rapidly as they could brokers were putting out anchors to windward, for they knew that the storms which had ravaged the Street for a decade had not really abated, even though the record-breaking volume of business, occasioned by the bull market of 1975–1976, was filling their coffers as never before.

But despite Wall Street's revolution, despite the ever-growing dominance of the big institutional customers in the stock market, the average individual investor could still count on doing business with his friendly broker in almost any bigger-than-average town in the United States. And there was even the chance that he would get friendlier and friendlier as the new competition between member firms of the New York Stock Exchange grew keener in the years ahead. As long as business was good, no broker was interested in starting a commission price war, but once the bull market volume dried up, as someday it surely would in the ceaseless ebb and flow of the stock market, then rate-cutting was likely to begin in earnest. And then the average investor might once again find himself king for a day.

CHAPTER 10

How the Stock Exchange Works

WHAT actually happens on the New York Stock Exchange when a broker gets an order to buy or sell stock? How is the transaction completed with another broker so that both buyer and seller are assured of the best price possible on the exchange at that moment?

Consider first the physical layout of the stock exchange. It is a big building at the corner of Wall and Broad streets in New York City. (The probability is that the exchange will continue to do business in that building at least through the seventies, despite the fact that it signed a letter of intent with the city to build a new exchange, at least three times bigger, on landfill to be created in the East River at the other end of Wall Street.) The trading room looks somewhat like an armory, with a high ceiling and a *trading floor* about three-fifths the size of a football field.

All around the edge of the trading floor are *telephone booths,* as they are traditionally called, although today they might as appropriately be called teletype booths. These booths bear no resemblance to any other phone booths you have ever seen. Most of them are open at both ends, and along the two sides there are spaces at which a dozen or more clerks, representing various brokers, can work. At each clerk's space, there is a narrow shelf at which he stands and does his paperwork, and above the shelf there is a bank of telephones connecting him with his home office. These phones were once the nerve ends of the entire stock exchange business, for it was through them that all public orders to buy or sell stocks came to the floor of the exchange. The phones are still used, but as part of its modernization program, the exchange permitted most

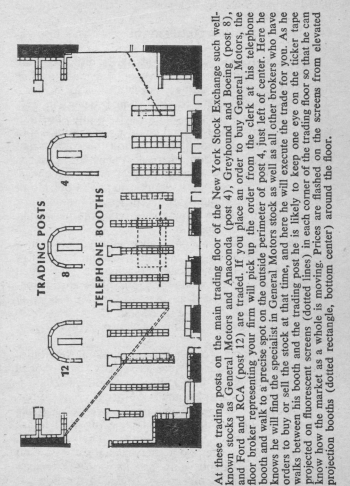

TRADING POSTS

4

8

12

TELEPHONE BOOTHS

At these trading posts on the main trading floor of the New York Stock Exchange such well-known stocks as General Motors and Anaconda (post 4), Greyhound and Boeing (post 8), and Ford and RCA (post 12) are traded. If you place an order to buy General Motors, the floor broker representing your firm will pick up the order from the clerk at his telephone booth and walk to a precise spot on the outside perimeter of post 4, just left of center. Here he knows he will find the specialist in General Motors stock as well as all other brokers who have orders to buy or sell the stock at that time, and here he will execute the trade for you. As he walks between his booth and the trading post he is likely to keep one eye on the ticker tape projected on fluorescent screens (dotted lines) in each corner of the trading floor so that he can know how the market as a whole is moving. Prices are flashed on the screens from elevated projection booths (dotted rectangle, bottom center) around the floor.

large brokerage firms to install teletype equipment in or near the telephone booths so that they could receive orders direct from their branch offices. This eliminated the necessity for relaying orders by phone from the home office to the floor clerk, and since teletype orders are printed, the possibility of error was also reduced.

Spaced at regular intervals on the trading floor are *twenty-two trading posts,* twelve on the main trading floor and six in the "garage," or annex, and an additional four in the new trading room opened in July 1969, called the "blue room." Each trading post, or station, is a horseshoe-shaped counter, occupying about 100 square feet of floor space. Behind the counter, inside the post or station, there is room for a dozen clerks and for several paid employees of the exchange.

All buying and selling is done around the outside of the trading post. About 90 different stocks are assigned to each post in different sections around the perimeter, ten or so to each section.

Little placards on a board above the counter show just which stocks are sold in each section, and below each placard is a price indicator showing the last price at which a transaction in that stock took place and whether this price represented an increase or decrease from the last different price—a plus sign or *up tick* if it represented an increase, a minus sign or *down tick* for a decrease.

When an order is received at the headquarters office of any brokerage firm in New York City, it is phoned over to a clerk in that firm's telephone booth on the exchange floor (unless, of course, the order comes direct to the floor by teletype). Some firms have booth space for only one or two clerks, while one big wire house has about 40 spaces in nine booths. When the clerk gets the order over the phone, he writes it out in a kind of shorthand and hands it to his *floor broker* to execute, because only members can trade on the floor. If the broker is not at the booth, the clerk can summon him by means of a pocket-sized radio receiver, which brokers started carrying in 1971, or by pushing a button located in the firm's booth. Every broker has a number, and when the clerk pushes the button, the broker's number is flashed on large *annunciator boards* in each of the trading rooms.

If the clerk knows his broker is busy with other orders, he employs the services of a so-called *two-dollar broker,* an independent member of the stock exchange who is not connected with a member firm. There are about 100 of these men who own their own seats on the exchange and make their living by executing orders for other brokers or for wire houses who are sometimes too busy to transact all of their business. The two-dollar broker got his name in the days when he received that fee for every order he executed. Nowadays his commission, called *floor brokerage,* is negotiated. For executing an order to buy or sell 100 shares of a $20 stock, he probably would make about $3.50.

Let's assume that with the passage of years Rod & Reel, Inc., has grown to the point where its stock is listed on the New York Stock Exchange, and that the order which the clerk gives his broker is a *market order* to buy 100 shares of Rod & Reel. A market order is one that a broker must execute as soon as he can at the best price he can get. As soon as the broker has the actual order in his hands he walks—no running is permitted on the floor—over to the trading post where Rod & Reel is traded and where he knows he will find any other brokers who might have orders to buy or sell Rod & Reel.

As he approaches the post, he looks at the price indicator and notes that the last sale of Rod & Reel took place at 18¾, which means $18.75 a share. However, some broker may now be willing to sell it for less than that price, and so as he enters the *"crowd"* of other brokers—two, three, or more of them at the trading position—he simply asks, "How's Reel?" He doesn't disclose whether he wants to buy or sell; he just asks the question. Another broker may answer, "Eighteen and three-eighths to eighteen and three-quarters," or simply, "Three-eighths, three-quarters." This means that 18⅜ is the best bid, the most any broker is then willing to pay, and 18¾ is the best offer, the lowest anyone will sell for.

Our broker will try to get the stock cheaper if he can; so he waits a few seconds for other offers. Finally he decides to tip his hand and make a bid. So he says, "One-half for a hundred," by which he means that he will pay $18.50 a share for 100 shares.

If he gets no response, he may raise his bid by ⅛ of a point. This is the minimum fluctuation in the price of most stocks. So he announces, "Five-eighths, for one hundred." At this point, perhaps, the first broker, who was offering the stock at 18¾, may have decided that he can't get that price. Or another broker, who may have entered the crowd later, will decide to accept this bid of 18⅝. If either one of them decides to "hit" the bid he says, "Sold," and the transaction is concluded, simply on the basis of that spoken word. Conversely, if a broker decides to accept an offering price announced in the course of an auction, he simply says, "Take it." No written memoranda are exchanged by the brokers. Each broker simply makes his own note of the other broker to whom he sold and from whom he bought and the price agreed on.

The rules of the New York Stock Exchange provide that all bids to buy and all offers to sell must be made by open outcry. No secret transactions are permitted on the floor of the exchange. Furthermore, a broker cannot conclude transactions between his own public customers without presenting their orders to buy or sell on the floor. For instance, the broker may have a market order to buy 100 shares of Rod & Reel and another market order to sell 100. He can't just *"cross"* these orders privately and effect a transfer of the stock between his two customers. He must send both orders to the floor, where the appropriate bids and offers must be made. Only in very rare cases, usually involving thousands of shares, are off-the-market crosses permitted, and even in these cases, both buyer and seller must know that the cross is being made, and the stock exchange must grant permission.

No broker is permitted to execute any orders on the floor except during the official trading hours of the exchange. These are from 10 A.M. to 4 P.M., New York time, Monday through Friday, excepting holidays.

(From mid-1968 to mid-1970, when brokers were struggling with an unprecedented volume of orders which they were then not equipped to handle, the exchange operated on a reduced schedule of trading hours, but by 1976, efficiency had so improved that the exchange did not have to resort to early closings despite the record-breaking volume.)

As soon as a transaction such as the Rod & Reel purchase at 18⅝ is completed, the broker who bought the stock and the broker who sold it have their clerks report back to their respective home offices so that the buyer and seller may each be advised that the transaction has been concluded and be told what the price was. Brokerage firms with teletype order service direct to the floor simply send the information from the floor back to the originating office.

After the market closes, the two brokerage firms involved in the Rod & Reel transaction must arrange for the actual transfer of the stock and the payment of the amount due. Actually these two firms might have concluded many transactions with each other in the course of the day, and, in turn, each of them might have dealt with dozens of other brokers.

Thus one firm might have sold 1,100 shares of Rod & Reel for its customers on a given day and bought only 1,000 shares for other customers. The transfer of 1,000 shares from its customers who sold the stock to the customers that bought the same number of shares is purely an internal bookkeeping problem for the firm to settle. But it would still owe some other broker 100 shares.

Time was when the broker who owed shares at the end of the day would deliver the actual certificates to the *Stock Clearing Corporation,* where other brokers to whom shares were due would pick them up. Later, all member firms simply kept a supply of all stocks at the clearing corporation, and the transfer of shares between brokers would be accomplished simply by debiting or crediting each broker's account; dollar balances—the net amounts due them—were settled in the same fashion.

Now, the *Depository Trust Company* (a subsidiary

of the New York Stock Exchange, formerly known as Central Certificate Service) has eliminated nearly all of that shuffling of certificates back and forth by its handling of more than 75% of all clearing operations. It conducts a central certificate operation, which relieves its participants—broker-dealers, banks, clearing corporations, insurance and investment companies, among others—of the burden of handling hundreds of pieces of paper each day in both the receiving and delivery functions.

In the vaults of major banks and in the Depository Trust's own vault are stored about 1.75 billion shares of stocks, including those sold on the exchange and those traded elsewhere, and they are worth more than $75 billion. Including registered corporate bonds, more than 3,500 issues are involved.

When certificates are deposited, they are held in nonnegotiable form until it is necessary to transfer them out in the name of a customer or a firm. The participants do not have to handle or even to see the certificates until they are delivered upon request, through a delivery system known as "PDQ."

Computers make daily bookkeeping entries to reflect changes in the participants' position after the securities have been traded. All of this has obviously reduced the number of securities under a participating broker's care to a minimum and has freed valuable space and personnel. At the end of the business day, only one check need be delivered or received from each active participant.

Ultimately, the problems involved in handling stock certificates may be further simplified by the introduction of a certificate like an IBM card on which all the essential data necessary for clearance or transfer can be "read" by a computer. Another proposal would involve adding a half inch to the width of the present 8″ x 12″ certificate and incorporating into that half-inch extra margin all the essential data in characters that could be read electronically by an *optical scanner*. But either one would be only a stopgap measure, for in 1975 Congress directed the S.E.C. to take steps to eliminate stock certificates as a means of settling securities transactions. A system of computerized book-keeping entry would probably be substituted; thus, one of Wall Street's most cherished and often colorful traditions will have vanished from the scene.

To return to our Rod & Reel order, after the sale took place at 18⅝, one of the *floor reporters,* paid employees of the exchange who stand outside each trading post, would see that the price indicator on the post was changed from 18¾ to 18⅝. And since this sale was below the preceding sale, he would be sure that a minus sign showed beside the price figure.

For unnumbered years, the reporter then used to write a report of the sale—the name of the stock, the number of shares involved, and the price—and hand it to a page boy, who would take it to the pneumatic tubes that lead directly from each post to the ticker room. There a notation of the sale was typed onto the *ticker tape,* and it was carried by wire to the *tickers* in every broker's office throughout the country.

Here again, modern technology has come to the rescue of the beleaguered exchange and vastly speeded up operations, thanks to optical card-scanning and the ever-present computer. Now when a transaction is completed all the reporter has to do is draw pencil lines through the appropriate coded boxes—stock symbol, number of shares, price—and insert the card into the electronic scanner. The machine automatically "reads" the essential data from the card and transfers the information to the computer, which itself is used to drive the ticker and produce the printouts, showing each transaction on the tape, or electronic screen. Thus, in a matter of seconds the public knows about every transaction.

With these significant steps toward automation of floor operations, some brokers are wondering seriously if the day might not come when computers would take over virtually the entire trading function and render both them and the exchange itself obsolete. After all, they have seen what a revolution computers have wrought in just a few short years in the accounting, bookkeeping, traffic, and even research departments of their home offices.

On the tape the name of every stock appears only as initials or a combination of letters, such as C for Chrysler Corporation, CP for Canadian Pacific and CRR for Carrier Corporation. The single-letter symbols are, of course, the most highly prized and the best known. Thus A stands for Anaconda, F for Ford, T for American Telephone & Telegraph, and, probably the best known of them all, X for U.S. Steel.

Rod & Reel might have the symbol RAR, in which case the sale of 100 shares at 18⅝ would appear on the tape simply as:

RAR
18⅝

If 200 shares instead of 100 shares had changed hands, the transaction would be noted this way:

RAR
2S 18⅝

If 1,000 shares had been involved, it would appear on the tape this way:

RAR
1000S 18⅝

When sales volume is so heavy that the ticker, which can print 900 characters a minute, almost the limit of readability—falls as much as one minute behind in reporting transactions, the price information is abbreviated to the last digit plus a fraction, except when that digit is a zero, as in 20 or 30. If the ticker was one minute later, our sale at 18⅝ would appear as:

RAR
8⅝

It is assumed that people who are following the stock closely on the ticker will be able to supply the missing first digit. If the stock were to go up to 20 or above, hence involving a new first digit, this price would be noted in full, such as 20⅛, on the first such sale.

When the ticker falls two minutes behind in reporting, the volume of sales is deleted also. Thus, even if 1,000 shares of Rod & Reel were sold at 18⅜, the transaction would still appear:

RAR
8⅜

The ticker rarely falls three minutes or more behind and then only on big volume days—25 to 30 million shares—but it did happen with increasing frequency in 1975 and almost daily in January-February 1976 when the turnover soared to record highs. Therefore, whenever the tape is late by three minutes or more, *repeat prices* are omitted. In other words, succeeding transactions in the same stock at an identical price are not printed. As soon as the tape recovers lost time, it returns to usual routines.

If the tape can't keep up with the pace of trading, you may wonder why the exchange doesn't simply introduce a faster ticker. The answer is that anything above 900 characters a minute would be "blurred," almost impossible to read. Although a high-speed data processing ticker is planned for the future, it will be available only to financial vendors and to press associations.

When most people think of buying or selling stock, they think of doing it on the basis of a market order, one to be executed as soon as possible after it reaches the floor and at the best price then prevailing. Actually, an individual very often wants to buy or sell a stock only if it can be done at a certain price or better. Thus, you might want to buy 100 shares of Rod & Reel if you didn't have to pay more than 18½. You could place an order to this effect with your broker. It's called a *limit order,* and you can tell him whether it's good for a day, a week, or a month, or "good till canceled." All limit orders are treated as day orders and are cancelled if they are not executed by the end of that day's trading, unless they are clearly marked for a longer period of time.

The stock will be bought for you only if it can be bought at 18½ or less. Perhaps when the order is actually executed, your broker will be able to get the stock at 18¼. On the other hand, the stock may actually drop to 18½, and your order won't have been filled. That's because other orders to buy at 18½ were placed ahead of yours, and the supply of the stock offered at that price was exhausted before your order was reached. In that kind of situation, if you asked your broker why your order wasn't executed, he would tell you that there was *"stock ahead."*

Limit orders can also be used in selling stock. Thus, if you owned Rod & Reel stock, you might be willing to sell it, but only if you could get $19 for it—$19 or more. You could place a *sell-limit order* to that effect with your broker. Sometimes, you might like to place a day limit order to buy or sell at a specified price, but you would still like to have your order executed that day even if the stock didn't quite reach the price level you set. You could accomplish that by having the order marked for *execution at the close* regardless of the market level at 4 P.M.

There's still another kind of suspended order, and that is known as the *stop order*.

Suppose you had bought Rod & Reel at 12 or 13, and the stock had risen to a level where you had a nice profit—perhaps to 19 or 20. You might want to protect that profit in case the market dropped sharply, and you could do so by instructing your broker to sell the stock if it declined to 18, let's say. This would be a *stop order to sell,* and your broker would see that it was executed if Rod & Reel ever fell as low as 18. Whenever it hit that mark, your stop order would become a market order to be executed at the best price then possible. Again, because other people might have placed orders ahead of yours to sell at the 18 figure, the price might slip to 17¾ or 17½ before your order could be executed.

Conversely, you might not want to buy Rod & Reel when it was selling at 18 because you felt it might fall further, but on the other hand if there were a sharp rally, you wouldn't want to miss your opportunity to pick up the stock before its price got out of hand. In that case you might place a *stop order to buy* by instructing your broker to buy Rod & Reel for you at, let's say, 19. ·

Occasionally, the exchange will exercise its authority to prohibit stop orders in individual stocks, but such action is taken only when the stock has followed a very volatile pattern of price movements and when the exchange fears that the execution of stop orders to sell would trigger a sharp sell-off.

In theory these fixed-price orders, both limit orders and stop orders, look pretty attractive as a means of controlling your profit or losses. In practice, however, they don't work as well for the average investor as you might think. To have any real utility, a limit order has to be fairly close to the prevailing market price. For instance, if Rod & Reel is selling at 18½, there might not be much point in placing an order to buy it at 16 or even 17. And if you place a limit order at 18, you might just as well buy it outright at 18½. The same logic applies in reverse when it comes to selling stock.

In short, decisions to buy or sell that turn on getting an extra point or fraction of a point, above or below the market price prevailing at the time the order is entered, are usually not apt to be sound decisions for the average investor.

CHAPTER 11

How a Market Is Made

WHENEVER you place an order to buy or sell stocks, your brokerage firm is responsible for executing it at the best price possible, the highest price if you are selling, the lowest if you are buying. Often this responsibility would require the firm's floor broker to spend far more time on your order than he can afford to spare if he is going to attend to all his other duties. Thus, for instance, if you were to place an order to buy Rod & Reel at the specified price of 18 and the stock was then selling at 19, you could hardly expect your broker to spend all his time keeping an eye on Rod & Reel, waiting to see if it dropped to 18.

In a case like that, he would turn your order over to another broker who, as his agent, would watch the stock for you and execute the order if he could. This agent is usually the *specialist* in Rod & Reel stock.

A specialist is a broker who has elected to confine his buying and selling activities to a particular stock or several stocks that are traded at one spot around the perimeter of a trading post. He never moves away from that spot; he is always there to accept orders from other brokers and, for a negotiated commission known as floor brokerage, to assume responsibility for their execution. The individual investor does not pay anything extra for the specialist's services.

A specialist must not only function as an agent for other brokers, executing orders that they leave with him, but must also be willing to buy and sell for his own account those stocks in which he specializes. In fact, this is his primary responsibility if he fulfills the obligation imposed upon him by the exchange to maintain a "fair and orderly market" in these stocks.

All told, there are about 380 members of the exchange who operate as specialists, and they work for 68 separate specialist organizations—mostly partnerships or two or three firms working together—that handle the stocks of all the 1,559 companies listed on the exchange. Some big specialist units handle as many as 150 stocks; some only a few.

No member can operate as a specialist except with the approval of the stock exchange, and he must be a man of substantial means, for every specialist unit is required to have enough capital to buy as many as 5,000 shares of the common stocks and 1,000 shares of the convertible preferred stocks in which he is authorized to deal. In the case of a common stock priced at $50 a share, a specialist unit would thus need capital of a quarter million dollars just to handle that one stock.

Moreover, each specialist firm must have at least $500,000 readily available for its use, or 25% of whatever funds it would need if it had to buy 5,000 shares of all the common stocks and 1,000 shares of all the convertible preferreds that it was authorized to deal in, whichever of these two amounts is the greater.

This means that the big specialist firms that handle dozens of stocks must have access to many millions of dollars. Some specialists rely principally on their own resources, but most specialists supplement their own capital through private financing arrangements. Some specialist firms are so well-heeled that they can buy as many as twenty or thirty thousand shares of one or more of the stocks they handle, if a seller offers such a block of stock and if the specialist thinks the stock's prospects are good.

When a specialist executes orders for other brokers, he is himself operating as a broker. For technically, that is what the word broker means, a man who acts as agent for others. But when a specialist buys or sells for his own account, he is acting as a *dealer*. That is the whole distinction between a broker and a securities dealer. A broker simply bargains *for* you; a dealer bargains *with* you and acts as a principal in the transaction. He sells securities to you that he owns himself, or buys such securities from you at an agreed price.

When a member firm broker (about 700 in number on the New York Stock Exchange) comes to the trading post with an order to sell a stock and there are no other brokers with buy orders for that stock at the post, the specialist will make a bid for the stock himself. Similarly, when a broker wants to buy a stock and there are no other sellers, the specialist will offer it for sale himself.

Normally, about 30% to 40% of stock exchange volume results from this kind of buying and selling by specialists for their own accounts. And normally, they count on making about half their income from it; the other half comes from executing orders for other brokers.

On each of the stocks in which he specializes, the specialist keeps a book, and in this *specialist's book* are entered all the limit or stop orders that other brokers have given him for execution whenever possible. These are orders that cannot be executed at the time because they are "away from the market"—that is, either too high or too low in relation to the price at which the stock is then being traded. If a specialist gets two or more orders to buy a stock at the same price— or to sell it at the same price—he enters them in his book in the order in which he receives them. Those that are received first are executed first, whenever the price auction permits, regardless of all other conditions or circumstances.

Thus, if your order for Rod & Reel at 18 was the first one in the specialist's book, and if the stock was offered at that price, your order would be filled first. Even if he wanted to, the specialist couldn't buy the stock for his own account at 18 until your order and all others in his book at that price were executed.

Whenever the last sale of Rod & Reel was made at 18½, the specialist's book might typically show one or two limit orders to buy at 18⅜, one or two others at 18¼, and perhaps three or four at 18, since most customers place limit orders in round figures rather than fractions. On the sell side, his book might show a couple of orders to sell at 18⅝, a few at 18¾, and several at 19 or higher. These might be either limit orders or stop orders, and would be so marked in his book.

In that situation, if a broker came to the trading post with a market order to buy Rod & Reel and there were no other brokers there with stock to sell, his query "How's Reel?" would be answered by the specialist. The specialist would reply, "Three-eighths, five-eighths," meaning 18⅜ bid and 18⅝ offered, since 18⅜ was the highest buy order and 18⅝ the lowest sell order that he then had in his book. This would be the *bid-and-asked* quotation as of then.

Actually, the specialist's book may eventually become a thing of the past, being replaced by a cathode ray tube. In 1969, the exchange began experimentation with a system of electronic storage and display that could relieve the specialist of the burdensome clerical task of keeping his book. When he received orders to buy or sell he would enter them into the electronic system by punching a few keys, and he could see what his "book" looked like on any stock by looking at a TV-like tube.

The major problem is how to make the system work so only the specialist can see the electronic book. A specialist's book, after all, is a highly confidential document. If other brokers knew that there were heavy orders either to buy or to sell Rod & Reel just a little away from the market, that knowledge could have a marked influence on the handling of their own orders. It seems more likely, therefore, that it will be replaced eventually by some form of a *composite book* that will feature competing market-makers and specialists.

Since a specialist's primary responsibility is to see that there is no violent fluctuation in the price of any stock he handles, he usually undertakes to see that the difference between the bid and the asked price is only ¼ of a point or so, although it might be more on high-priced issues.

Because specialists are generally faithful to their obligation of maintaining orderly markets, well over 90% of all transactions on the exchange take place at prices which show a fluctuation of ¼ or less from the next previous transaction. Whenever there is a more than normal gap between bid-and-asked quotations, the specialist, under the rules of the exchange, is expected to do something about it. Specifically, to narrow the gap he is expected to make appropriate bids or offers of his own—to buy or sell the stock as necessary, for his own account.

Furthermore, if one of his stocks is moving rapidly up or rapidly down, he is expected to *stabilize* the market in that stock. If there is heavy pressure of sell orders which pushes the price down, he is expected to buy the stock for his own account. Conversely, if buy orders are pushing the price up too rapidly, he is expected to sell the stock from his own inventory. He may even be forced to sell stock he doesn't have, and if he does, he can only hope that somewhere along the line he will be able to buy an offsetting amount of the stock at a lower price because he knows he will have to make good the stock he has sold to other brokers.

The obligation to maintain a fair and orderly market can indeed impose fearsome and expensive responsibilities on a specialist. Important news developments can drastically affect a company's prospects and result in a sudden torrent to buy or sell orders. Sometimes such a development will delay the opening of a stock for half an hour or more after trading is supposed to begin at 10 A.M.; sometimes it will force suspension of trading for a much longer period of time. In such situations, the specialist will consult with floor officials and one or two directors of the exchange, and they will decide what constitutes a fair price quotation, and when trading in the stock begins again, that's the price at which the specialist is obligated to buy or sell.

A classic illustration of the kind of a dilemma that frequently confronts specialists is that which resulted from the news break in early 1964 that Lockheed had developed the A-11, a jet plane whose performance, in the words of President Johnson, far exceeded that "of any other aircraft in the world today." The President made that announcement on a Friday, and Lockheed had closed that day at 38. What price would it open at Monday? That morning the Lockheed specialist was confronted with market orders to buy 30,000 shares, and in his book, he had offsetting sell orders that totaled only 17,000 shares—13,000 less than were needed. Floor traders were willing to sell 3,200 shares, and the specialist had 5,600 in his inventory. As for the remaining 4,200 shares, the specialist had no choice but to sell shares he didn't have in the hopes of being able to cover his shortage by buying 4,200 shares later at a reasonable price.

After conferring with floor officials, the specialist set an opening price of 40⅞—$2.75 above Friday's close —and trading opened on a block of 30,000 shares at that price. Lockheed closed that day at 40⅞, after 299 individual transactions valued at some $5,500,000, but the most significant thing is that the specialist ran such an orderly market that not one of those transactions took place at a price that varied more than ¼ from the preceding transaction.

Occasionally, there may be such an overnight accumulation of buy orders for a stock that the specialist is unable to arrange an opening price, even with the help of floor traders or the floor officials. On Monday, January 27, 1975, for instance, after an appeals court decision favoring IBM in a major antitrust action was announced over the weekend, the stock wasn't traded at all on the New York Stock Exchange, although it did manage to open later that day on the Midwest Stock Exchange—twenty points above its previous closing price.

In addition to stabilizing the market and being willing to buy or sell when there are no brokers with offsetting orders, the specialist performs another important service, which is called *stopping a stock*.

Suppose your broker came to the trading post with your market order for Rod & Reel when the best offering price in the specialist's book was 18⅝ and when there were no other brokers there with better offers. Anxious to get a lower price for you if possible, and yet not wanting to miss the market if it went up, your broker would ask the specialist to "stop" 100 shares for him at 18⅝. If another broker came up then and

offered Rod & Reel at 18½, the specialist would buy
it for your broker and earn a floor brokerage commission. On the other hand, if the stock was not offered at a lower price but sold again the next time at
18⅝, the specialist would execute your buy order at
that figure. He could not execute your order at more
than 18⅝, for when he was asked to stop the stock, he
agreed that 18⅝ would be the maximum price your
broker would have to pay. He'd try to buy it cheaper
if he could, but 18⅝ would be the top price.

After every sale a wholly new auction starts. Thus,
if a transaction in Rod & Reel had just been concluded at 18⅝, other brokers in the crowd who might
be trying to buy 100 shares apiece would immediately
restate their bids, maybe the same bid—18½. These
simultaneous bids would have parity, and if a broker
then came up and offered 100 shares of the stock at
18½, the brokers who wanted to buy at that price
would settle the matter as to which one would get the
stock by tossing a coin.

The brokers who lost out might then report to their
customers that they had *matched and lost*. Customers
who get such a report often wonder why they never
win. The answer is that the broker never reports
when he matches and wins; the customer simply gets the
stock.

In the case of simultaneous bids, if one broker has
an order for 200 shares while the others are trying to
buy only 100 shares apiece, the larger order takes
precedence if the seller offers a block that big or bigger. If the seller offers 200 shares, the broker who
wants 200 will get them all. If the seller has 300
shares, the broker who wants 200 will get his first, and
the others will have to match for the remaining 100.

Very often, before placing a market order a customer wants to have a pretty exact idea of what he
might have to pay. To accommodate such a customer, the floor broker will try to "get *the market and
the size*." This means that he will ask the specialist for
the current bid-and-asked prices and for the size of
the orders at these prices. The specialist will tell only

the highest bid and the lowest offer, such as on Rod & Reel. "Three-eighths, five-eighths," or 18% bid, offered at 18%. He is not permitted to reveal any of the lower bids or higher offering prices shown on his book. As far as the size of the orders is concerned, he might say, "One hundred either way," by which he would mean that he has 100 shares to buy at 18% and 100 to sell at 18%. If he had 100 to buy and 500 to sell, he would say, "Three-eighths, five-eighths, one and five."

The specialist is not required to divulge the size of the orders on his book at either the bid or asked price if he feels that it would not be in the best interests of the buyers or sellers.

Because the specialist's book gives him a feel of the market that no other broker or investor can possibly have and because he not only can but *must* buy and sell for his own account to maintain an orderly market, he is obviously in a position to affect the trend of prices in a very important way.

To be sure that the specialist does not abuse his privileged position or manipulate prices in any way to his personal advantage, the exchange has circumscribed his operations with a set of highly technical rules, which have become steadily more stringent over the years.

In 1973, the specialists again found themselves under fire from the staff of a Senate subcommittee. Questions were raised about how vigilant the stock exchange was in enforcing the minimum net capital requirements for specialists and in policing the operation of specialists. Specifically, the New York Stock Exchange was criticized for not providing an automated system that could provide almost instantaneously a complete record of the trading activities of specialists and make monitoring of them more efficient.

Despite the fact that various surveys, including the S.E.C.'s own, have not turned up any evidence of wrongdoing by specialists on the New York Stock Exchange and have even demonstrated what a useful service they render, the S.E.C. continues to regard their operations with grave suspicion, and there is no doubt of the fact that those operations will be kept under much closer surveillance by both the exchange and the S.E.C.

Specialists are now required to submit to the exchange—about eight times a year—details of their dealings for various one-week periods, selected at random by the exchange and not revealed in advance. These reports make it possible for the exchange to study the orderliness of the market in an individual stock, the continuity of price, and the spread in quotations, and to render a judgment about how well the specialist is fulfilling his obligations.

Specialists must also report weekly to the stock exchange every trade they make for their own account—stating the time, the *"tick"* (whether up or down in price), and the number of shares involved. They are then graded on their stabilizing record—meaning whether they bought on down ticks and sold on up ticks, as they are expected to.

In addition, the exchange maintains an on-line price surveillance program based on trading data obtained from the exchange's computers which run the stock ticker. This program monitors all trades reported on the ticker throughout the market session. When the price movement of a stock exceeds preset standards, the computer calls attention to that fact. The transaction—stock symbol, time, and price—is reported on a teletypewriter machine in the exchange's surveillance section. The surveillance section then retrieves from the computer's memory bank the chronological sequence of sales, before and after the suspicious transaction, and analyzes the record. If there is no apparent cause for the fluctuation, the surveillance section alerts a trading floor official in the area where the stock is traded. The official will then speak to the specialist to find out just what happened—and why.

Whenever the hue and cry is raised that specialists ought not to be allowed to trade for their own accounts, that their functions should be restricted to running the book and executing orders for other brokers, specialists ask what would have happened to the stock market if they had not been able and willing to step into the breach at the time of President Eisenhower's heart attack in 1955 or the day when President Kennedy was assassinated in 1963.

On Monday, September 26, 1955, when the market opened, after the news of Eisenhower's heart attack had broken over the weekend, sell orders far outnumbered buy orders. It was virtually impossible to open trading in any stock. The sell orders would have depressed prices beyond all reasonable levels before buying sentiment could be generated. The specialists met the challenge. They bought steadily for their own accounts at prices only moderately below the levels that had prevailed at Friday's close. All told, one-quarter of the stock purchases that day were made for specialists' own accounts—1,759,360 shares with an estimated market value of $80 million. Eisenhower's recovery enabled the specialists as a group to work off the stock they bought without loss—indeed, with profit —but when they took the risk, they did not know whether or not they would be wiped out.

"How," ask the specialists, "could you get a computer to do that kind of job?"

On November 22, 1963, the performance of the specialists was equally noteworthy. The story can be summarized in terms of what happened to 25 key stocks between 1:40 P.M., when news of President Kennedy's assassination hit the exchange floor, and 2:07 P.M., when the exchange was closed down by the governors. At 1:40 P.M. specialists in these 25 issues held 126,000 shares worth over $7 million in their own inventories. When panic selling engulfed the floor, the specialists stepped in to buy, risking their own personal solvency. In the following 27 minutes, 570,000 shares of these 25 stocks were traded on the floor, and of this total, the specialists bought more than 144,000, increasing their inventories to almost 230,000 shares, then worth $12,348,000. And it should be noted that the floor traders also helped stabilize the market in these stocks, buying 31,000 shares on balance. True, again, the specialists sustained no loss, thanks to a rapid market recovery, but that's something they couldn't count on when they took their big gamble.

The S.E.C. contends that specialists have not always behaved in such exemplary fashion on other crucial occasions, notably in the sharp decline of May 1962, but, then, perhaps no one can be a hero all the time.

CHAPTER 12

How Large Blocks of Stock
Are Handled

SUPPOSE you owned a sizable block of stock in a company. Maybe you acquired the shares as part of your retirement benefits from that company. Maybe you inherited the stock. Or maybe you simply bought the block bit by bit over a long period of time. Now, for any one of a dozen good reasons, you decide you want to sell 5,000 shares, or 10,000 shares, or more. How would you go about selling that much stock?

Obviously, if you just dumped it on the market all at once, it would depress the price and you wouldn't get as much for the stock as you should. Moreover, it might be a period of days or weeks before you could dispose of all that stock in ordinary trades of one or two hundred shares at a time.

In a situation of this kind you would be well advised to let your broker solve the problem. And the first thing he would do is try to "find the other side of the market," to uncover a buying interest in the stock that would match your own desire to sell. The department of his firm that specializes in block business would then contact various sources to find a buyer for your block. These sources would naturally include other member firms, but also nonmember firms, mainly those known to have an interest in the stock. If the stock was not popularly traded in the market, your broker might see if the company itself was interested in buying back its own stock, as many large companies often do.

Your broker might also turn to the specialist who handles that stock and who, in his role as market-maker, buying and selling it all the time for his own account, very often performs a notably useful service in helping brokers dispose of sizable blocks.

Time was when a broker could turn a block order over to the specialist to execute on a *not-held* basis. On this basis the specialist would be free to exercise his own best judgment about when and how to feed the stock into the market. He might, for instance, hold the stock back in the expectation that prices would rise. If instead they dropped before he finished executing the complete order—if other orders were filled at prices higher than what he finally realized on his not-held order—he was at least assured that the broker for whom he was acting would "not hold him to the tape," that is, would not hold him responsible for failing to sell at those better intervening prices.

For some years, however, the S.E.C. has insisted that specialists cannot accept not-held orders, and this makes the handling of them difficult for the broker. About all he can do is try to get the customer to change his order into a limit order. If he succeeds, the broker can then turn the order over to the specialist to execute as best he can at prices above the minimum set in the limit order.

In the last analysis, the specialist is as interested as your broker is in disposing of your block with the least possible impact on his market. The specialist might, for instance, know some floor traders who would be interested in buying all or part of the block. Or the specialist might be willing to buy it outright for his own account, thus assuming the entire risk that he would be able to sell it at a profit.

If he took on a block on this basis, it would be known as a *specialist block purchase*. However, under stock exchange rules such a transaction may take place only when the stock cannot be sold in ordinary exchange transactions without disturbing the market; it must be considered as contributing to the performance of the specialist's duty to maintain a fair and orderly market. (A *specialist block sale*—just the reverse of a block purchase—is, of course, subject to the same restriction.)

Occasionally, a broker with a big order will be able to find buyers or sellers for the whole block among his own customers and handle both sides of the transaction. This is called a cross because the broker actually crosses the buy and sell orders on the floor in a regular trade. The biggest block handled in this fashion in N.Y.S.E. history involved the sale of 5,240,000 shares of American Motors on March 14, 1972; the biggest trade in terms of dollar value was a $76,135,026 transaction in American Standard (Pfd. A. stock) on June 13, 1968.

In this kind of an "in house" transaction, if a broker can't find enough buy orders among his customers to equal the sell order, he will often buy the balance of the shares for his own account and assume the risk of selling them later at a profit.

If a member firm takes on a big block—too big for it to handle alone—the technique it is most likely to use to sell the block is the *secondary distribution* (secondary, as distinguished from an original underwriting, or primary distribution). A secondary distribution, like a new issue, can be handled either by a member firm of the New York Stock Exchange or by a securities dealer who is not a member, and will usually involve the participation of member firms as well as nonmembers. A record 140 "secondaries" involving nearly 65 million shares of stock were effected through the New York Stock Exchange in 1972, but in 1973–1974 they receded drastically both in number and in the volume of shares involved, due to the bear market.

If the block offered in a secondary is a listed stock, an announcement of the impending offering is made on the exchange ticker on the day of the sale, and the actual offering to the public generally takes place after the close of the market. This advance publicity that a sizable block of stock is hanging over the market can, of course, have an untoward effect on the price of the stock during the day's trading. Actually, if the exchange community is in any way concerned about the overhanging block, the price may already have drifted downward for a day or two, because news of an

impending secondary gets around as soon as the broker
or dealer who is handling the sale sets about organizing his underwriting group.

The underwriters participating in the secondary buy
the block outright from the seller and assume the risk
of reselling it to the public, often inviting other brokers and nonmember dealers to join them in the selling
group. The underwriters charge the seller a *gross
spread,* which typically will amount to three or four
times the going commission rate, although it can range
from as little as two commissions to as much as six
commissions. This spread covers the manager's fee,
the underwriting commission, and the *selling concession,* which normally runs from a third to a half of the
gross spread. Since negotiated commissions became effective, the spread or cost to the seller has generally
been reduced in order to meet competition.

The price at which the block is offered in a secondary
distribution involving a listed stock is usually the price
at which that stock is sold in the last transaction on the
floor that day, although it might be either lower or
higher depending on the attractiveness of the offering.

If you had no particular desire to buy a given stock
at the close of the market, you may wonder how you
could be interested in buying that same stock at the
same price just a little later the same day. The answer
is simple: to induce you to buy, the underwriters offer
the stock on a commission-free basis, no matter how
many shares you buy. The seller pays all the costs, and
that's why the gross spread is so big.

On a secondary distribution the underwriting group
usually undertakes to stabilize the market with S.E.C.
sanction, just as they do on an original underwriting.
Obviously, it would not be possible for them to sell
their stock at the price fixed in their agreement with
the seller if the same stock was being offered in the
open market at substantially lower prices—prices that
more than offset the commission saving to the buyer.
In such cases, the underwriters would have to buy up
the stock offered at the lower price and add it to their
own block. If large quantities of the stock appear at
considerably lower prices, they may have to give up

their *price stabilization* efforts, withdraw the block, and wait for a better market, a happier day.

The largest secondary offering of common stock was the Ford Foundation's first public offering of stock in the Ford Motor Company in 1956. This was handled by seven securities firms operating as *joint managers,* and it had a gross value of $657,900,000. The next-largest secondary—and the largest ever handled by a single firm—was the sale by Merrill Lynch, Pierce, Fenner & Smith in 1966 of Howard Hughes's holdings in TWA—a block of 6,584,937 shares worth $566,304,-582.

A second technique for distributing a large block of stock is the *special offering.* A special is handled the same way as a secondary, except that participation is limited to members of the New York Stock Exchange and takes place on the floor of the exchange during regular trading hours. However, there were none at all between 1963 and 1972; only quite recently has the special offering had an occasional play on the exchange.

A third technique—the *exchange distribution*—is also available, although it too has lost substantially in popularity. Such a distribution is usually handled by a single brokerage firm, and the block is disposed of wholly by its own sales organization to its own customers. It is, in effect, nothing but a giant cross. The seller gives the broker what amounts to a market order, and the broker's sales force then seeks to develop buying interest among their customers on the assumption that the stock will be available at or near the price then prevailing on the exchange. When the sales organization has developed buy orders which in the aggregate match the size of the block, the broker checks the seller a last time to be sure he is satisfied with the price then prevailing, and if he is, the floor broker will then offer the block on the exchange and simultaneously bid for it, usually at the last sale price or at a price between the bid-and-asked quotations.

There are two chief advantages to an exchange distribution from the seller's point of view. Since there is no public announcement of the offering and since the entire transaction is usually handled within a single broker's organization, there is little likelihood that news of the impending block sale will depress the price of the stock before the offering is made, as often happens with secondaries or specials. Again, since there is no need to organize an underwriting syndicate or a selling group, the cost to the seller is lower—characteristically, only about half of what he would have to pay on either a secondary or a special. The buyers, of course, get their stock without paying any commissions, since all costs are borne by the seller.

Banks, insurance companies, and other institutions are more apt to encounter a serious problem in selling a large block of securities than they are in buying one, but institutional business has grown so rapidly that it is sometimes also difficult for these big purchasers to acquire the stock they want at a fair price and without disturbing the market. To meet this situation, the stock exchange in 1956 also established a mechanism known as the *exchange acquisition,* which works exactly like the exchange distribution, except in reverse. The broker who handles such a transaction solicits sell orders from his customers at a net price, free of all commission, until he accumulates shares equal to the buyer's order, and the buyer usually pays at least a double commission.

The exchange acquisition has never proved popular —there has been only one in several years—and it isn't hard to see why. It's one thing for a broker to ask a customer if he wants to buy a stock commission-free; it's another—and more awkward—thing to ask him if he wants to sell a stock commission-free. The customer is immediately suspicious. Why, he asks himself, should his broker want him to sell that stock, particularly if it is one the broker recommended that he buy in the first place?

While the New York Stock Exchange has developed all these techniques for handling the purchase or sale of blocks of all sizes—and almost automatically grants the required approval for any secondary, special, or exchange distribution—many an institution in recent years has found it simpler and easier to take the block to the third market and sell it in toto to a securities dealer who is willing to position the stock and assume the entire risk of selling it. Obviously, for assuming such a risk, the dealer expects to buy the stock at a substantial discount from the prevailing market price. If he is selling a block instead of buying it, he expects to get a price concession on that side.

The marked success that nonmember dealers have enjoyed in developing block business for the third market has induced more and more member firms to follow the same tactics. Instead of resorting to the machinery of the stock exchange in order to move a block of stock, they buy the block outright from the seller, position the stock, and then devise ways and means of selling it, just as a nonmember would in the third market with one small difference. If a member firm wanted to dispose of all or part of the block to a nonmember, he was required—at least until January 1977—to be sure that all limit orders for the stock on the specialist's books at the same or higher buying price were satisfied first.

Institutions also have available to them a fourth market—the Institutional Network, or "Instinet," as it is called—to help them trade big blocks of stocks.

Instinet is a privately owned computerized network, and subscribers can notify Instinet of their interest in block purchases or sales via a cathode ray tube. If a seller announces that he wants to sell a particular block and if another subscriber indicates an interest in buying that stock, the two of them can negotiate prices and terms with each other through a computer terminal. Instinet claims that some of its subscribers have been able to save up to 70% of the commission they would have had to pay under the exchange's old fixed-rate system. Instinet makes its money not by collecting commissions but by charging each subscriber a flat annual fee.

Once a subscribing institution has indicated its interest in selling a block of some stock, that indication of interest is placed in the Instinet Network file. Perhaps a little later another subscribing member decides on the basis of its own information that it would like to buy that stock. When it reports that interest to

Instinet, the file is checked and the would-be buyer is put into computer contact with the organization that has decided to sell it. Since the whole transaction is handled privately, there is no chance that a rumor about such-and-such an insurance company wanting to sell a block can depress the price of the stock and hence reduce the amount the seller might hope to get for his stock. Conversely, the potential buyer doesn't show his hand publicly and run the risk of bidding up the price.

While institutions are the principal sellers of large blocks, sizable offerings are sometimes made by the directors, officers, or principal stockholders of a company, and such blocks often pose a difficult problem for the broker, for the S.E.C. rules provide that no one in a *control* position can sell stock unless it has been registered with the commission. The whole question of just who is and who isn't a control person is not susceptible of easy definition; so most brokers play it safe and insist on S.E.C. approval before undertaking to sell a block of stock for any company executive.

CHAPTER 13

How Small Orders Are Handled

ALL stocks bought and sold on the stock exchange are traded in round lots, units of 100 shares, with the exception of a few relatively inactive stocks that are sold in 10-share units.

But what if you want to buy or sell just 20 shares of our hypothetical Rod & Reel Company on the exchange? The answer is that you can do it; you can buy an *odd lot*—anything from 1 to 99 shares—of any stock listed on the New York Stock Exchange, but chances are that your cost of buying or selling it, figured as a percentage of the total value of your order, will be slightly higher than it would on a round-lot trade.

One reason for that, of course, is that brokers generally charge higher commission rates on smaller orders. How much higher depends on your broker. Since the abandonment of fixed commissions, brokers have adjusted their commission schedules either to encourage or discourage the small investor. Generally speaking, you will find that the brokers who do a broad public business will charge you less to handle an odd-lot order than houses that cater to an exclusive clientele or the ones that specialize in institutional business.

But there's a second reason why it will probably cost you proportionately more to buy and sell odd lots, and that is that historically the odd-lot customer has been obliged to pay a kind of service fee, over and above the commission. The charge was mandatory under the rules of the New York Stock Exchange, but on January 23, 1976, competition entered the picture and the mandatory service charge rule was broken. Thus, another time-honored monopoly was shattered.

To understand the significance of that development, it is necessary to understand just how the odd-lot system formerly operated.

For many years there were two *odd-lot brokers*— Carlisle & Jacquelin and DeCoppet & Doremus—and they handled 99% of all the odd-lot orders that reached the floor of the exchange, and in 1969 they merged to form the firm of Carlisle, DeCoppet & Company. This odd-lot brokerage firm wasn't really a broker at all; it was a security dealer. If you bought 20 shares of Rod & Reel, the odd-lot house would supply your broker with the 20 shares from its own inventory. If you sold 20 shares, the odd-lot house would buy the odd lot from your broker and put it in inventory. If you ordered 20 shares of Rod & Reel and the odd-lot broker didn't have it in his inventory, he would buy a round lot of the stock, sell you your 20 shares, and put the other 80 shares in inventory—an inventory which in the aggregate might run to many millions of dollars.

Under the rules of the exchange, as they existed just before fixed commissions were abolished, the odd-lot broker had to fill your market order for any stock at whatever price prevailed on the next round-lot transaction after your order reached the trading post. For this service the odd-lot broker charged a fee, known as the *odd-lot differential,* which was ⅛ of a point or 12½¢ a share on every share of stock that the customer bought or sold.

If you bought an odd lot, you paid ⅛ above the price at which the next round lot was sold after your order got to the trading post, and if you sold, you got ⅛ less than that price. At an earlier time, the odd-lot differential had been ¼ of a point or 25¢ a share on stocks selling at $40 or above, and later that ¼ of a point was changed to apply only to stocks selling at $55 or more. The odd-lot house never dealt directly with the customer, only the customer's broker. In that sense, the odd-lot house was really a broker's broker, but in the sense that he was always trading on his own account, positioning stocks, and buying for his own inventory or selling from it, he was a securities dealer.

In January 1976, this time-honored system of charging an odd-lot differential was challenged. Over the objections of the stock exchange—but with the obvious blessing of the S.E.C.—Merrill Lynch, Pierce, Fenner & Smith announced that it would buy and sell odd lots out of its own inventory and, in certain circumstances, not charge the odd-lot differential on market orders.

That was a body blow as far as Carlisle & DeCoppet was concerned, for Merrill Lynch, which accounted for about a quarter of all odd-lot business on the exchange, was by all odds the biggest customer of the odd-lot broker.

Here is what the Merrill Lynch plan offered the odd-lot customer:

(1) If you place an odd-lot order with the firm on a given day and don't mind waiting until your stock opens on the exchange the following day, Merrill Lynch will fill your odd-lot order at the price which prevails on that first round-lot transaction, and it will charge you only its regular commission. No odd-lot differential.

(2) If you place an odd-lot market order for immediate execution during a trading day, Merrill Lynch will execute it for you at the bid or asked price then being quoted by the specialist in your stock. If you are buying, you will get the asked price—the lowest at which any round-lot owner is then willing to sell. If you are selling, you will get the bid price—the highest any round-lot buyer is then willing to pay. Either way, you pay only Merrill Lynch's regular commission—no odd-lot differential.

If you pick the first option, you realize a clear and obvious saving of 12½¢ a share, but you do have to wait for the next day's opening to have your order executed. That could work either in your favor or against you, depending on which way the market moved after you placed your order. Almost a quarter of Merrill Lynch's odd-lot customers appeared willing to take this gamble in the first few months of the plan's operation.

As for the second option, if the spread between the

bid and asked prices is only ⅛ of a point, as it often is on heavily traded stocks, you have a 50-50 chance of saving that 12½¢, depending on whether the next sale takes place at the bid or the asked price. Suppose Rod & Reel is quoted at 30½ bid, 30⅝ asked when you give Merrill Lynch your order to buy 20 shares. Your order will be filled at 30⅝. If the next round-lot sale takes place at that price, you will indeed have saved yourself ⅛ of a point, the odd-lot differential you would have had to pay under the old system. But if the next round lot is sold at 30½, you come out even, for you paid just what you would have under the old system—30½ plus ⅛ differential, or 30⅝. So if the spread is only ⅛ of a point, and you trade at the bid or asked price, you may or may not save money, but at least you know you can't lose any.

If the spread is more than ⅛ of a point, the odds on saving the odd-lot differential aren't quite so good. Suppose Rod & Reel were quoted at 30½–30¾. Your odd-lot order to buy would be executed at 30¾. The next round-lot transaction could take place at any one of three prices—30½, 30⅝, or 30¾. At 30½, you would lose ⅛, compared to what you would have had to pay under the old system. At 30⅝, you would break even. At 30¾, you would be ⅛ of a point ahead of the game.

As the spread between bid and asked prices widens, your chance of saving that odd-lot differential by trading on the bid-and-asked prices diminishes. Thus, if the spread were ⅜ of a point, you would have one chance of saving the odd-lot differential, one chance of breaking even, and two chances of paying more than you would have under the old system.

If a Merrill Lynch customer doesn't want to place an order to buy or sell at the bid-or-asked price, he doesn't have to. He can insist that his odd-lot order be executed in the traditional manner—at whatever price prevails on the next round-lot sale—but if he does, he will pay the standard ⅛ point differential.

As a matter of fact, this conventional method is the way Merrill Lynch announced it would handle all odd-lot limit orders—through Carlisle & DeCoppet. The execution of an odd-lot limit order differs from the execution of an odd-lot market order in one particular. A buy order for 10 shares of Rod & Reel at a limit price of 18½ is filled on the next round-lot transaction at 18⅜, so that when the differential is added the buyer gets his stock at the 18½ limit and the odd-lot broker is assured his ⅛. Conversely, an odd-lot sell order is executed when a transaction takes place ⅛ above the limit price.

Although Carlisle & DeCoppet retained some of Merrill Lynch's business, the Street was guessing that sooner or later Merrill Lynch would handle all its own odd-lot business.

For one thing, there might not be an odd-lot broker on whom Merrill Lynch could rely to execute its limit orders or other orders for customers who preferred the traditional method to Merrill Lynch's. At least, there might not be any Carlisle & DeCoppet, for the first reaction of the exchange, when it was faced by the competitive threat from its single biggest member firm, was to announce that it would buy out the Carlisle firm and use its computer facilities to go into the odd-lot business itself, relying on the floor specialists to supply the required odd lots from their round-lot inventories.

Then second thoughts set in. Maybe the Merrill Lynch odd-lot system didn't pose as big a threat as it seemed to at first. Maybe competition would be a good thing for the odd-lot business. Maybe the old and new methods of odd-lot trading could co-exist. Or, if worst came to worst, the exchange itself could adopt the Merrill Lynch system—something the exchange obviously had in mind, for it ordered Carlisle & DeCoppet, even before it had actually acquired the firm, to execute odd-lot orders at the market opening without charging a differential shortly after Merrill Lynch announced its system.

With Merrill Lynch competing for odd-lot business and with the New York Stock Exchange handling odd-lot orders itself, it appeared that even the small investor might get something of a break in the new era of competition.

How important is the odd-lotter in the overall brokerage picture? One answer to that question is to say that he is both more important and less important than he used to be. With the great growth in the number of shareholders between 1950 and 1970, he became numerically much more important, and yet collectively has accounted for a steadily decreasing percentage of the volume of total shares traded.

In the era that culminated in the bull market of 1929, the little man represented almost 20% of stock exchange volume, and twenty years later, odd-lot trading was still accounting for about 15% or 16%. But from then on it headed pretty steadily downward to a level of less than 10% in 1968 and below 5% from 1972 through 1974. Interestingly enough, however, the dollar value of odd-lot transactions reached an all-time high in 1967, thanks to the fact that odd-lot customers usually buy higher-priced stocks than round-lot customers do. But with the drying up of trading in the 1974 market slump, the total value of odd lots fell to its lowest level in almost two decades, and the little man was slow making his reappearance when the 1976 bull market got under way.

For whatever significance it may have, odd-lotters generally bought more than they sold in the forties and fifties, but in seven out of ten years through the sixties and all through 1970–1975, they were sellers on balance. Even in the first quarter of 1976, when the market was heading up sharply, they still remained on the selling side. There was not a single day when odd-lot purchases topped sales. Observing this scarcely believable situation, one is almost tempted to agree with the cynics that the time to sell is when the little man is buying and vice versa.

CHAPTER 14

M.I.P. and Other Accumulation Plans

UNTIL January 1954, the smallest amount of stock that anyone could buy was one share. In that month, however, member firms of the New York Stock Exchange initiated the Monthly Investment Plan—commonly known as M.I.P.—under which it was possible to buy a fractional share of stock, a fraction figured out to the fourth decimal point. The plan wasn't formulated, of course, for that reason—just to permit an investor to buy part of a share. It was designed to permit people to invest a set sum of money every month—or every quarter if they preferred—and to acquire for that money full or fractional shares of any stock listed on the New York Stock Exchange, except those few sold in ten-share units.

By this method of systematic saving and systematic investing, a person is thus able to acquire a worthwhile interest in the stock of some company on a regular budget basis. He does not have to wait to become an investor until he acquires several hundred dollars, enough to buy five or ten shares of some stock.

The Monthly Investment Plan, in short, is geared to the tempo of life today, since most American families are used to settling their bills and making their installment payments on a monthly budget basis.

M.I.P. is a method of buying stock by the dollar's worth, regardless of how the price may change from month to month, just as you buy $4 or $5 worth of gasoline, regardless of what the per-gallon price is.

In March 1976 the exchange announced that it was abandoning its sponsorship of the Monthly Investment Plan, but many individual member firms continue to offer small investors the opportunity to buy stocks on an M.I.P. basis or through various accumulation plans of their own devising. The exchange withdrew its sponsorship simply because it did not want to handle the business itself, as it would have had to do after its acquisition of Carlisle, DeCoppet & Co., for that odd-lot house had handled some 17,000 M.I.P. plans for a number of small brokerage firms that lacked the computer equipment needed to operate a plan of this kind efficiently. Although Carlisle, DeCoppet's M.I.P. business was only 5% of the total, it was more than the exchange wanted to cope with, and so it disowned its own brainchild.

Under the M.I.P plan, the buyer signs a "contract" —it is actually nothing more than a declaration of intent—with a member firm of the exchange, under which he agrees to accumulate shares of a particular stock listed on the exchange and to invest a regular sum of money—anything in excess of $40—every month or every quarter toward the purchase of that stock.

Since M.I.P. contracts can be canceled by the buyer at any time and are so drawn that the buyer can skip payments without penalty, they are in no sense of the word binding or obligatory.

Here's how the plan works: Suppose you want to buy shares in Rod & Reel at the rate of $50 a month. Out of each payment, the broker gets a commission, and with the balance the operator of the M.I.P. plan buys whatever number of full and fractional shares he can for you, at whatever price prevails at the opening of the market the day after each payment is received.

When the buyer closes out his M.I.P. contract, he gets a stock certificate for whatever full shares he has purchased, and any fractional share that may remain is sold at the prevailing price and the proceeds remitted to the buyer. The broker may levy a minimal extra charge for stock certificates representing anything less than 100 shares.

Dividends become due and payable on all shares, including fractional shares, from the moment any shares are bought; and these dividends, as they are received by the broker, are credited to the customer's account and can be automatically applied to the purchase of additional shares. This is one of M.I.P's unique features, for the investor can automatically reinvest the dividends he collects in any one of the 1,534 common stocks available through M.I.P. on the New York Stock Exchange in mid-1975.

Although the small investor always pays the highest commission rates percentagewise—and no investor can be smaller than an M.I.P. customer—many brokers, since the arrival of negotiated commissions, have shaved their charges on M.I.P. business, partly to encourage new, small investors and partly because computerized operations have made it possible to cut handling costs. Thus, Merrill Lynch, Pierce, Fenner & Smith, which does better than a quarter of the M.I.P. business, cut its commission about 25%. Nevertheless, because they may get a better commission break on purchases involving larger dollar amounts, some M.I.P. customers let their funds accumulate for three months, in order to buy bigger dollar amounts on the quarterly basis.

No matter how high commission costs may be, M.I.P. does have the advantage of helping investors establish regular habits of thrift. Then, too, consistent buying of the same stock provides protection for the small buyer in the event of a decline in price. If he continues buying in the same dollar amount while the price declines, the average cost of all the shares he owns will be reduced, and if the market rises again, he stands to make a tidy profit. Of course, if he stops buying in a downtrend and sells out when the value of his accumulated shares is less than their purchase cost, he will incur a loss.

In 1975, there were 371,115 active accounts in the Monthly Investment Plan and in M.I.P.-like variations offered by different member firms. The big reason why M.I.P. finally caught on is that in 1965 several brokers began pushing M.I.P. as a means by which listed companies could initiate *employee stock purchase plans* on a voluntary, payroll-deduction basis. Hundreds of companies joined forces with brokers to promote such plans, and tens of thousands of their employees thus became stockholders in their companies for the first time.

There is nothing new, of course, about company-sponsored stock purchase plans—200 or more N.Y.S.E.-listed companies have them in some form—but the M.I.P. angle has been attractive to many managements primarily because the broker carries the onus of selling the plan, and management feels less responsible for the price action of its stock. The plan is attractive to the employee because he acquires his stock commission-free, since the company usually picks up the commission tab. Again, the employee escapes payment of virtually all fees that may be charged for purchasing in small lots, since the company purchases the stock for all the employee accounts monthly in a single block and hence acquires practically all the stock at the cheaper commission rates that apply to bigger orders.

Certain banks too have initiated accumulation plans or variations of M.I.P. for the benefit of their customers. The Chase Manhattan Bank, for instance, offers an *Automatic Stock Investment Plan* through which depositors can agree to have funds withdrawn automatically from their checking account each month and applied toward the purchase of any or all of a selected list of stocks; anywhere from a minimum of $20 per stock to a maximum of $500 per stock. The bank then combines the funds that are allocated to particular stocks, makes bulk purchases, and divides the shares up in proportion to individual payments. The stock accumulation plans of other banks all operate in essentially the same way.

Since the *Pension Reform Act* was signed into law in 1974, *Keogh Tax-Shelter Retirement Plans* have become popular. The Keogh law permits self-employed individuals to postpone payment of taxes on 15% of their earned income up to a maximum of $7,500 annually. The income tax on such funds as a man may put into a Keogh plan—as well as taxes on capital gains and dividend or interest income to be earned in the future—is deferred until he retires. Since his tax bracket then is likely to be a whole lot less than it was during his high-earning years, he will pay a lower tax on all the money he set aside than he would if he paid it when earned. Meanwhile, he has also had the use of all that tax money for years. The basic concept of the Keogh plan is to defer taxes as long as possible; to build a nest egg for the future.

The growth of tailor-made accumulation programs and other similar regular investment plans demonstrates the willingness of investors—individuals, as well as small institutions and corporations—to pay premium prices for new and special brokerage services that are offered in package form. Their appeal lies in their streamlined, automatic operation and their minimum transaction costs.

Many M.I.P. investors have become regular brokerage customers, having learned to accumulate their own money until they can afford to buy an odd lot in a regular brokerage account. But others, many others, have fallen by the wayside. They found it easy to drop out of M.I.P. because there was no compulsion, actual or implied, to keep up their payments.

If M.I.P.'s performance has been somewhat disappointing, reasons are not hard to find. Since M.I.P. began, the market has been extraordinarily active, especially as stocks began to recover from the bear market of 1973–1974. And brokers' sales representatives are generally too busy attending to their regular customers to undertake much missionary work on behalf of M.I.P. It is no overstatement to say that M.I.P. is seldom sold by the brokers; it is bought by the customers.

There is a second explanation for the disinclination of brokers' sales representatives to push M.I.P. Many of them feel that it is not right to impose relatively higher commission rates on the investor who characteristically is least able to pay them. On the other hand, it can be argued that the high commission cost is justified because America has to pay a price to learn thrift. Consider the high interest charged nowadays for mortgage money; indeed, for any variety of loan. Consider the high carrying charges which are levied on the buyer to finance all installment purchases. The pay-as-you-go man is used to paying both as he goes and as he comes.

CHAPTER 15

Other Exchanges – Here and in Canada

ALTHOUGH they differ somewhat in rules, regulations and operating mechanics, the other ten registered exchanges in the United States function fundamentally in much the same way as the New York Stock Exchange.

All told, the securities of some 5,000 corporations are listed on the organized exchanges, but on the basis of the dollar value of all stocks traded on these exchanges, about 70% of the business is done on the New York Stock Exchange—the *Big Board,* as it is called —with 2,122 common and preferred stocks listed on January 31, 1976.

In recent years other exchanges have been steadily increasing their volume at the expense of the New York Stock Exchange—twenty years ago it had 85% of total exchange volume—and the Big Board, despite its still overwhelming dominance, complains loudly.

But those complaints from Wall and Broad streets are apt to seem mere whispers compared to the cries of real anguish that will almost certainly be heard from the Big Board when it feels the full effect of the Securities Reform Act of 1975. When the national market becomes a reality and brokers are free to trade on any exchange or negotiate with other securities dealers wholly outside of all exchanges, the New York Stock Exchange, lacking the protection of old Rule 394, which assured it almost monopolistic control of all trading in the nation's premier stocks, is bound to suffer a marked reduction in its share of the total trading volume. Indeed, there are some in Wall Street who wonder if there will be any real place for the New York Stock Exchange—or any other organized exchange—in the securities world of the future.

These concerns are obviously shared by the American Stock Exchange, which has been this country's second biggest stock exchange for generations. With about 1,300 listed stocks, the Amex, as this exchange is called, normally handles about a third to a half as much volume as the New York Stock Exchange. But, because the average price of its shares is much lower, it accounts for only about one-eighth of the total dollar value of all stock transactions on the Big Board.

Rightly or wrongly, the American Stock Exchange has long been regarded as a kind of prep school for the New York Stock Exchange. Many important companies like General Motors and the various Standard Oil companies had their start on the old Curb Exchange. But there are still many other well-known companies such as Hormel, Horn & Hardart, Prentice-Hall, and Syntex, which remain faithful to the American Stock Exchange.

Until 1953, the Amex was known as the New York Curb Exchange. It got its name from the fact that it actually began as a curbstone market, first on Wall and Hanover streets in New York City and later on Broad Street. It remained an outdoor market until 1921, when it finally moved indoors, thus depriving the city of one of its most colorful spectacles. Most of the trading was done by hand signals, and orders were relayed to the brokers in the street by shouts and whistles from clerks perched on the windowsills of their offices in adjoining buildings. Even in its spacious headquarters today, far more modern than the New York Stock Exchange, orders are relayed from the clerks at their phones to floor brokers by hand signals.

Included among the 650 members of the American Stock Exchange are all of the nation's major brokerage firms. With increased activity in recent years, seat prices rose steadily—to an all-time high of $350,000 in 1969. But the market decline of 1973 hit the American Stock Exchange, just as it did the Big Board, and seat prices tumbled that year from a high of $100,000 down to $27,000—the lowest since 1958.

The two New York exchanges operate in rather similar fashion. On the American Stock Exchange odd lots were always handled by specialists, just as they are now on the New York Stock Exchange, instead of an odd-lot broker. An odd-lot differential was always charged by the Amex until January 1976 when Merrill Lynch, Pierce, Fenner & Smith went into the odd-lot business and established a new schedule of fees. The American Stock Exchange decided to meet that competition at once and initiated the same rates as those quoted by Merrill Lynch. If you want to place an order through your broker for an odd lot on the Amex to be filled at the opening on the following day, it will be filled at the price of the first round-lot transaction in your stock, and you will not be charged any odd-lot differential. If you place a market order during the trading day, it will be filled at the bid price in the specialist's book if you are selling or the asked price if you are buying. By paying the ⅛ odd-lot differential, you can always have your order executed at whatever price prevails on the next round-lot sale. You also pay the ⅛ differential if you place a limit order to be executed at a set price. Because the average price per share is much lower on the American Stock Exchange, a greater proportion of its traders buy and sell in round lots rather than odd lots.

Although it was a price-manipulation scandal involving two specialists on the American Stock Exchange that touched off the whole S.E.C. investigation of the market and led to the 1964 securities legislation, it can fairly be said that this exchange moved more rapidly than the Big Board did to put its house in order and conform to S.E.C. standards of self-regulation. The reforms were pushed through by the American Exchange in 1963 as part of its complete reorganization program.

It can also be said that the American Stock Exchange moved more rapidly than the New York Stock Exchange to automate its procedures and to maximize computer application in the conduct of business—including a stock-watch technique to spot unusual trading patterns for prompt study by the staff. The American Exchange also installed electronic equipment to speed reports of transactions from the floor to the ticker before the Big Board did. Moreover, it introduced its own market averages one month sooner in 1966.

In 1975, it scored another "first" when it introduced trading in odd-lot quantities of certain United States government securities on the floor of the exchange, and later augmented this with trading in government agency issues. The Amex also provides a marketplace for all 75 outstanding issues of U.S. Treasury bonds and notes.

But in a spirit of cooperation rather than competition, the two big exchanges in 1969 announced that they would undertake to combine many of their key services and computer operations. Not only did they consolidate their stock-clearing systems but they developed joint automation programs on the trading floors of both exchanges that can save member firms an estimated $5 million annually in duplicate costs.

Such cooperative efforts gave rise naturally to the proposal that the New York and American exchanges be merged into one market, and a study of the feasibility of such a merger was given top priority by both exchanges in 1970. Although neither exchange expressed any great enthusiasm for the idea of a complete merger, they did form the jointly owned *Securities Industry Automation Corporation* in 1972 to consolidate their entire technical facilities and agreed to pursue still further the idea of combining the two exchanges into one. However, in July 1975, the death knell was sounded for the merger concept when the Amex board of directors voted unanimously against it. But no one would be surprised if the proposal was resurrected someday.

The third biggest United States exchange, the *Midwest Stock Exchange,* came into being in 1949, when the Chicago Stock Exchange undertook to effect a consolidation of its activities with those of other exchanges in Cleveland, St. Louis, and Minneapolis–St. Paul.

Other *regional exchanges* include: the Pacific Stock Exchange, located in both Los Angeles and San Francisco; the Philadelphia Stock Exchange, which opened a Southeastern Stock Exchange division in Miami in 1974; and the stock exchanges in Boston, Cincinnati,

Detroit, Honolulu, Salt Lake City (Intermountain Stock Exchange), and Spokane.

All of these exchanges are registered with the Securities and Exchange Commission, which means in effect that the S.E.C. has approved their rules and regulations and adjudged them adequate for the discipline of any member who violates his public trust.

The regional exchanges were organized originally to provide a marketplace for the stocks of local companies, but as these companies grew and acquired national reputations, many of them wanted their securities listed on an exchange in New York City, the nation's biggest money market. And so, naturally, did the Big Board. As it succeeded in luring many issues to New York, the regional exchanges languished.

But in recent years the regional exchanges have managed to turn the tables on the Big Board. They trade many of the same securities that are listed on the New York Stock Exchange, and in recent years the business they did in these stocks accounted for 75% to 85% of their total volume. It was a business that kept growing every day, and local or regional-type issues steadily account for less and less of their volume.

To get this business in Big Board stocks, the regional exchanges induced some of the big companies to list their securities on one or more of the local exchanges as well as on the New York Stock Exchange, and if a company didn't want to go to the expense of *dual listing,* the regional exchanges made their own arrangements to trade in those securities without formal listing. Such arrangements have to be approved by the Securities and Exchange Commission, but in view of the S.E.C.'s determination to break up the Big Board's monopoly, such approval has never proved hard to get.

More than half of all the Big Board stocks are now also traded on one or more regional exchanges, and in the main these are the most popular stocks, those that account for over 80% of Big Board volume. (The American Stock Exchange has not shared in this bonanza, because under S.E.C. rules a stock cannot be traded on two exchanges in the same city.)

The reason for the great growth of trading in Big Board stocks on the regional exchanges isn't hard to find. It traces back to the old Rule 394 of the New York Stock Exchange, the rule that for years forbade a member firm to split commissions with a nonmember.

When a big securities dealer who did not belong to the Big Board had a sizable block of some Big Board stock to buy or sell, he often arranged to have the order executed on a regional exchange by a firm which had memberships both on the Big Board and on the regional exchange and which undertook to develop the other side of the order—a purchase to match the dealer's sell order or a sale to match his buy order. The nonmember dealer and the member firm split the commission, and everybody was happy, everybody except the New York Stock Exchange.

A 1965 amendment to Rule 394, permitting member firms to deal with nonmembers, made it seem likely at the time that some of the regional exchange business in Big Board stocks might dry up, but such was not the case. Under the 1975 securities law, the Big Board and all other exchanges were required to scrap any rules that restricted off-board trading by member firms, and this meant that all exchanges—principally, of course, the Big Board—were bound to suffer.

Though the Big Board did offer to ease Rule 394 in an attempt to offset more radical moves by the S.E.C., the commission turned a deaf ear and set a deadline of April 1, 1976, for lifting all restraints on the freedom of a member firm to execute a customer's order for a Big Board stock wherever he pleased—in the over-the-counter market, on a regional exchange, or the New York Stock Exchange.

The exchange made one last try. It argued that at least it had a right to compel a member to execute an order that had already been recorded in a specialist's book on its own floor and nowhere else. The commission was adamant, but it did allow the exchange an extra 11 months to end that requirement.

Additionally, much of the competition that faces the New York Stock Exchange comes not only from the regional exchanges in the United States but from the exchanges north of the border, where the big boom after World War II stimulated worldwide interest in the ownership of Canadian stocks.

Of the five Canadian exchanges, by far the largest is the Toronto Stock Exchange. From the standpoint of the dollar value of shares traded, Toronto does more than twice the business of all the other Canadian exchanges combined, and almost 30% of its business is in securities listed also on these other Canadian exchanges. In 1974, the Toronto Stock Exchange ranked fourth among all North American exchanges in the dollar value of securities traded: $4.5 billion, compared with more than $99 billion for the New York Stock Exchange.

The other Canadian exchanges are in Montreal, Alberta, Vancouver, and Winnipeg. Interest in oil and mining shares runs especially high in western Canada, while industrial shares are still the prime attraction on the more staid market in Montreal, which used to dominate the Canadian securities scene until the boom after World War II gave Toronto its chance to take over the leadership.

Many of the common stocks listed on the Toronto and Montreal exchanges are on a dividend-paying basis, but the typical buyer of Canadian stocks—or shares, as he and his British counterpart usually call them—isn't so much interested in dividends. He buys common stocks because he wants to share in the dynamic growth of the country and its industry, and he expects his shares to pay him a handsome profit over the years ahead as a result of price appreciation.

In the main, stocks are traded on the Canadian exchanges very much as they are in the United States, but there are several significant differences.

For one thing, floor trading is not restricted exclusively to member brokers. Thus, on the Toronto Exchange, authorized nonmember brokers are entitled to split commissions. Again, there are significant differences in the units of trading. On the Toronto Stock Exchange, stocks selling at less than 10¢ a share—and believe it or not there are some—and those selling at more than 10¢ but under $1 are traded in units of

1,000 and 500 shares, respectively. If the price is at least $1 but under $100, the trading unit is 100 shares, and stocks selling above $100 are traded in 10-share units. All of these different units are known as *board lots,* rather than round lots.

Moreover, the minimum allowable price fluctuation is not just ⅛ point (12½¢) as on the New York Stock Exchange. On stocks selling below 50¢, the minimum spread is ½¢; at more than 50¢ but under $3, it is 1¢; at more than $3 but under $5, it is 5¢; at $5 and over, it is 12½¢.

Odd lots are also bought and sold in Toronto, but they are called *broken lots,* and whether a particular order is classified as a broken lot or a board lot depends on how many shares constitute a board lot of that particular stock.

If a floor broker has a broken lot to sell, he cannot look to either an odd-lot dealer or a specialist to help him, for there is no such person on the Toronto exchange. He turns instead to a registered trader, the nearest equivalent to a specialist. A registered trader has a responsibility for maintaining a market in certain stocks, and a broker with a broken-lot order in his hands can compel the registered trader in that stock to take it off his hands. If it is a buy order, the registered trader must supply the stock at the current quotation, plus a premium. If it is a sell order, the trader must buy the stock, but he is allowed a discount from the current quote.

Canada does not have a national agency like our own S.E.C. to regulate the securities business. Instead, each province has its own commission, and the control they have exerted over the securities business has been something less than rigorous. As a consequence, *boiler shop* operations involving the sale of questionable oil and mining stocks flourished in Canada for many years. Typically, a promoter of such a stock would offer an unsuspecting prospect the "chance of a lifetime" to buy some new issue of stock at a price below that at which it was presumably scheduled to be offered to the public.

The promoter would try to high-pressure the prospect by long-distance telephone and assure him that he had to "act now" if he wanted to get in on the ground floor. And the promoter would glibly cite "engineer's reports" that established the value of the mineral deposit or oil field that the new company intended to work, but the prospect would rarely be able to lay his hands on a printed copy of any such report, much less a prospectus. As a matter of fact, whether the company actually proceeded with its venture very often depended on how many suckers the promoter was able to find.

Many of these boiler shops used to operate in Ontario and prey on prospects in Boston, New York, and other big eastern cities, but they have generally been put out of business as a result of the Ontario Securities Acts—enacted in 1966 and 1970 as a result of widespread public complaints.

But there's always a chance, especially with the big speculative boom in western Canada, that you'll be invited someday to buy a block of stock at a bargain price in the Pipe Dream Mining Company. If you are, check with some reputable broker first, and don't worry about missing out on your big chance by failing to say yes right away. If the stock is worth buying, it will probably be as good a buy tomorrow as it was today.

CHAPTER 16

How the Over-the-Counter Market Works

IF you can buy stocks and bonds of only about 3,000 companies on the registered stock exchanges, where, you may ask, can you buy or sell the securities of the tens and tens of thousands of other companies that exist in this country?

Where, for instance, would you have bought the stock of the Rod & Reel Company in the days when it was growing up and before it could ever hope to be listed on any exchange?

The answer is that you would have bought it in the *over-the-counter* market, and that's where you buy or sell all of the other unlisted securities today—about 40,000 of them. Actually, this market isn't a place; it's a way of doing business, a way of buying or selling securities other than on a stock exchange. Buying interest is matched with selling interest, not on a trading floor but through a massive network of wires linking together thousands of securities firms.

The over-the-counter market is difficult to define or describe, because transactions that take place in this market have few common characteristics.

You might, for instance, conclude a purchase or sale with a securities dealer who operated a one-man shop in some small town, or you might deal with one of those large securities firms in Wall Street who used the facilities of the over-the-counter market to create the third market where institutions could trade large blocks of stock at lower cost.

You might buy an unlisted stock, or one that is regularly traded on the Big Board, the Amex, or a regional exchange.

You might buy a security that the dealer himself

owned and sold to you from his inventory, or you might buy a security that he bought from another dealer just to fill your order.

You might pay a negotiated commission, or you might pay a flat price. You might buy a highly speculative $2 stock in some little-known company, or you might buy the stock of such well-known corporations as Anheuser Busch, Cannon Mills, or Tampax. You might even buy stock in some well-known foreign company by purchasing an *American Depositary Receipt*. (An A.D.R. certificate is simply the evidence that the shares you buy in such a company are deposited to your credit in a foreign office of an American bank or one of its correspondent banks abroad. Such certificates are traded in the over-the-counter market—only a few are listed on the exchanges—just as American stocks are bought and sold.)

You might buy stock in a new company like Rod & Reel, for this is where all companies first offer their securities to the public, or you might buy stock in a bank that has paid dividends for over 190 years—fifty years longer than any New York Stock Exchange security can boast—because the stocks of all but a score of major banks are bought and sold exclusively in the over-the-counter market, as are virtually all insurance companies—life, fire, and casualty.

Finally, your over-the-counter transaction might not involve stocks at all. It might involve the purchase or sale of a bond. More than 99% of all United States government bonds, all municipal bonds, and the great bulk of corporate bonds are traded in the over-the-counter market, not on the exchanges.

The over-the-counter market is, indeed, all things to all men, whether they be conservative investors or wild-eyed speculators, and whether they have millions or simply hundreds of dollars to put in the market.

Despite the diversity of this market, all over-the-counter transactions have about them one common characteristic. The price arrived at in any transaction is not determined by a two-way auction system, such as prevails on a stock exchange; it is a price arrived at by negotiation—negotiation between the securities dealers on both sides of the transaction and negotiation between the dealer and you, his customer.

Probably the most common kind of over-the-counter transaction is one that takes place on a net price basis. A net trade is one in which no commission is charged. Instead of a commission, the securities dealer expects to make a profit by selling the stock to you at more than he paid for it, or by buying it from you at less than he expects to get by selling it to somebody else.

Suppose you got interested in Rod & Reel when it was a new company and decided you would like to buy 50 shares of it. You can buy any number you like in the over-the-counter market, because there are no round lots or odd lots—no standardized trading units.

Now, it might happen that the securities dealer to whom you gave your order was able to fill it from his own inventory, since he had bought some shares recently from another customer who had wanted to sell Rod & Reel. So, he would be able to quote you a price and conclude the sale on the spot.

At the time you made that purchase the prevailing quote might be 18 bid, offered at 18½. Your dealer might quote you that same offering price of $18.50 a share, or he might offer it cheaper, say $18.25, if he were anxious to move it out of his inventory, especially if he had been able to purchase the stock at $17.00 or $17.50 originally.

Now, let's suppose he doesn't have 50 shares of Rod & Reel in his inventory. In such case, he would have to buy the stock from another dealer in order to fill your order. So he checks with other dealers and finds that the lowest price at which he can buy the stock is 18¼, or $18.25. That's the price to him, the price one dealer quotes another, and such price is called the *wholesale price* or *dealer price*—sometimes the *inside price*. It is not the price at which he will sell the stock to you. That price, the *retail price,* might be $18.75 or $19.00 a share, perhaps even more. The difference between what he paid the other dealer for the stock and the price he charges you is his *markup,* and since this is a net trade, it is this markup that he takes, instead of a commission, that constitutes his profit on the transaction.

If you were selling the stock instead of buying it, the dealer would simply reverse the procedure. If he knew that 18¼ was the best inside price, the highest price at which another dealer would take the stock off his hands, he might offer to pay you 17¾ or 17½ for your stock, and the difference, or *markdown,* would represent his profit.

Of course, once he bought the stock from you, he might decide not to sell it. Instead, he might decide to hold it in his own inventory. In such case, he would take a position in the stock. If he then began to trade the stock actively, buying and selling it in substantial volume, he would be *making a market* in the stock.

Price differences or spreads between the wholesale and retail, such as those on your Rod & Reel transaction, are fairly typical of the spreads that might prevail on an average net trade on a low-priced stock that wasn't too well known in the over-the-counter market. If you were buying or selling one of the actively traded stocks in the market, the spreads between the retail and wholesale prices might narrow to ¼ of a point on low-priced stocks, and the difference between the bid and asked quotations might be only ½ a point.

On the other hand, if the over-the-counter stock you wanted to buy or sell was almost unknown, if it did not enjoy any public market to speak of, there might be a spread of a full point or more on the wholesale market and of several points between the retail bid and asked quotations.

Suppose, for instance, you were in New York and wanted to dispose of some stock you owned in a little lumber company out in Oregon, a company that was virtually unknown outside its hometown. Your dealer would try to find a bid for the stock by contacting other dealers, principally in New York, where most of them are congregated. He might then try his luck in Chicago or San Francisco or Portland by calling or teletyping dealers in those cities. Ultimately, to promote a bid, he might wire or phone local banks in the area to see if they knew of any possible buyers. He might even phone the company itself to see if it wanted to buy back any of its own stock. For such special service the dealer is obviously entitled to a special extra profit.

In ordinary transactions, trades that involve no special effort on the part of the dealer and in which he assumes no risk, the *National Association of Securities Dealers* (*N.A.S.D.*) has long taken the stand that the dealer should restrict his markup to a maximum of 5%. Thus, if the inside market for Rod & Reel were 19 bid, offered at 20 when you placed an order to buy, your dealer would be entitled to mark the offering price up 5%, or 1 full point, and his retail price to you could be $21 a share. Another less greedy dealer might have quoted you a retail price of $20.50 or $20.75, but this is not something you are likely to know unless you shop around. The S.E.C. has long looked with disfavor at that 5% markup on a *riskless transaction* and feels that the customer is well advised to demand that his dealer reveal the amount of his markup. As a result, some securities firms now voluntarily disclose the amount of their markup on the trade confirmations that they send their customers.

Remember, when you buy a stock from a dealer on a net price basis, you are negotiating or bargaining with him. You are asking, "How much will I have to pay?" And the dealer, in effect, is asking, "How much will you pay me?" He is not acting as your broker or agent, trying to buy or sell something for you at the best price possible, plus a commission; instead, he is dealing with you as a *principal* in the trade. As a dealer, he doesn't collect a commission; he expects to make a profit.

While the great majority of over-the-counter transactions are handled on a net price basis, it is possible, especially if you are dealing with one of the big national brokerage firms, to buy or sell over-the-counter securities on an *agency basis*. Operating as an agent, your broker would seek the best possible inside price, and he would buy or sell the stock for you at that wholesale price and charge you a commission, just as he would if he were buying or selling a stock on an exchange for you. The commission he charges is usually the same as he would charge for buying or selling the same number of shares at the same price on an exchange.

In the big brokerage firms, over-the-counter business is handled by a separate *trading department* located in the headquarters office, but sales representatives in the firm's offices across the country handle orders for both stock-exchange and over-the-counter securities. Most firms that operate both as dealers and as brokers usually make a market in a specified number of over-the-counter stocks, and that number may run into the hundreds in the case of really big firms. If you buy or sell one of these stocks, the transaction will almost certainly be handled on a net price basis. On other over-the-counter stocks in which he does not make a market, he is generally willing to act as your agent or broker in concluding a trade.

Whenever you buy an over-the-counter stock, you may wonder whether your dealer really did get the best possible inside price for you. Nowadays, you can get a clear-cut, instant answer to that question if you are buying or selling any one of several hundred most popular and widely held over-the-counter stocks, thanks to the development in the late sixties of an automated quote system by the Bunker Ramo Corporation, a company specializing in all kinds of quotation equipment for the securities business, and the National Association of Securities Dealers, the industry's self-regulatory agency, which represents 4,300 dealers in the over-the-counter market and operates under the authority of the Securities and Exchange Commission.

Before the development of the National Association of Securities Dealers' *Automated Quotation System,* popularly known as *NASDAQ,* there was no way in which a dealer himself could be absolutely sure that he was getting the best possible price on a particular stock, because there was no way in which he could know all the firms throughout the country that might be making a market in the stock or what their current price quotations were. He might be able to contact the principal *market-makers* in New York and Chicago, maybe even San Francisco, but at any given time some dealer in Cleveland or Atlanta or Denver might actually be making a better market in the stock.

For a long time, the *National Quotation Bureau* has provided at least a partial solution to that problem. Every day this privately owned price reporting service publishes in its *"pink sheets"* the wholesale prices on 10,750 over-the-counter stocks and 4,300 bonds. These are the prices at which hundreds of different dealers announce their willingness to buy or sell various securities in trades between dealers.

Any dealer who wants to have his prices quoted supplies them every afternoon to the bureau. The quotation sheets are printed overnight and distributed nationwide prior to the opening of the N.Y.S.E. Since any dealer who has an important position in a stock wants to stimulate inquiries about it from other dealers, the pink sheets, subscribed to by almost every important dealer in the country, render a valuable service. But in its study of the over-the-counter market, which preceded the 1964 Securities Acts Amendment, the S.E.C. expressed its concern about how dealers used—or abused—the pink sheets.

The S.E.C. wants to be sure that every dealer stands behind the prices he announces in the sheets, that they are not used to create a false impression of value or market activity. If a dealer announces a price he is willing to pay for a given stock, he may get away with a refusal to buy the stock that is offered to him at his announced bid on any one particular day—he might defend himself by saying that the market had moved away from his bid—but if he publishes the same price the next day, he has to take stock offered to him at that price or run the risk that an official complaint will be lodged against him.

When the 1964 act was under consideration, the commission made it clear that it felt automation was in order for the over-the-counter market. It wanted a computerized electronic system, operating on a national scale, that would assure a more accurate and more rapid exchange of price and market information. And that is how NASDAQ was born.

Beyond question, NASDAQ has revolutionized the

over-the-counter business. By hooking the dealers together in one wire system, capable of providing exact, instantaneous wholesale price quotations of all dealers who make markets in important over-the-counter stocks, NASDAQ has virtually eliminated the vast jumble of telephone wires on which the business previously had to depend. NASDAQ has become, in effect, a new kind of securities exchange in which the computer and assorted electronic gear represent a 3,000-mile-long trading floor stretching from coast to coast to which securities dealers in some 6,000 offices have immediate access.

NASDAQ began operations by supplying bid-and-asked quotations on 2,500 over-the-counter stocks, and it has been gradually increasing that number ever since, although it will not put any stock into the NASDAQ System unless there are at least 100,000 shares in the hands of 300 or more stockholders and unless the company has total assets of at least $1 million and net assets of a half million.

At any time during the trading day, a market-maker can feed into NASDAQ the price at which he is willing to buy a particular stock and the price at which he is willing to sell it, changing these prices during the course of the day as competition may dictate. NASDAQ records all of these thousands of different entries in its memory bank, and whenever a dealer wants to know at what price other dealers will buy or sell a stock, he simply turns to his NASDAQ machine.

NASDAQ provides different levels of service. Level 1 is a quote machine for the use of securities salesmen. Simply by pushing buttons for the alphabetical symbol of the stock on his desk-model machine (ABUD for Anheuser Busch, for instance), the salesman can get a *representative bid* price and a *representative asked* price on that stock; the data appear on a small fluorescent screen, which is part of the machine. The representative bid is the median wholesale bid of all the firms making a market in the stock. Thus, if five dealers quoted bids on a particular stock of 40, 40¼, 40½, 40¾, and 41, the representative bid would be 40½.

Since every dealer has also entered the price at

which he is offering to sell—a price somewhat above his bid—the average spread between the bid and asked prices can be calculated. If it were 1½ points in this particular case, NASDAQ would show a representative asked price of 42; a price arrived at by adding the average spread of 1½ points to the representative bid of 40½.

If a customer finds a representative quotation to his liking, he may decide to make a purchase or a sale. With the order in hand, the salesman now turns to the Level 2 machine in the trading department, and again by punching out the stock symbol, he gets the actual quotes of five firms making a market in that stock. The names of those firms are shown beside their quotes by symbols on the screen. There may be less than five market-makers in the stock, but if there are more than five, the indication MOR appears on the screen, and when the MOR button is pushed, the bid and asked quotes of the other dealers, ranked in order of best price, appear. Once a trader knows what firm offers the best quotation, he contacts that market-maker by phone or wire and concludes the purchase or sale in the usual manner. All trades in over-the-counter securities are settled and cleared through the *National Clearing Corporation,* a wholly owned subsidiary of the N.A.S.D., which has facilities in 11 cities to serve nearly 300 clearing members.

The N.A.S.D. does not attempt to dictate what the spread should be between bid and asked prices on any stock, it leaves that to be determined by the competition of the marketplace. But, the automatic quotation system is geared so that each time a market-maker enters a bid-and-asked quotation it is checked by computer against the *"representative spread"*—the average spread of other market-makers in that security. If this representative spread is half a point and the market-maker enters a spread which is a point or more, he is notified instantly that his spread is excessive. This report of excess spread is forwarded from the computer to the N.A.S.D., which may then take disciplinary action against the market-maker.

A company whose stock is included in the NASDAQ system generally must register under a section of the Securities Exchange Act of 1934 and meet the same disclosure requirements as a listed company. Furthermore, there must be at least two dealers who make a regular market in the stock, and each dealer must have a net capital of $50,000 or $5,000 for each security in which he is registered as a market-maker, whichever is less.

Once he registers with the N.A.S.D. as a market-maker in a stock, a dealer must be willing to buy it or sell it at any time and to announce through NASDAQ the prices at which he will trade.

Perhaps the single most dramatic reform which the S.E.C. brought about after the 1964 act was the publication in the newspapers of more accurate and dependable quotations on over-the-counter stocks, thanks again to NASDAQ.

Over-the-counter quotes were not—and are not today—actual prices. They have always been only indications of the price range within which the customer might expect to trade. Prior to 1966, quotes on the bid, or buy, side furnished to newspapers by the National Association of Securities Dealers were always reasonably accurate, but the asked, or offering, prices were characteristically inflated by 4% or 5%, sometimes even more. Thus, a stock with a published quote of 21 on the asked side might actually have been available at 20—and the customer who was asked to pay only 20½ would have been delighted at the "bargain" he thought he got.

The S.E.C. took a dim view of this practice, and after a bitter fight with many small dealers in the industry, the commission forced the publication daily of more realistic quotes on the 2,500 stocks that are considered to have national or regional markets. As a result, virtually all prices for over-the-counter stocks that are now published in newspapers are reliable quotes, not inflated on either side. Throughout the trading day, NASDAQ releases to the press lists of closing representative bid-and-asked quotations for all issues quoted in NASDAQ. These lists also indicate the trading volume and the price change, if any, in the bid from the previous day's close.

Quotations and trading volume figures for securities on the national NASDAQ list (approximately 1,400 issues) are published in more than 200 newspapers across the country. In addition, over 130 local N.A.S.D. quotations committees select securities with local investor interest, and newspapers are supplied with additional NASDAQ quotes on these. The NASDAQ system also computes a number of market indexes and trading statistics which are furnished to newspapers and radio and television stations.

In addition to the publication of reliable wholesale quotes, many other reforms have flowed from the enactment of the 1964 and 1975 legislation. One of the most important is the requirement that companies whose stocks are sold over-the-counter (except insurance companies, which are regulated by state insurance commissions) must make annual reports to the Securities and Exchange Commission and their shareholders if they have assets in excess of $1 million and more than 500 stockholders.

One of the main pillars of the S.E.C.'s long-envisioned central securities market, that would link stock exchanges and the over-the-counter market, is a *composite quotation system* for securities transactions. At the S.E.C.'s request, the exchanges eliminated the rules and practices that formerly restricted the use of stock quote information. The stage was set, but the choice of a cornerstone for the system was delayed initially by control struggles between the exchanges and the many complexities of the system itself.

Slowly but surely over the years, the Securities and Exchange Commission has forced on the over-the-counter market most of the regulations that have long been imposed on stock exchanges and their member firms. Thus, provision has been made for the regular inspection of all dealer organizations by the N.A.S.D., with authority to compel compliance with all rules and regulations to assure fair dealing to customers. Salesmen of both member and nonmember firms must take tougher examinations, and controls have been established to assure the honesty of advertising and sales literature.

Since the 1964 act gave the S.E.C. the authority to suspend trading in any over-the-counter stock for ten days, it now has the necessary power to control the so-called *hot issues*. These are the stocks, often little-known, in the over-the-counter market that in past bull markets skyrocketed in price in a relatively short time only to plummet back to their starting point, or lower, just as rapidly and all without any provable price manipulation.

Intent on preventing such shenanigans, the Securities and Exchange Commission since 1966 has been using a computer to help it police its over-the-counter beat. The computer makes regular surveys of the market, and it can scan 32,000 quotations in 90 minutes. Regularly, it turns up 300 or 400 suspicious price jiggles, a sharp rise or a drop that suggests the need for further investigation. In each such case, the computer supplies the name of the dealer involved, and unless investigation proves that there was good and sufficient reason for the price movement, that dealer becomes a marked man. From then on, his name can be fed into the computer regularly and all his trades subjected to close scrutiny.

Despite this improved climate of regulation, the phrase "over-the-counter" will probably continue to suggest to some investors the kind of questionable dealing associated with the phrase "under-the-counter." The unfortunate label—which goes back to colonial times when the few securities that existed were often traded by a merchant, just like other merchandise, right over his store counter—will not die, despite concerted efforts to substitute other terms, such as unlisted or *off-board* or *off-exchange*.

However, as more people have become familiar with the over-the-counter market and come to have more confidence in it, thanks to S.E.C. reforms, business continues to increase, and nowadays share volume in the market is apt to be a third of Big Board volume, although the dollar value of shares traded is apt to be somewhat less because of the lower-priced stocks.

Because the over-the-counter market is essentially a negotiated market instead of an auction market like the New York Stock Exchange, day-to-day price fluctuations may not be as pronounced, but the long-term trend is usually pretty much the same in the two markets. The 1973–1974 bear market in over-the-counter stocks reached its final low two months before the Big Board; by July 1, 1975, the NASDAQ composite index had recovered 57.3% from its bear market low, while the Dow Jones *industrial average* was up 51.9%.

Unlike the Big Board, however, the over-the-counter market always seems to have a few glamour stocks that perform surprisingly well even in a bear market. Thus, the *Over-the-Counter Securities Review* reports that in 1973, when 2,381 stocks declined by more than 50%, there were actually 236 issues that advanced by 50% or more. In 1974, there were still almost 200 issues that went up 50% or more, while a record 3,700 plunged more than 50%. It's that kind of performance that makes life exciting in the over-the-counter market.

CHAPTER 17

Investing — Or What's a Broker For?

SUPPOSE you decide that the time has come for you to put some of your extra savings into securities. What do you do next? How do you go about buying stocks or bonds?

You might go to your local banker and ask him how to proceed. He'll know several investment firms in your general community and probably at least one man in each of them. But don't forget that the banker is actually in competition with those security houses for your savings. He may buy government bonds or other securities from them himself, but the typical banker outside the big-city banks is quite apt to look with a jaundiced eye on *your* buying securities. He would rather see you add to your savings account or employ your money in other ways through his bank—in a local business, in real estate, or in mortgages, for example.

Again, don't forget that most bankers are extremely conservative. It's their business to be. When it comes to investing the bank's own money, they have been legally compelled to confine investments largely to government and other high-grade bonds. They may have little familiarity with stocks and understandable misgivings about them. They don't realize that the individual's investment problem is apt to differ considerably from a bank's problem.

And what is true of a banker is apt to be true of a lawyer too. He's likely to be almost as conservative, because he thinks of investments principally in his role as a trustee, a man legally responsible for the administration of an estate.

So where else may you turn for help if you want to buy securities?

The answer to that is: a broker, because he's obviously the man best qualified to help you with your investment problem. That's his whole business. If you don't know the name of a broker, one of your friends or associates surely does. And if you don't want to ask, look in the financial section of your daily newspaper. You'll find brokers' advertisements there. Study those advertisements for a while; decide which firm seems to have the kind of policy you like and the service you need. Then visit the firm. You don't need a letter of introduction.

But can you trust brokers' advertising? After all, advertising is special pleading, notoriously given to overstatement, exaggeration, and excessive claims. But while that may be generally true, it is a matter of fact that you can place much greater confidence in brokers' advertising than you can in the advertising for virtually any other product or service. And that is equally true of all their sales promotion literature, because under the rules of the New York Stock Exchange all forms of communication with the public by member firms must be approved by the exchange before publication. Furthermore, almost all member firms submit their advertising and their sales literature to the scrutiny of their own legal counsel as well as to the exchange because any misstatement can subject a broker to expensive lawsuits.

In its censorship work for more than thirty years, the exchange has adhered to the general standards of truthfulness and good taste, and in judging the acceptability of any advertisement or published report the exchange has concerned itself not only with what was said but with what was omitted and should have been said, with implications as well as overt statements.

In the early sixties when the S.E.C.'s study of the securities industry pointed the need for many reforms, the exchange tightened up its regulation of advertising and all other forms of communication, spelling out its standards in meticulous detail. Specifically forbidden are language that is promissory or flamboyant or contains unwarranted superlatives; opinions not clearly labeled as such; forecasts or predictions not stated as estimates or opinions; recommendations that cannot be substantiated as reasonable; testimonials; boasts about the success of past recommendations unless they meet a set of exacting requirements; and any evasion of a broker's responsibility to disclose any special interest he might have in any given security he recommends.

Shortly after the exchange adopted its standards, the National Association of Securities Dealers adopted roughly similar regulations which apply to all over-the-counter dealers in that association, and both the N.A.S.D. and the exchange are continually tightening those regulations—strictly enforcing them and adding new ones. They can't afford not to.

Yes, you are justified in placing greater faith in the advertising of the securities business today than in almost any other advertising you are likely to encounter in newspapers, magazines, radio, or television.

Lots of people still shy away from the broker for a variety of reasons. Some of them feel embarrassed about the amount of money they have to invest. Maybe they have only a few hundred to put into stocks, perhaps only $40 or $50 a month, and they figure a broker wouldn't be interested.

Maybe some brokers wouldn't be, but the big wire houses are spending millions of dollars in advertising every year to tell the smaller investor that they definitely are interested in him and in helping him invest his money wisely.

And still people hesitate. Perhaps they think of the broker as a somewhat forbidding individual who gives his time only to Very Important People, people who are well-heeled and travel in the right social circles. That's not true. There's nothing exclusive about the brokerage business today. No spats or striped pants. The club rules are all changed, and coffee and hamburgers are more popular items on the club menu than champagne and caviar.

Another thing that stops a lot of people is the jargon that brokers talk. You know that there's nothing mysterious about words like "debenture" or "cumulative preferred" or "stock dividend." True, they're specialized words, because they apply to very specialized things, but there's nothing difficult to understand about either the words or the things they stand for, if you take the trouble to learn them.

Finally, some people don't want to go to a broker because, frankly, they distrust him. They're afraid of being sold a bill of goods, a block of stock in some worthless company. That happened back in the twenties. Nobody can deny it. Maybe it happened to people you know—your father, your uncle, some other member of your family.

Can it happen today? Yes, it *can* happen, because no law or regulation has ever been devised that will put every crook and swindler in our society behind bars. Occasionally—very, very occasionally—you may still encounter one of those gyp artists in the securities business intent on unloading some stock on you and other unsuspecting investors so he can run the price up and then sell out his own holdings at a fat profit, leaving you to hold the bag when the price subsequently plummets.

Occasionally—but again, very occasionally—you might be sold such a stock at a highly inflated price by a thoroughly honest but somewhat naïve and irresponsible broker who himself has been taken in by the propaganda that the gyp artist always spreads. The S.E.C. and the exchange are constantly on the alert to track down and scotch such false and misleading *tips* or rumors, for their circulation is a clear-cut form of illegal price manipulation or outright fraud, but, alas, brokers—like all human beings—can fall prey to propaganda that promises an easy dollar, a quick profit.

A broker may logically and legitimately try to sell you on the idea of buying stocks because he believes in investing, but unless his firm is involved in an underwriting of a stock or the sale of a large block, he hasn't any selfish reason to try to sell you any one particular stock on the New York Stock Exchange, because his only return is a percentage of the commission that his firm charges. Even if he works on a salary basis, his salary in the long run will depend mainly on the commissions he generates. As far as the commission is concerned, there is usually not much difference in what his firm makes whether you put a given amount of money into one stock or the other. So it doesn't matter to him which you buy.

Of course, when you buy stocks on a net price basis —over-the-counter stocks—there is more of a chance that you can be sold something the dealer has an interest in unloading at a profit. But that doesn't happen too often. Few businesses are as competitive as the American securities business today, with every broker and dealer in the country anxious to get customers and keep them for a good many years to come. In that kind of situation there's not much room for the second-story operator who plays fast and loose with the customer's best interests.

Credit the Securities and Exchange Commission, if you wish. Or credit the stock exchange's own house-cleaning. Or credit the moral influence of a healthy competition.

But credit also the fact that the men in the securities business are, in the vast majority of cases, men of conscience and probity, responsible to a standard of ethics as high as prevails in any business you can name.

What it all comes down to is this: the safest way to begin investing is to choose some listed stock through a member firm of the New York Stock Exchange and study that stock, and the company behind it, before you buy.

If there's no member firm near you, you can write to one and buy by mail. But, since negotiated commissions became effective in May 1975, you should request a copy of any particular broker's commission schedule and inquire about possible extra charges— what they are for and what added cost they could mean to you. Or you can order stock through virtually any bank or securities dealer in the country, although you will probably have to pay an additional handling charge. Such a charge is wholly legitimate.

One last word of caution: If any broker or securities dealer tries to dissuade you from buying stock in some well-established company, if he tries to switch you into

Wildcat common or Pipe Dream preferred or some other dubious stock, you had better check with another house.

To help protect investors against the high-pressure, "fast-buck" peddlers of dubious stocks, the S.E.C., with the cooperation of industry trade groups and the Better Business Bureau, has issued an investor's guide which makes these ten recommendations to all investors:

(1) Think before buying.

(2) Deal only with a securities firm you know.

(3) Be skeptical of securities offered over the telephone from any firm or salesman you do not know.

(4) Guard against all high-pressure sales.

(5) Beware of promises of quick, spectacular price rises.

(6) Be sure you understand the risk of loss as well as the prospect of gain.

(7) Get the facts. Do not buy on tips or rumors.

(8) Request the person offering securities over the phone to mail you written information about the corporation, its operations, net profit, management, financial position, and future prospects, and save all such information for future reference.

(9) If you do not understand the written information, consult a person who does.

(10) Give at least as much thought when purchasing securities as you would when acquiring any valuable property.

CHAPTER 18

How You Do Business with a Broker

LET'S assume you finally make up your mind to buy some stock, like General Motors or General Electric, and you go to a broker, a member firm of the New York Stock Exchange, to place your order.

What's likely to happen? What's a broker's office like? What do you say and what do you do? How does he operate?

A lot of people go in and out of a broker's office all the time, people who want to know how the market is doing, and people who just like to watch the passing show or want to take refuge from rain, snow, or heat. So if nobody pays any attention to you when you walk in, don't feel that you're being neglected. Just walk up to the first person who looks as though he works there and tell him you would like to talk to somebody about buying some stock. That will get action fast.

Maybe that person will take you to the manager, who in turn will introduce you to a *registered representative* with whom you can discuss your situation in more detail. Maybe you'll skip the manager and be referred directly to some registered representative.

What's a registered representative? In the twenties he was called a *customer's man*. That's not a title in favor anymore, because the customer's man got a bad reputation as a fast-work artist with a glib line when it came to selling bonds to old college chums or clubhouse cronies. Today's registered representatives bear little resemblance to that character.

Again, the old customer's man used to "play the market" a good deal himself. Most brokerage firms now are happy to see their employees invest in securities, but they frown on too much "in and out" trading by a registered representative for his own account. And they can keep close tabs on that because of a New York Stock Exchange rule which, with rare exceptions, forbids any employee of a brokerage firm to buy or sell securities except through the firm for which he works.

Many a customer refers to the registered representative as "my broker." Actually, of course, he isn't. He is an employee of the brokerage firm, and he simply represents the firm's floor broker, who will actually execute your orders on the exchange. That's why he's called a representative. The "registered" part of his title means that he has been licensed by the S.E.C. and approved by the exchange as a man of good character and one who is thoroughly informed about the operations of the securities business. In fact, he has had to pass a searching examination on the subject administered by the New York Stock Exchange. The National Association of Securities Dealers gives the same kind of examination to representatives of nonmember dealers.

Registered representatives—also called *customer's brokers* or *account executives* by some firms—come in all kinds and qualities. Some are young, and some are old. Some are Democrats and some are Republicans. Some have been in the business for years, and some are comparative newcomers.

These newcomers deserve a special word, because their entrance into the field is itself an evidence of how the business has changed. From the time of the depression to the end of World War II, only a handful of college graduates went into Wall Street. They looked for greener pastures—the big corporations.

But nowadays, except in periods like 1969–1970 and 1973–1974 when the market languishes, the securities business can count on getting its share of topnotch men—and women too—from every graduating class. Many an old customer's man coasted for years on his reputation as an all-star halfback. His successor's career is apt to be based much more solidly on a record of real scholastic achievement, plus extracurricular leadership. Often, he will have earned a degree at some university's graduate school of business.

Again, the customer's man of yesteryear rarely bothered to acquire any formal training in the business; he just picked it up as he went along. The present-day registered representative has usually put in a much more painstaking apprenticeship. More often than not, he will have attended some firm's training school, plugging away eight hours a day for several months at basic lessons in accounting, economics, security analysis, and investment account management. It costs a sponsoring firm about $15,000 to train each representative. He or she has to be good!

The registered representative is "your broker" in the sense that he's the man you deal with when you do business with a brokerage firm. He's usually assigned to you by the manager of the office, and if at any time you find his service less than satisfactory, all you have to do is ask the manager to be assigned another man.

And if you don't like the brokerage firm itself, try another. There are plenty of them, some big and some little, some offering a wide variety of special services and facilities, and some specializing in just one phase of the securities business, such as municipal bonds or institutional investment.

All of them can buy and sell securities for you, and all of them will execute your orders faithfully; they won't "bucket" them. A *bucket-shop* operator is a man who accepts your order to buy a stock at the market —and your money—but he doesn't execute the order; instead he pockets your money and gambles on his ability to buy the stock for you sometime later at a lower price and make a profit for himself on your order. He reverses the method on a sell order. Needless to say, all such operations are thoroughly illegal, and today they are virtually nonexistent, thanks to the vigilance of the Securities and Exchange Commission and the stock exchange.

You can talk to your registered representative with complete candor, because whatever you tell him about your affairs will be held in strict confidence. A broker never reveals who his customers are, much less anything about their circumstances.

The more you tell him about your finances—your

income, your expenses, your savings, your insurance, and whatever other obligations, like mortgage or tuition payments, you may have to meet—the better will he be able to help you map out an investment program suited to your needs.

It is a part of his job to see that you get information or counsel whenever you need it. Don't be embarrassed about asking him the simplest kind of question about investing—about a company, about some financial term, or about the way your order is handled.

At the same time, you should remember that you have certain obligations to your broker, just as he has to you. You should pay promptly for any securities you buy. You should inform him of any change in your address and whether the securities you buy and pay for are to be transferred into your name and mailed to you, or held by the broker in your account.

If you give him an order to buy or sell, be sure there is no misunderstanding about what you want to do. The broker may seem overly meticulous and careful about your order. This is not only because he wants to give you prompt and efficient service but also because the cost of correcting possible errors has gone up too, just like everything else. Moreover, the firm he works for very likely penalizes him for any error, and that error might very well be attributable to you. Indeed, the phrase common to most boardrooms for many decades, "Put it in the error account," today has been translated to mean "Charge it to the registered representative."

The ticker tape itself is no longer what it was in the days when conquering channel swimmers, visiting statesmen and astronauts rode up Broadway through paper snowstorms. As a matter of fact, the last official ticker tape parade was in October 1969 to celebrate the Met's World Series victory.

Paper ticker tape began to fade from the scene over a quarter century ago when the eight-foot *Trans-Lux* screens became a standard fixture of brokerage offices. The tape itself, printed on cellophane, was magnified and projected on the screen, and quotations marched across the screen from right to left, so that the brokers, customers, and boardroom loafers could all watch the market action on both the New York and American exchanges.

The Trans-Lux screens were supplanted in the late sixties by electronic screens on which the stock symbols and prices, projected in brilliant neon-lighted characters, marched across a black background, as in an animated electric sign. Trans-Lux Corporation itself developed the first of these electronic tapes and called it the *Transjet.* The Ultronic Systems Corporation then introduced its *Lectrascan,* but because its tape had to be read from left to right and because the quotations didn't move but were replaced, one at a time, by later transactions, brokers had some difficulty in getting used to its unconventional operation. Ultronic then brought out its *Ultrascan,* which is read in conventional manner like the old Trans-Lux.

Another competitor in the field is the Bunker-Ramo Corporation, which sought to go its rivals one better by developing the *Telequote Ticker* in which transactions appear on an electronic screen in vertical fashion, so that the tape is read from top to bottom. Best known of these machines was the *Telequote 3,* but now it has been eclipsed by the company's new *Market Decision System 7,* which provides the same information as Telequote 3, but displays it all simultaneously, rather than having to push separate buttons for the specific data required. All of these various services and devices give brokers and their customers ready and convenient access to an almost bewildering array of last-second market information, all right at their fingertips.

Gone with the paper ticker tape is the old-fashioned *quote board* on which board markers, often teen-age girls, used to chalk up quotations for various stocks as they came in on the ticker. The electric quote board known as *Teleregister,* now a part of Bunker-Ramo, grew into a standard fixture across the front of every boardroom. As the prices for a stock changed, little figures clicked electrically into place under the appropriate stock symbol, showing the last sale, the opening price, the high and low for the day, and yesterday's close. Some brokers once had Teleregisters on which hundreds of stocks, as well as a dozen or more commodities, were boarded, but their number steadily dwindled as the Teleregister, like the chalk board, headed down the trail toward oblivion.

What has made Teleregister virtually obsolete was the development in the late sixties of highly sophisticated, computer operated, *desk model quote machines* by Bunker-Ramo, Scantlin Electronics, and Ultronic Systems.

The desk models are available in a variety of styles and degrees of sophistication, but on all of them the registered representative, simply by pushing a few keys, can get almost a sorcerer's lineup of statistical information on thousands of different stocks—all those listed on the New York and American exchanges, as well as many on leading regional and Canadian exchanges, plus many hundreds of leading over-the-counter stocks and mutual funds. On most stocks, he can instantly obtain the latest price, with an indicator to show whether it is an up tick or down tick, the bid-and-asked prices, the open, high, low and previous close, the volume of trading, earnings, dividend and percentage yield per share, the price-earnings ratio, and the time of the last sale. Some machines will also provide essential news or a brief appraisal of the stock. Equally comprehensive information on the trend of the market as a whole can be obtained on the desk-model screen, and on some models the current tape is projected.

With the development of computers and various electronic gear to provide instantaneous price and market information for thousands of stocks, listed and unlisted, it was only logical that the securities industry should develop a *consolidated ticker* system covering all major markets.

Under the sponsorship of the *Consolidated Tape Association,* composed of the principal exchanges and the National Association of Securities Dealers, a pilot version of the consolidated stock tape was introduced in October 1974 with 15 N.Y.S.E-listed stocks. After various deadline extensions caused by technical snags, the tape made its formal debut in June 1975.

Today, it consists of two sections—*Network A* and *Network B*. Tape A reports all transactions on 2,122 Big Board stocks—both common and preferred—regardless of the exchange where the trade took place. Thus, when a transaction is effected in any Big Board stock on a participating exchange, in the over-the-counter or third market, or in any other market such as that operated by Instinet, the stock symbol printed on the New York Stock Exchange consolidated tape is followed by "&" and then a letter identifying the marketplace: M (Midwest), P (Pacific), X (Philadelphia), C (Cincinnati), B (Boston), D (Detroit), T (Third Market), O (Other Markets, including Instinet). Transactions in Big Board stocks that are executed on the New York Stock Exchange, of course, have no identifying letter since that is the primary market for those listed stocks.

For instance, a trade involving 1,600 shares of Ford Motor that took place in the third market at a price of 37 would be reported on the upper line of the consolidated ticker tape by the letters "F & T," followed on the lower line by "1600S37." In order to report trade executions of N.Y.S.E.-listed issues on the Pacific Stock Exchange, which remains open an hour and a half later than the Big Board, the tape runs until 5:30 P.M., E.S.T.

Here's a sample section of the consolidated tape, showing transactions made in Occidental Petroleum (N.Y.S.E.), Northern States Power (Third Market), Fluor Corp. (Philadelphia), du Pont (Midwest), and Transamerica (Philadelphia).

OXY		NSP&T	FLR&P	DD&M	TA&P
3S7⅞	4S⅝	4⅞	39⅛	118⅝	4S8⅜

Whenever the volume of trading is so heavy that the tape runs late, a kind of shorthand is used. If the tape runs a minute late, all full-number digits are eliminated except the last digit and the fraction, unless that last digit is a zero, in which case the full figure is shown. When the tape runs two minutes late, volume figures are omitted for all sales of less than 1,000 shares. And when the tape runs three minutes late, only transactions that involve a price change are reported. As the tape catches up, these deletions are restored in reverse order until the tape is running normally again.

Tape B follows exactly the same system in reporting transactions that are effected on the American Stock Exchange and the regional exchanges.

Since all brokerage operations have become generally more streamlined and efficient, it is easy for the average broker to visualize the day when a central securities market and a national clearance and depository system would be introduced. He could also anticipate the time when the traditional broker's boardroom might disappear completely, because there would no longer be a board nor any reason for having one—just the quote machines, which in many brokerage offices are operated by the customers themselves if they want the latest price information on a stock.

These and other innovations will inevitably change the character and atmosphere of the broker's office, so that it will more closely resemble that of his professional counterparts, the banker or the insurance executive.

Far more important than the change in physical appearance will be the improvement in the quality of service that the broker will be able to supply his customers —instant comprehensive information on any stock or on the market as a whole, and instant information on his transactions and on the exact position of his account, whether cash or margin.

CHAPTER 19

How You Open an Account

EVERY new customer of a brokerage firm must open an *account* with that firm before he can either buy or sell securities.

Opening a *cash account* with a brokerage firm is very much like opening a charge account at a department store. It simply involves establishing your credit so that the broker is sure you can pay for whatever securities you order. The New York Stock Exchange has a rule, widely known as the "know your customer rule," which it requires that all member firms enforce strictly. If the broker doesn't know you, he will probably ask you to make a *good faith* deposit on opening an account, but most times he will be satisfied with a bank reference.

He has to be sure of your credit responsibility for one simple reason. When you place a market order for a stock, neither you nor the broker can know to the exact penny just what you will have to pay. You may know that the last sale took place at 18½ a share, but when your order is executed, even a few minutes later, the price may have gone up or down by an eighth of a point, a quarter of a point, or even more. So when the purchase is made the broker assumes the responsibility of paying for the stock and sends you a bill, a bill that you are supposed to pay in five business days, not counting Saturdays, Sundays, or holidays, because your broker must settle his account within that time.

Because no one can know just when an *open order* —a limit order or a stop order—may be executed and because the customer may be away from his home or office at the time of execution, brokers can in their own judgment extend the payment date to seven business days after the transaction, but if payment is not received then, a further extension can be granted only by the exchange because by your delay you will have violated the Federal Reserve Board's *Regulation T*, governing all matters of credit on stock transactions.

In the case of a Monthly Investment Plan account or similar plan originated by various brokers with the advent of negotiated commissions, the broker has no credit problem, because the customer makes his payment in advance of the purchase.

If your first transaction with a brokerage firm involves the sale of some stock that you already own, instead of a purchase, you will still be required to open an account, because the brokerage firm must still comply with the stock exchange rule which compels every broker to know his customer in order to protect himself against fraud or other illegal practices. For one thing, the routine of opening an account provides the broker with some assurance that the securities you offer for sale are really yours.

A bearer bond, for instance, can be sold by anybody who holds it, and the broker doesn't know but what it might be a stolen certificate. Even a registered bond or a stock with your own name on it presents a problem to the broker. It may be made out in the name of John Smith, and John Smith may bring it to a broker to sell it; but if he hasn't done business there before, how's the broker to know that he really is the Smith named on the security?

Many husbands and wives prefer to open *joint accounts* with a broker, just as they may have joint checking accounts. In case one of them dies, the other can generally sell the securities without waiting for the courts to unsnarl the legal problems that are involved in settling any estate, but because of tax considerations and variations in state law, a married couple may well want to consult an attorney before opening a joint account. Joint accounts are also used by individuals who are not related to each other but who have pooled their resources in a cooperative investment venture, often just for the sake of reducing commission costs on their trades.

People frequently want to open accounts for their own children or for the children of relatives, and historically this always presented a thorny problem, for in the absence of state legislation specifically authorizing such gifts to children, brokers incurred a measurable risk in selling stock that was registered in the name of a minor; a minor is not legally responsible for his acts, and if brokerage transactions were carried on in the name of a minor, he could, on coming of age, repudiate them, and the broker would have no redress.

Beginning in 1955, the various states began enacting laws permitting an adult, acting as a custodian without court appointment, to handle investments for a child. Such a custodian can buy stocks as a gift for a minor; he can sell them for a minor; and he can collect any dividends in the child's name. With the New York Stock Exchange and the entire brokerage fraternity plumping vigorously for the enactment of such laws, by 1961 all 50 states had laws permitting gifts of stock to minors. As a consequence, stock ownership among minors increased at a faster rate than in any other age group before 1970. In 1962, 450,000 minors owned stock; by 1970, the number had increased to 2,221,000. However, according to the last census, this total dropped to 1,818,000 in 1975.

It has, of course, always been possible for parents or other relatives to buy stock for children by setting up trust funds and getting a court order appointing them as trustees so that they could legally buy or sell stock for the children. This is an expensive and cumbersome procedure, although it does permit wealthy people to realize important tax savings. It is generally much simpler for the parents or other relatives or friends to give stock to minors under the provisions of the states' laws.

If you want to open a *margin account* instead of a regular cash account, so that you can buy securities by paying only a portion of their purchase price, the broker will want to be especially certain about your financial solvency. After all, when you pay only part of the cost, the broker has to pay the balance, and that money may be on loan to you a long time with interest payments coming due regularly.

Once you have opened an account—cash, joint, or margin—you can buy or sell whatever you want simply by phoning your representative—or writing or wiring him. Probably 90% of a broker's business comes to him by phone.

If you live outside New York and give an order for a Big Board stock to a registered representative or a correspondent of some brokerage firm, that order is teletyped into the New York headquarters of the firm, where it is either switched automatically to that booth on the exchange floor nearest the post where it will be executed or is phoned over to that booth. In either case the order is executed as promptly as possible by the floor broker. Then the process is put in reverse. The floor broker gives his clerk in the booth a report on the order and the price at which it was executed, and this information is transmitted instantly back to your representative—and then to you.

The entire operation can be accomplished literally while you may still be on the phone talking to your representative about other matters. On a market order for immediate execution, one involving an actively traded stock, the round trip from California to the exchange and back again, including the transaction on the floor, can be made in about one minute. Actually five minutes or so is more like par for an average transaction, and if the stock you are buying is one that doesn't trade frequently or if the whole market is very active and your broker's wires are flooded with traffic, it may take longer.

In any event, once your order is executed, your representative should report to you. But whether you get the information by phone or not, you'll know the next day or so just what price you got on the order, because you will receive in the mail your broker's formal *confirmation* of the transaction.

If you have bought stock, this will be your bill, unless you have bought and paid for it in advance as you would under the Monthly Investment Plan or any other prepayment plan.

If you have sold stock, the confirmation will be a report on how much money you realized from the sale, and the proceeds will automatically be credited to your account on the *settlement date,* five business days after the transaction.

Instead of having the proceeds credited to your account, you can, of course, ask that payment be made direct to you by check. In very special circumstances, you might possibly be able to arrange for immediate payment, instead of waiting for settlement date, but brokers are extremely reluctant to make such advance payments because, after all, they don't get their money from the other broker till settlement date. Furthermore, advance payment can open the door to sharp practice by unscrupulous customers—a practice known as *free-riding.*

A free-rider is a person who places a purchase order for a stock with one broker and then, if the stock goes up before he is forced to pay, sells the stock through another broker, demands immediate payment for some ostensibly good reason ("I can't get my wife out of the hospital till I pay the bill"), and uses the proceeds of the sale to pay for his original purchase. The result is that he has realized a profit without putting a cent of his own money at risk. He has had a free ride. If the stock goes down, chances are that he will attempt to repudiate the original order ("I said sell—not buy") or simply vanish and leave the broker holding the bag. This is one good reason for the exchange rule that every broker must know his customer.

Of course, if you sell stock in a regular cash account, you must see that the stocks are delivered to the broker. Since you have an account with him, he will know what stocks you own, and he will sell any of them for you on instruction, even if he does not have the certificates actually in hand. But he expects you to deliver the certificates, properly endorsed, immediately after a sale, because he in turn must settle within five days with the broker who bought the stock.

So that they won't have to bother with delivery problems, many security owners find it advisable just to leave their stock certificates or bonds with their brokers. They are right there then when the owner wants to sell. Such securities are carried in the customer's account just as cash might be, and every month he gets a statement showing just exactly what securities and what funds are credited to him.

On stocks that are left with him, the broker will collect all the dividends that are due and credit them as cash to the customer's account. Similarly, on bonds he will see that the interest is paid, clipping the coupons, if it's that kind of bond, and he will credit the payments to the customer's account. Further, brokers will mail to the customer the regular financial reports on those companies whose securities he owns as well as all proxies and official notices of meetings, dividends, stock rights and conversion privileges, as those materials are supplied to him by the individual companies.

When the customer leaves his securities with his broker, the actual shares of stock are sometimes segregated and kept in his individual account, very much as they might be if he rented a safe-deposit box. As a general rule, however, this kind of *custodian account* is available only to those who own large amounts of securities. In all other cases, if a customer leaves his securities with his broker, they are held in *street name*. This means that all the shares of a given security owned by all that broker's customers are lumped together and held in the broker's name; he keeps his own records of just what each individual customer owns. Thus, a broker might hold 100,000 shares of U.S. Steel for 2,000 or 3,000 individual customers. The shares would be made out in the broker's name—not the name of the individual stockholder unless he requested it—but the broker would send each customer a monthly statement showing just how many of those shares belonged to him. Shares held in street name and those held in the stockholder's own name must be kept separate under federal law.

There is one big advantage to leaving your stocks with your broker: if you want to sell any of them, all you have to do is phone him and give him instructions. You don't have to bother with delivering or endorsing the certificates.

But is it safe to leave your securities with your broker, as you might leave cash with your banker?

The answer is that it's probably safer to leave them with a broker than it is to try to take care of them yourself, unless you rent a safe-deposit box. He handles all of the safekeeping and storage problems and he carries insurance on them. When they are left with him, they can't be lost or misplaced, and the risk of loss by fire or theft is probably much less than it would be if you kept them in your home or office.

Furthermore, the broker cannot borrow money on those securities nor can he sell or lend any of them except on express authorization. Those securities belong to his customers. The surprise *audits* which are sprung on all member firms at different intervals by the New York Stock Exchange further help to make sure that the broker is faithful to his trust, because every single share of stock held in street name and every dollar in his customers' accounts must be accounted for.

In addition, to insure financial solvency the exchange insists that member firms have substantial capital reserves. Thus, the amount of money owed to a brokerage firm, principally on margin accounts, can never be greater than 15 times a firm's capital. The exchange may even require a member firm to reduce its business if its *net capital ratio* should exceed 12-to-1, and it may prohibit a member firm altogether from trying to expand its business if the ratio exceeds 10-to-1.

In 1970, the S.E.C. put the full weight of its authority behind these capital requirement rules of the exchange, and it undertook to see that the 15-to-1 ratio also applied to nonmember firms that had previously operated on a 20-to-1 standard.

But what if a broker goes under, despite all the regulations of the stock exchange and the S.E.C.?

For years, an adequate answer to that was that brokers didn't go bankrupt. Despite 1929, member firms of the New York Stock Exchange boasted a solvency record over a 50-year period that was around 99%— better than the solvency record of state and national banks.

But in 1963, an event took place that shook the

brokerage fraternity's confidence in its financial stability to the very foundations. In November of that year, one of Wall Street's most respected houses, Ira Haupt & Company, did go under to the tune of almost ten million dollars, and a second firm, J. R. Williston & Beane, was bailed out in the nick of time and absorbed by another firm.

The Haupt bankruptcy was brought on by the inability of Anthony De Angelis, a big speculator in soybean oil and president of the now defunct Allied Crude Vegetable Oil Refining Company, to meet an obligation to the Haupt firm in the amount of $18 million, and its doom was sealed when it was discovered that warehouse receipts which De Angelis had given Haupt as security were fraudulent. The receipts were supposed to stand as evidence that millions of gallons of soybean oil were stored in tanks in New Jersey, but the tanks were empty.

Ironically, Haupt's relations with its securities customers conformed impeccably to all requirements of the law and of the exchange, and these were the people—people who were in no way involved in Haupt's commodity mess—who stood to get hurt, because Haupt obviously could not meet its own loans from the banks.

To save those customers in particular and to preserve investor confidence in general, the exchange devised a plan over one critical weekend which obligated all members to make good Haupt's loss. All told, after the liquidation of Haupt's assets, the bill, which was shared by members in proportion to the amount of their exchange business, came to $9,600,000.

But Wall Street's troubles were far from over. In fact, they had barely begun.

First, the Street was engulfed by the great bull market of 1968, when volume some days soared far above the historic highs recorded in the days of late October 1929. Despite the advent of computers and other forms of mechanized record keeping, many brokers and transfer agents found themselves unable to keep abreast of the operational work load. Because of the resultant mess, *"fails to deliver,"* reflecting the inability of one broker to settle his trades with another broker by delivering securities that had actually been sold in a floor transaction, rose to a record high of $4.1 billion at year-end, and many of the "fails" were months old because of the difficulties brokers encountered in trying to untangle their confused records.

For many brokers, 1968 was a year of profitless prosperity. Not only were brokers forced to expand personnel to handle the volume, but as business had grown over the years, they had failed to control costs in many vital areas. Thus, as they competed with each other to hire salesmen who could produce the biggest amount of business, particularly the big-block business, they let the cost of compensating salesmen get out of hand. In 1958, this cost had represented an average of only 26% of a broker's gross income. By 1968, it had risen to 32%. As a consequence of all these factors, gross income for all member firms in 1968 increased 26% over 1967, but total expenses were up 39%, and net income dropped proportionately.

Then came 1969 and 1970. Stock prices went into a tailspin. Volume contracted sharply, falling to an average of only 11,400,000 shares a day in 1969, when the New York Stock Exchange estimated that the *break-even point* for its member firms was a daily average of 12,000,000 shares.

Worst of all, many firms that had invested their own capital in stocks suffered such losses as stock prices fell that they were unable to meet the New York Stock Exchange capital requirements. Some 50 firms closed their doors while they were still solvent, and 65 others managed to sidestep disaster only because "shotgun" mergers were arranged with other, stronger firms.

But there was no way to stave off the debacle, and before the storm abated the New York Stock Exchange had not only exhausted the $25 million in a special trust fund, which it had set up after the Haupt disaster, but had been compelled to pump an additional $43 million into its rescue operations—funds it could raise only by assessing its hard-pressed members.

All told, the exchange intervened in the affairs of almost 200 brokerage houses, but despite its best efforts 15 firms went under, including such well-known ones as McDonnell & Company, Orvis Brothers, Dempsey-Tegeler, Blair & Company, and Hayden, Stone. The exchange had to supervise the liquidation of these businesses and provide the necessary funds so that the customers could get the securities and cash out of their accounts without waiting for the bankrupt firms' affairs to be untangled.

Nor was the collapse of these 15 firms a full measure of the extent of the disaster. Just when it seemed that the worst of the storm might be over, two of Wall Street's very largest firms found themselves in such dire straits that they could be saved only by a minor miracle. In the case of Dupont, Walston & Co., the third largest firm in the business, that miracle seemed to have come to pass when the firm dug up an angel in the form of a Texas financier, H. Ross Perot, who together with a few associates put $10 million into the Dupont firm just ahead of the fatal deadline when Dupont would have had to close its doors because of its failure to meet the capital requirements of the New York Stock Exchange. Many more millions were pumped into the firm in 1971, but the salvage effort proved ill-fated in the end. Perot and his associates could afford to put no more money in Dupont, and the firm folded up in March 1974.

If Dupont's collapse was a disaster, the plight of Goodbody & Company, the fifth largest firm in the business and one of the oldest and most respected names in Wall Street, had in it the makings of real tragedy for the entire exchange community. Goodbody was in such dire trouble and its affairs were so tangled that no one knew the full extent of its liabilities. All the exchange knew was that the firm had to be rescued, for its collapse might so undermine public confidence that the entire brokerage business would suffer drastically. Finally, Merrill Lynch, Pierce, Fenner & Smith—not only the nation's largest firm but by all odds its strongest, with over $280 million in capital—was induced by the exchange to take over Goodbody.

Merrill Lynch agreed to put $15 million of its own capital into Goodbody, but only on condition that the exchange membership would indemnify it to the extent of $30 million if it developed that Goodbody's total liabilities, including pending lawsuits, were of such staggering proportions, and indeed, the liabilities turned out to be all of that—and more.

The desperate stopgap measures that the exchange had to take—at a total cost to its members of $100 million—in order to preserve the integrity of the business made clear the fact that some far more reliable machinery was needed to insure investors against loss in the event of the failure of any firm in the securities business. And that necessity was clear not only to every man in the business but also to the Securities and Exchange Commission, most members of Congress, and millions of individual investors. Hence, the proposal was made to create a federal insurance system for investors comparable to that provided by the Federal Deposit Insurance Corporation to insure bank savings.

With Wall Street wreckage standing in plain and tragic view, Congress moved with unaccustomed speed in the last half of 1970 to establish the *Securities Investor Protection Corporation* on December 30, 1970. Only then could the investor—and Wall Street, too—breathe a sigh of relief in the certain knowledge that he did not have to worry about the possibility of losing either cash or securities as a result of the failure of any securities firm with which he did business. He could, of course, lose money in the market—and plenty of it in bear markets, as he discovered in 1973–1974—but at least he now knew he couldn't lose it because his broker went broke.

The Securities Investor Protection Corporation, known as S.I.P.C. and called "Sipic," will advance as much as $50,000 for every customer account in case of the liquidation of any S.I.P.C. member—and that includes every member firm of every securities exchange and every nonmember securities dealer, excepting those who do only a mutual fund business. Cash in an account is insured only to the extent of $20,000.

S.I.P.C. is empowered to disburse as much as one billion dollars of federal funds to insure investors, but when any of the fund is used, the S.E.C. imposes a fee of 20¢ per $1,000 on the purchase of securities in excess of $5,000, and by this means the Treasury can be reimbursed.

Quite obviously, the federal government could not be expected to insure investors against the collapse of securities firms unless it had some very definite say in how those firms were operated, and the S.E.C. is the agency that really exercises that power, although theoretically S.I.P.C. writes its own rules. One of the rules requires all securities firms to maintain adequate cash reserves against their customers' credit balances—the cash they have in their accounts—and another rule requires brokers to keep separate and apart all the securities owned by the customers but held by the securities firm in street name.

S.I.P.C. is run by a board of directors consisting of seven men, one appointed by the Secretary of the Treasury, one by the Federal Reserve Board, three representing the securities industry but appointed by the President, and two representing the general public, also appointed by the President. Originally, the industry fought to get a majority of the directors on this board, but it gave up without too much argument because it realized that regardless of who was on the board, the S.E.C. intended to be the power behind the throne. And the industry had resigned itself to the certainty that the S.E.C. was going to be an increasingly tough taskmaster in the years ahead—as the Securities Reform Act of 1975 certainly gave it the authority to be —poking its nose as far as it could into matters of firm management to insure the solvency of S.I.P.C. members.

During the first four years of its life only one N.Y.S.E. member firm went into S.I.P.C. liquidation, and this was due to fraud. This record was all the more remarkable considering that volume on the New York Stock Exchange for many days in the bear market of 1973–1974 was substantially below the 17–18 million shares that member firms were then estimating to be their break-even point.

While the federal insurance program, supplemented in the case of many big firms by the purchase of private insurance coverage beyond what the S.I.P.C.

might provide, has obviously lifted a tremendous weight off Wall Street's shoulders, the industry knows that the long-range solution to the basic problem of financing its own business lies in attracting large chunks of permanent new capital and in restoring investor confidence in the financial community in general.

For generations the brokerage business thought of itself as a business of individuals or *partnerships* of individuals who could be held personally responsible in the exercise of what almost amounts to a fiduciary responsibility. This—the old "family counselor" kind of approach—was the way brokers said that customer confidence in the investment business could best be built. But with the spread of public shareownership of stocks, the adoption of modern merchandising methods, and the arrival of computers, the business rapidly outgrew its old concept of itself. And the exchange membership had to recognize that.

In 1953, the exchange took a first step toward liberalization of its rules by permitting the voluntary *incorporation* of member firms. One advantage of incorporation lay in the fact that corporations are subject to a maximum federal tax of 52%, while individual partners in a firm might find themselves having to pay a considerably higher income tax. Thus, by incorporation the owners of a firm might be able to retain as capital a much higher proportion of the firm's earnings.

More important, incorporation provided a much greater permanence of capital. In a partnership, a partner can decide to withdraw and take his capital with him, and when a partner dies, even if his heirs are willing to leave his capital in the firm, a large part of it inevitably has to be withdrawn to pay estate taxes. With incorporation, a firm can spread its ownership among many more people by selling shares to hundreds of key employees. This technique not only gives the employee a piece of the action and hence stimulates morale, but it reduces measurably the risk of having large hunks of capital precipitously withdrawn.

In the decade following the exchange's abandonment of partnership rule, more than a third of the member firms, including most of the biggest firms, transformed themselves from partnerships into corporations and thus strengthened their financial positions.

In June 1969 the exchange took a second important step. It authorized member firms to raise additional capital by issuing bonds for sale to the public.

And only a few months later the aggressive young firm of Donaldson, Lufkin & Jenrette, which specialized in institutional business, forced the exchange's hand by applying to the S.E.C. for registration and sale of an issue of its own common stock. The exchange had no alternative. It had to amend its rules to permit Donaldson, Lufkin & Jenrette and all other member firms to "go public" if they wanted to.

It was inevitable that many member firms would follow suit because it was the only way in which they could raise the capital they needed. Only one thing deterred them from taking immediate action, and that was the bad earnings record that many firms showed during the 1969–1970 market slump. One notable exception to that was Merrill Lynch, Pierce, Fenner & Smith, and in April 1971 the biggest firm of all announced it too would go public. It has since been followed by Bache & Co., E. F. Hutton, Dean Witter, Paine Webber, and Reynolds Securities—all listed on the New York Stock Exchange.

disclosure requirements as a listed company. Further-more, there must be at least two dealers who make a regular market in the security. The dealer must have a net capital of $50,000 or $5,000 for each security in which he makes a market, whichever amount is less.

CHAPTER 20

What It Means to Speculate

SPECULATING is an inevitable part of the business of buying securities. But then speculating is an inevitable part of just living.

Whenever you are confronted with an unavoidable risk—as indeed you are in many of your actions every day—you must speculate. You must meet the risk; you must take your chances. Often you are presented with a choice of risks; when you make up your mind about which one you will take, weighing the good and the bad features of each, you arrive at a speculative decision.

The businessman who *must* be in another city at a given time often has the choice of flying or driving. He can figure on getting there faster if he flies, but there's always the possibility of bad weather, mechanical failure, or other delays. Those risks may be somewhat reduced if he drives himself, but in that case he faces other hazards—a breakdown, an accident, traffic tie-ups. Faced with that kind of choice, the man must inevitably speculate.

The retailer who decides to stock up on a lot of goods is speculating on a rise in wholesale prices. He figures he can buy those goods cheaper now than he can some months later—and that he can sell them ultimately.

The manufacturer who must pick Jones or Smith for a key job must speculate on which will be the more able man.

And the farmer's whole operation is one vast speculation. When he puts the seed in the ground, he is speculating on his ability to grow a crop and sell it at a profit despite bad weather, pests, blight, and changing market prices.

When a man takes a risk he cannot avoid, he is speculating. But when he takes a risk that he doesn't have to take, he gambles.

That is one distinction between speculation and gambling, and there is another. Speculation involves an exercise of reason, while gambling involves nothing but chance. The man who speculates can make an intelligent forecast of the hazards of his course. The gambler stands or falls on the flip of a coin or the draw of a card.

In the purchase of any stock or bond, even a government bond, there is an element of speculation, because the risk that it might decline in value cannot be avoided. For that matter, there is a risk just in having money—the risk that it won't buy as much sometime in the future when you want to spend it as it will if you spend it today.

But when a man buys securities, he doesn't have to operate exclusively on chance. He can make a fairly intelligent estimate of just how much risk he assumes on the basis of the record. And he has a wide range to choose from—all the way from a government bond to the penny stocks of those companies whose assets may be made up principally of hope.

The word "investments" is technically applied only to government bonds, municipal bonds, and first-quality corporate bonds. To an ultraconservative buyer of securities for a bank or an insurance company, all stocks are considered too risky to be classed as investments, despite the fact that some stocks have proved safer than many corporate bonds, particularly the debentures and secondary bonds of weak companies.

But because most preferred stocks and a good number of common stocks have shown themselves to be so stable, even the conservatives refer to them nowadays as "investment-type" securities. These are apt to be the stocks of utilities or food firms or banks or chain stores —industries that have shown themselves to be comparatively steady earners, come boom or depression.

Of course, what is one man's speculation is very often another man's investment, and below the level of topflight securities is a vast assortment of stocks which

many men of sound judgment consider good investments primarily because of the liberal dividends they
pay.

Often these are the stocks of companies whose for-
tunes rise and fall more sharply with the business cycle
—companies in the automobile, steel, construction, or
clothing industries. When business is good, they pay
excellent dividends, and when it slumps, those dividends
may be reduced or eliminated. Early in 1975, for instance, although the market was recovering sharply after a steep fall in 1973–1974, good quality companies
such as General Motors, Libbey-Owens-Ford, and du
Pont trimmed their dividend payouts, while others, including Chrysler and American Distilling, omitted the
dividend entirely.

As a rough—very rough—rule of thumb, the degree
of risk which you assume in buying one of those "cyclical" stocks can be measured by the liberality of the
dividend. The larger the dividend as a percentage of
the selling price, the greater the risk.

Then there are other stocks—thousands and thousands of them—that must be frankly classified as speculations. But even here there is a wide range of quality. At the top of the list are those stocks that might be
described as "good growth situations." They are the
stocks of companies, often paying little or no dividend,
which are regarded as attractive because of future prospects. Fifty years or so ago, many of the automobile
and radio stocks might have been so classified. More
recently, electronic, office equipment, cosmetic, computer, drug, and aerospace stocks have often been
placed in this category. In recent years, these growth
stocks have been the darlings of the investing public.
Such has been the demand for these glamour stocks
that in 1972 prices were pushed up to a point where
some stocks were selling at 40 or 50 times current
earnings.

Some speculative securities are attractive not because the future is so glowing but simply because it
looks a lot better than the past. A company may have
had to pass some dividends or miss interest payments
during a difficult period of reorganization, but once it

starts to hit the comeback trail, its securities are apt to take on new life. Many a sizable fortune has been made out of buying bonds that were severely depressed in price because the company had to default on bond interest payments for a period. And that's also true of many preferred-stock issues on which dividend payments have accumulated for a number of years and ultimately been paid off. But these are strictly long shots and must be so regarded.

The most popular kind of speculative stock is apt to be issued by an aggressive small company, operating in one of the growth fields. Characteristically, these are over-the-counter stocks selling at relatively modest prices, unseasoned securities issued by companies that are so new they have no record of consistent earnings. They are long on hopes, short on cash. Rank speculations though they be, they attract interest because everyone knows that Xerox and Polaroid and IBM—and Rod & Reel—were just such stocks once not so many years ago.

Finally, there are the outright penny stocks. A few of these may be the listed securities of old-line companies that have fallen on evil days. Their business has declined steadily, and their stock seems virtually worthless. But a significant number of these low-priced stocks, selling at 50¢, $1, $2, maybe as high as $5, are issued by new ventures—stocks in questionable oil or mining companies that are peddled by high-pressure salesmen who expect to make as much as 50¢ on every dollar's worth they sell. Often by direct mail and even long-distance phone, the prospect is told that a block of 100 or 300 shares has been reserved in his name at a special bargain price, but he must buy within 24 hours or lose this chance of a lifetime. People who have charge accounts at expensive stores and professional people, such as doctors and lawyers, are particular targets for this kind of promotion, because their names and addresses are so easily available from direct-mail firms.

The most devastating thing is that these glamorous sales stories often have an element of truth about them. The men who put their money in the oil property "right next to our land" may actually have made 1,000% on their investment already, but the fact remains that anyone who takes a flyer on this kind of deal is much more apt to lose everything he puts into it than he is to make a whopping profit.

Although there is an obvious difference between this kind of rank speculation and the solid investment that a government bond represents, it is also true that the distinction between investing and speculating frequently gets hazy as soon as you move away from either of these two extremes. Actually, the difference between investing and speculating is not to be measured so much in terms of the individual security as it is in terms of the motive of the buyer.

The investor is a man who puts his money to work in a company in the expectation of earning a reasonable and regular return on it, both in dividends and price appreciation, over the long pull. The speculator takes a short-term view. He is not interested in dividends; he is interested in making a quick profit on his money and selling out while he can get it. Often he takes a big risk in the process, but if he hits it right, he stands to make a lot of money.

Furthermore, under present federal tax laws he may be able to keep more of that money than he would if he made the same amount of money in dividends, salary, or other income.

Risk capital—the money that a man puts at risk when he buys or sells almost any kind of property—has played such an important role in building this country that Congress for more than a quarter of a century has always given favored tax treatment to profits realized in such ventures. These are called *capital gains,* and they include the profits realized on the purchase and sale of securities.

For many years our federal tax law provided that a man who made a capital gain on any security that he owned for more than six months—a *long-term* capital gain—would not have to pay a tax of more than 25% of that profit. That was the absolute maximum. Actually, the tax might be considerably less, for instead of paying 25% on the entire gain, he could, if he chose, pay a straight income tax on only half the gain at whatever regular income tax applied in his case. Thus, if a stockholder's maximum tax bracket was only 40% on regular income, the effective rate he would pay on a long-term capital gain would be only 20%. If a man made a profit on a security he owned for less than six months, that *short-term capital gain* was taxed as though it were ordinary income.

In recent years, particularly in the recessions of 1969–1970 and 1973–1975, there has been a widespread demand that Congress close the tax loopholes which have enabled wealthy men to pay only minimum taxes, and one of the loopholes which the reformers attacked was the capital gains tax.

Yielding to that pressure, Congress raised the tax rate on capital gains exceeding $50,000 in 1972 from 25% to 35%—one-half the maximum income tax rate then in effect—and in 1976 also increased the length of time that an investor must hold a security in order for any profit on it to be classified as a long-term rather than a short-term capital gain. The so-called holding period was increased from six months to nine months in 1977 and to a full year beginning in 1978.

Nor was that all. Capital gains were also included as one of several different kinds of income which Congress classified as "preference income," because it was income that escaped the full tax rate that applied to ordinary income. Hence, it is possible under the complicated formula that relates the amount of preference income to a taxpayer's total income for an investor to pay an additional 15% tax on one half of his long-term capital gains. Thus the maximum tax on long-term capital gains can go as high as 42½%.

For many years, the tax law has offered another special treatment of capital gains and losses that investors and speculators have found attractive. An investor who sustains substantial capital losses on some investments but also realizes capital gains on other investments can use his gains to offset his losses—in full or in part.

Further, if an investor has realized losses, either short-term or long-term, he can even offset some of that loss against his ordinary income, thus reducing his tax. For many years only $1,000 of such loss could be offset against ordinary income, but Congress increased the amount to $2,000 in 1977, and $3,000 in 1978 and succeeding years. If the stockowner's losses exceed the allowable deduction in any tax year, he is permitted to carry the loss forward year by year and use it as an offset against income until his total loss has been offset.

However, if the stockowner has capital gains, either short-term or long-term, as well as capital losses, either short-term or long-term, he must use those capital gains to offset his capital losses on a straight dollar-for-dollar basis. If after doing this, he still shows a short-term capital loss, he can offset $2,000 of it against ordinary income in 1977 or $3,000 thereafter on a straight dollar-for-dollar basis. But if his remaining capital loss is long-term, he can offset it against ordinary income only on a 2-for-1 basis; that is, $2 of long-term capital loss are required to offset $1 of ordinary income up to that ceiling of $2,000 in 1977 or $3,000 thereafter. If his losses, either short-term or long-term, still exceed the amount he can charge off against ordinary income, such balance can be carried forward to the next tax year and succeeding tax years until all his loss has been offset against capital gains or ordinary income.

A few illustrations may make clear how this system works. Suppose the year is 1978 or later, and the investor has a short-term capital loss of $5,000 and no capital gains; he can deduct $3,000 from his ordinary income that year and carry $2,000 forward as a short-term capital loss. If that $5,000 capital loss is long-term and he again has no capital gains, he can deduct only $2,500 from ordinary income, and he has no loss to carry forward.

Now suppose the investor has a short-term capital gain of $10,000 and losses, either short or long-term, of $15,000. He first offsets $10,000 of his losses against the $10,000 of capital gains, leaving him with a $5,000 loss. If that loss is short-term, he can offset it, dollar for dollar, against ordinary income up to

$2,000 in 1977 or $3,000 thereafter and carry forward the balance of the loss to the next tax year. If the $5,000 remaining loss is long-term, he can deduct only $2,500 from ordinary income. This means that in 1977, he would use $4,000 of losses to offset the $2,000 maximum deductible from ordinary income, leaving him with a $1,000 loss to carry forward. In 1978, when the deductible maximum is $3,000, he could charge off all his long-term capital loss against ordinary income in that tax year.

Finally, suppose the investor has a $10,000 long-term capital gain, $5,000 of long-term loss, and $8,000 of short-term loss. Since he is compelled by law to use capital gains first as an offset against capital losses before deducting such loss from ordinary income, he first offsets that $5,000 of long-term loss against his capital gain, leaving him with a total of $5,000 of long-term capital gain. He then offsets $5,000 of his short-term loss, against that remaining $5,000 of capital gain, leaving him with $3,000 of short-term losses. In 1977, he could offset $2,000 of that against $2,000 of ordinary income, leaving him with a $1,000 loss to carry forward. In 1978 and thereafter, he could offset that $3,000 of short-term loss against $3,000 of ordinary income and come out even. In a situation like this, it is obviously to a taxpayer's advantage to offset his long-term losses first against any capital gains, because he can deduct short-term losses from ordinary income on a dollar-for-dollar basis, but it takes $2 of long-term capital loss to offset $1 of ordinary income.

Another recent change in the tax law takes away one of the advantages that accrued to the heirs of a man or woman whose estate included substantial capital gains at the time of death. Suppose at his death an investor held stock worth a million dollars that cost him only $100,000. The million dollars asset would, of course, be subject to regular estate taxes, but no tax would be paid on the $900,000 gain, and the heirs to whom he left that stock would own it at the million-dollar level—the price that prevailed at the time of the original owner's death. If they sold the stock at that price, they would escape all capital gains tax, but if they continued to hold it and the stock appreciated to $1,100,000, they would, of course, owe a capital gains tax on that additional $100,000.

In 1976 the law was changed. It provides that any capital gain that might have accrued on such inherited stock prior to December 31, 1976, is still exempt from the capital gains tax, but further it stipulates that the heirs *must* pay the capital gains tax on any further gain realized on that stock *after* December 31, 1976. Suppose a man bought $100,000 worth of stock in the 1950s, and on December 31, 1976, it was worth $500,000. His heirs would ultimately pay no capital gains tax on that $400,000 profit, but if the value of the investment were to have increased to $600,000 before the stock passed to his heirs and was sold by them, the $100,000 gain from December 31, 1976, to the time of sale would be subject to capital gains tax.

It is obviously only good sense for a stockholder to consider this matter of taxes on long-term and short-term capital gains (or losses) in deciding whether or not to sell. Thus, it would be ridiculous for a man in a high income tax bracket—say 60%—to sell a stock on which he had a substantial profit if he had owned that stock just a few days less than the required long-term holding period. Obviously, by waiting those few additional days he could establish his profit as long-term capital gain, and he would have to pay considerably less tax than he would if he realized a short-term capital gain and had to pay a tax of 60%. Only in the most unusual circumstances would his risk of loss in those few days be likely to outweight the extra tax liability he would incur by selling stock and taking the short-term capital gain.

On the other hand, too great a concern about taxes on capital gains can seriously warp investment judgment. Many a stockowner has refused to sell and take a profit because he didn't want to pay even a long-term capital-gains tax, and while he complains about being "locked-in," his profit may dwindle away in a declining market. One stock market authority calls this "taxation rigor mortis," and he contends that it costs stockholders a good deal more every year than all the dubious new issues of penny stocks and other outright swindles. The man with a 100% profit in a stock will complain bitterly about the long-term capital-gains tax, forgetting that when he bought the stock he would have been more than satisfied with his after-tax profit.

If you have a profit in a stock, you might as well reconcile yourself to paying a capital-gains tax on it and rule it out of all future investment considerations. You can, of course, hold on to the stock—and the profit, if you are lucky—till you die, but even then your executors and your heirs are going to have to worry about inheritance taxes. And there's always the chance that Congress may someday change the law and tax capital gains on stocks even when they are held until death and become part of an estate.

For years many people have advocated a kind of graduated capital-gains tax—in reverse—so that the percent tax one would pay would decline as the holding period lengthened over a number of years. Similarly, others have advocated that capital-gains taxes should be levied on stocks even in an estate. It is not unlikely that one or the other, or both, of these proposals will someday be enacted into law.

Of course, you do sidestep the tax by using your capital gain to offset a capital loss. This provision has served to stimulate a fair amount of speculation. A man with a capital gain will very often figure that he can afford a much greater measure of risk than he ordinarily would take, because if he loses Uncle Sam will cover a part of his losses.

The capital-gains tax constitutes the biggest paradox in the stock market. It stimulates speculation in the sense that it offers the high-income man a chance to build up capital at bargain rates, but it simultaneously acts as a deterrent on speculation, particularly among the amateurs, because it is human nature to resist the payment of any tax and to postpone that evil day as long as possible.

Curiously enough, the professional speculator does not so often try to make a profit—a capital gain—by putting his money into a really speculative growth stock as he does by speculating in the 50 or 60 active stocks —many of them topflight investments—that usually account for most of the transactions on the Big Board.

There is a reason for this. At any given time the price of a stock or the price of all stocks represents the combined judgments of all the people who are buying and selling. Most times a speculator is staking his judgment against the public judgment.

He may study the stock of a company in minute detail, and on the basis of that intensive analysis he may feel that he knows better than the public what it's really worth—or, rather, what the public will sooner or later accept as its real worth.

Again, he may think that he has a better feel of the market as a whole, knows better than the public does whether stock prices generally will advance steadily upward in what is called a *bull market* or decline for a period of time in a *bear market*. If he is right, the leading stocks—those that enjoy the widest public following—will probably provide the earliest confirmation of his judgment and hence provide the best opportunity for a quick profit.

On the assumption that his judgment is right, the speculator seeks to augment his profits—or protect them once they are made—by using various techniques of trading.

He may buy on margin.

He may pyramid profits.

He may sell short.

He may buy puts or calls.

And let it be noted that none of these techniques, discussed in the following chapters, constitutes in itself unfair or dishonest manipulation of the market. On the contrary, all these techniques make for greater trading activity and a more liquid market. Very often, the investor might find it difficult to sell some stock if it were not for a speculator willing to assume the risk that the investor wants to get rid of.

Periodically, there is public clamor about the ill-gotten gains of market speculators. People are apt to say "there ought to be a law" to curb them. In 1905, Oliver Wendell Holmes, Justice of the United States

Supreme Court, in one of his famous opinions delivered the definitive reply to all such critics. Said Justice Holmes: "Speculation . . . is the self-adjustment of society to the probable. Its value is well known, as a means of avoiding or mitigating catastrophes, equalizing prices and providing for periods of want. It is true that the success of the strong induces imitation by the weak, and that incompetent persons bring themselves to ruin by undertaking to speculate in their turn. But legislatures and courts generally have recognized that the natural evolutions of a complex society are to be touched only with a very cautious hand . . ."

CHAPTER 21

How You Buy Stocks on Margin

ONCE a security buyer has assured a broker of his financial responsibility and opened a margin account, he can buy stocks—any of the stocks listed on a United States securities exchange and some over-the-counter stocks as they are approved for margin transactions by the Federal Reserve Board—just by making a down payment on them. How big that down payment must be is governed by different rules.

First, the New York Stock Exchange says that no one can open an account to buy its securities on margin unless the down payment is at least $2,000 in cash, or its equivalent in securities. Until April 1966, only $1,000 was required, and so when the exchange doubled the minimum it made it applicable only to new accounts opened afterwards.

Occasionally, the exchange may be concerned about the market action of a particular stock because of sharp swings in its price or in its trading volume, and in such circumstances the exchange may require all those who buy or sell that stock to put up extra margin—a higher down payment. It can also forbid all margin trading in such a stock and has often done so, especially in periods of heavy speculative activity.

In addition to the rules set by the various exchanges you may encounter special margin requirements set by individual brokers. Some, for instance, will not permit a customer to buy any stock on margin unless it sells above $5 a share; others require a greater down payment than the exchange does.

Finally, and most important of all, there is the regulation exercised by the Federal Reserve Board, which has been empowered by Congress to say, in effect, just what the minimum *margin requirements* must be. Since 1934, when the board began to exercise its authority, it has set that minimum by saying that the down payment must represent a certain percentage of the total value of the stock that is being bought on margin. The percentage is changed from time to time, depending on the availability of credit—how tight or easy money is —and on how worried the board is about inflation and about the amount of stock trading that is done on margin.

The lowest figure which the board has ever set is 40%, and that figure prevailed for eight years, from 1937 to 1945. The highest figure has been 100%, and while that was in effect, from January 1946 to February 1947, nobody could buy on margin, for the minimum down payment required by the board was equal to the full purchase price.

In bull markets, such as that of the mid-sixties, the board will jack the rate up because it is concerned about overtrading and wants to cool down speculative fever. Conversely, in bear markets, when volume has dried up, the board is frequently willing to provide some stimulus to the market by reducing the minimum margin requirements.

Thus, in the bull market of 1968, the board raised the requirement to 80% and kept it there until May 1970 when prices on the exchange had dropped 36%; it then reduced the rate, first to 65% and then to 55% in 1971 but returned it to the 65% level in November 1972, when the Dow Jones industrial average closed above 1,000 for the first time in history.

In January 1974, with a bear market in full swing, the minimum requirement was reduced to a twelve-year low of 50%. By that time, according to one popular market indicator, stocks had dropped 26.6% from the record high they reached during trading on January 11, 1973, and the reduced volume of transactions had forced many brokers into red ink. But still prices and volume on the exchange continued downward until December 1974—a total decline of 46.6% from the trading peak of 1973.

With the bull market in full swing again early in

1976, it appeared inevitable that the Board would raise the rate again to keep the boom under control.

To simplify the explanation of how margin works, suppose the Federal Reserve Board requirement at a given time is 50%. This means that you can buy $10,000 worth of some marginable stock with $5,000; the broker lends you the other $5,000. Naturally, when he does that, he charges you interest on the money he lends. How much interest would depend on how much money he in turn would have to pay a bank—whatever the prevailing interest rate is on brokers' loans— if he had to borrow the $5,000 there, as he often does, to lend it to you. He'll charge you that prevailing interest rate plus, according to stock exchange practice, at least ½% to 1% for himself, and sometimes more. The total charge the broker makes may run anywhere from 4% to 5% in ordinary times up to 8% or 9% or even more when interest rates are high. That was the case in 1974 when the *prime rate,* the lowest on loans that commercial banks grant only to their best clients, rose to 12%, and the *discount rate,* which the Federal Reserve Bank charges its member banks for loans, hit a record 8%.

With these basic bank rates at such historical highs, the interest rate that brokers usually charged their margin customers was at least 13%, for brokers generally charge at least 1% above the prime rate. At such levels, brokers were concerned about violating state usury laws. Some states do exempt brokers from their usury laws, but where that was not the case, brokers argued that since their margin orders were executed in New York, the usury law of New York, which does permit a 13% interest charge, had to be regarded as controlling. In various cases, it appeared that state courts were generally inclined to accept this argument, but short of a U.S. Supreme Court ruling, no one would be absolutely sure of its validity.

If you think you might get a better deal elsewhere than you can from your broker on a margin account —perhaps your own bank might not require you to put up as much money—you can forget about it. Banks are not permitted to lend any more on stock purchases than brokers can lend. It is true that you can borrow a greater proportion of the down payment, up to 90%, from unregulated lenders, but you are not likely to get any break there; indeed, it is probable you will pay as much as 1% or 2% extra interest a month, and any broker or registered representative who helped you arrange such a loan would run afoul of the S.E.C.

When a broker borrows money at the bank and lends it to you so that you can buy stocks on margin, he has to give the bank some security on the loan. That loan security may be the very stock that you buy on margin. Hence, when you open a margin account, you must agree to leave your margined stocks with the broker and to let him *hypothecate* them, or pledge them as security for whatever bank loan he may need in order to carry your margin account or those of his other customers.

If you were to buy $10,000 worth of stock on margin, you would naturally pay all commissions on the full $10,000 worth of stock. But you would also be entitled to receive all the dividends on those shares, and this alone is sufficient to interest some investors in buying stocks on margin, when stocks are paying liberal dividends and margin interest rates are low.

But virtually all margin customers are interested in margin not because of the extra dividends but solely because of the speculative profit they hope to make.

For margin is the speculator's number one tool.

Suppose that a man with $5,000 to invest has picked out a stock selling at $50 a share which he thinks will go up. Under a 50% margin rule, he can buy 200 shares of that stock, instead of just 100 shares, with his $5,000. If it goes up five points, he makes $1,000 instead of just $500, a 20% profit instead of 10%. That kind of profit can make even an 8% interest charge on his margin loan look cheap.

But suppose the stock goes down in price? There's the rub.

It's then that he may receive a *margin call* from his broker, a call on him to put up more margin—that is, to increase his down payment. If he can't put up more money or more margin, the broker has the right to sell his stock—as much of it as may be necessary—to raise the required cash. This presents no problem to the broker, because all margined stock must be left on deposit with him.

How much more money may a margin buyer have to put up if his stocks decline? The answer to this is governed by the *margin maintenance* rules of the New York Stock Exchange and those of the individual broker. The Federal Reserve Board isn't in the picture at all after the original purchase; if a buyer meets its margin requirements then—say, of 50% cash—he is never compelled by the board to put up any more margin, even if it later raises its requirements to 75% or more.

Under the New York Stock Exchange rule, however, a broker must call on a customer for more margin whenever the amount that the customer would have left if he sold his stocks and paid off the broker's loan represents less than 25% of the current value of the stocks. (Some brokers have margin maintenance requirements that are higher than the minimums set by the New York Stock Exchange.)

To illustrate: Suppose a margin customer bought 100 shares of a stock selling at $60 a share at a time when the Federal Reserve Board required only 50% margin. In that case he would put up $3,000 and he would borrow $3,000 from his broker. Now suppose the stock dropped from $60 to $40 a share. If he were to sell out now, he would realize only $4,000 on his holdings, and after he paid his broker $3,000, he would have only $1,000 left, which would be exactly 25% of the current value ($4,000) of his stock.

If the stock fell below $40 in this instance, the broker would have to ask for more margin money so that the 25% ratio would be restored. Actually, he'd probably ask for a bit more so that he wouldn't have to make another margin call so soon again in case the stock continued to decline.

If a stock is bought on a 50% margin basis, it is evident that it can drop a full third in price—from 60 to 40, as in the example above—before a broker must call for more margin.

If the Federal Reserve Board's initial margin re-

quirement was 75% instead of 50%, the stock could
decline two-thirds in value and the customer would
still not have to put up more margin. Here's how that
works: The customer buys 100 shares of stock at $60
a share and puts up 75% margin, or $4,500. He bor-
rows only $1,500 from the broker. If the stock drops
from $60 to $20, his holdings are worth $2,000. At
that point, he could sell out, pay the broker $1,500
and still have $500 left, which would represent 25% of
the current market value of his stocks ($2,000).

These examples have assumed that the customer
bought only a single stock on margin. Actually, most
margin customers are likely to have positions in a
number of stocks in their margin accounts. In such
circumstances, the broker must compute exactly how
the customer stands on all of his stocks, and he will not
send out a margin call on some one stock that may have
fallen below the maintenance requirements if the customer shows a surplus on his other holdings sufficient
to offset the shortages. In short, the broker takes into
account the customer's overall position—the shortages
and surpluses in each stock—and sends out a margin
call only when the customer falls below the minimum
maintenance requirements on his total holdings.

Thanks to modern data processing and computing
equipment, something that wasn't available in the 1929
crash, brokers can compute the exact position of an
active margin account almost instantly in periods of
rapidly falling prices. At other more normal times,
weekly runs on all margin accounts are sufficient to protect the broker.

Incidentally, when a customer gets a margin call, he
doesn't have to pony up cash if he has acceptable
securities in a regular or cash account that he can post
as collateral.

A margin customer is also permitted to substitute
one stock for another in his margin account, but if the
stock he buys is higher in price than the one he sells,
he will have to deposit funds with his broker equal to
whatever the Federal Reserve initial margin requirement is on the difference between the purchase price of
the one and the selling price of the other.

Conversely, if proceeds from a customer's sale exceed his purchase cost, the amount that he can withdraw from his account is whatever excess there is above the Federal Reserve's current initial margin requirement, provided that his account is fully margined (unrestricted). If his account is restricted (margined below the current initial federal margin requirement), the customer can withdraw a minimum of at least 30% of the difference between the purchase cost and the sale proceeds.

The Federal Reserve Board's requirement governing the initial margin payment and the stock exchange rule on maintenance of margin explain why margin calls are comparatively infrequent today, except in very sharp market dips as in 1969–1970 and 1973–1974. In slumps like these, the margin buyer can be caught in a bad squeeze and forced to sell at a substantial loss in order to meet a margin call. That's why no one should trade on margin unless he has both the temperament and the resources that will enable him to accept his losses with reasonable equanimity. You can't be a margin trader—nor should you be—if you have only a widow's mite.

One other restriction on margin trading should be noted: the exchange has put a brake on the heavy trader who might move in and out of a given stock several times during one day's trading. Brokers are now required to see that such *day traders* operating on margin, as most of them do, have enough capital in their accounts to cover the initial margin requirement on the maximum position they held at any time in the day's trading—not just their position at the end of the day.

Not only have the regulations resulted in fewer margin calls than there were at the time of the 1929 crash, but they have also greatly reduced the proportion of margin accounts in relation to all accounts. In 1929 it is estimated that margin customers represented 40% of all customers, and they accounted for a considerably larger proportion of total commission business. Just how large a proportion no one knows exactly, but as the market boiled upward in the late twenties, the margin customers were always the big buyers, the people who kept *pyramiding* their *paper profits* and buying more and more stock.

Here's how pyramiding worked in those days: Suppose a man bought 200 shares of a $50 stock. Under the lax margin regulations which prevailed then, he might have had to put up only $2,000 of the $10,000 cost—maybe even less if he was a favored customer.

Now let's assume that his stock advanced to $75 a share. His total holdings would now be worth $15,000. If he sold at that price and paid off the $8,000 loan from his broker, he would have $7,000 cash; and on a 20% margin basis, this would enable him to buy $35,000 worth of stock. Actually, of course, he didn't have to go through the mechanics of selling out and buying afresh. The broker recognized the expanded value of his original holdings and accepted that added value as collateral on the additional purchases.

In this instance, the customer would have been able to own $35,000 worth of securities on a cash margin of only $2,000, thanks to that 50% increase in the value of his original 200 shares. If he continued to be that lucky, he could run his paper profits to a hundred thousand dollars, a half million dollars, a million dollars, many millions of dollars, all on just $2,000 cash.

And in the twenties many people did exactly that. But when prices started to decline and the margin calls came, many of them couldn't raise even a few thousand dollars cash except by selling securities. And when they sold, that very act of selling depressed prices further and resulted in more margin calls. Again they had to sell. And so the vicious circle kept swirling downward into the great abyss.

There's nothing illegal about pyramiding even today under the Federal Reserve Board rules, but it just can't work very effectively when you have to put up a margin of 50%, 70% or 90% instead of 20%. Only a substantial increase in the price of a speculator's stock will yield him big enough paper profits to permit a significant increase in his holdings.

And that's one reason why margin accounts aren't as popular as they used to be. It is estimated that by the end of World War II they had declined to less than 10% of their number in 1929. In December 1972, Big Board member firms had 750,000 margin accounts, but the big drop in the market through 1973–1974 whittled this number down to 465,000 shortly before the market hit bottom in December 1974.

Margin accounts increased again with the upswing in 1975–1976, but still margin trading at any given time is likely to account for only 10% or 15% of total trading on the New York Stock Exchange. However, because they are apt to trade more frequently and in larger amounts, margin customers today probably account for three or four times that percentage of total commission income that a broker derives from transactions by individuals.

So well protected are margin accounts today that if there were an even more serious decline in the market than there was in 1973–1974, it is unlikely that it could ever be turned into the kind of rout that made 1929 the debacle it was.

CHAPTER 22

What It Means to Sell Short

WHEN a man opens a margin account with a broker, he is asked to sign an agreement giving the broker authority to lend his marginable stocks to others. It is this lending or hypothecation agreement that makes it possible in most cases for other customers to sell stocks short.

Short selling normally accounts for only 6% to 8% of all the transactions on the New York Stock Exchange, and yet probably no other market technique excites so much public interest—or is so widely misunderstood.

A short sale is nothing but the reverse of the usual market transaction. Instead of buying a stock and then selling it, the short trader sells it first—goes *short* the stock (because he doesn't own it)—then buys it back at what he hopes will be a lower price.

If it is legitimate to buy a stock because you think it's going to go up, why isn't it just as legitimate to sell it because you think it's going to go down? Why shouldn't you be able to try to make a profit in either direction? It can be fairly argued that the right of a bear to sell, or go short, is just as vital to a completely free market as the right of a bull to buy stocks, or go *long*.

Regardless of the logic of the situation, most people think it just isn't morally right to sell something you don't have.

What about the magazine publisher who sells you a three-year advance subscription to his publication?

Or what about the farmer who may sell his whole crop to a grain elevator or to a miller when the seed hasn't even sprouted yet?

Both of them sell something they haven't got just on the strength of a promise to deliver. And that's all a short seller does.

Furthermore, it isn't really true that he sells something he doesn't have. He has to *borrow* the stock that he sells, and he has to give it back. This he hopes to be able to do by *covering,* or buying it back at a price less than he sold it for.

Where does he borrow his stock? From his broker.

Where does the broker get the stock to lend? Usually from his other margin customers, who signed the lending agreement when they opened their accounts. If a broker doesn't have among all his margin accounts the particular stock that a man wants to sell short, he will borrow it from another broker or from some individual stockowner who makes a business of lending stock. But the broker *cannot* borrow stock from the account of any of his regular cash customers without specific authorization.

Why should one broker lend stock to another? Because he gets paid for it by the borrowing broker, who retains all the proceeds of his customer's short sale until the transaction is closed out by an offsetting purchase. Sometimes if the stock is in heavy demand and is difficult to borrow, the broker will even pay a premium to borrow it. Any such premium payment is, of course, charged to the short seller. If the price of a stock on loan increases significantly, the lending broker will expect more money; if the price drops, the borrowing broker will expect a proportionate refund of the money he has paid. (Sometimes a lending broker will demand return of the shares, and if the borrowing broker can't locate them elsewhere, he is forced to buy them back from the customer and close out the short position, regardless of whether the customer likes it or not.)

A short seller operates under essentially the same rules that govern margin buying. If the Federal Reserve Board has a 50% margin rule in effect, the seller must put up cash equal to 50% of the market value of the stock that he borrows and sells. Under stock exchange rules, the minimum margin cannot be less than $2,000.

Suppose a man wanted to go short 100 shares of a stock selling at 60. If the Federal Reserve Board requirement was 50% at the time, he would have to put up $3,000 cash. If the stock dropped to 50, he could buy it back, cover his short position by returning the stock, and make a profit of $10 a share, or $1,000, less taxes and commissions.

But perhaps when the stock hit 50 he thought it would go lower. He could make more money if it did, but he wouldn't want to lose the profit he already had. In such a situation, he might place a stop order to buy at 52, and thus protect himself against a rising market. If the stock does go up to 52, his stop order to buy becomes a market order to buy at once.

If he buys back in at that price, he will still have a profit of $800, exclusive of all brokerage commissions and taxes. Additionally, he will also be liable for whatever dividends may have accrued on the stock during the operation, because the lender obviously was entitled to get them during the time his stock was on loan.

There is one important difference in the amount of margin required of the customer when he buys stocks on margin for a long position and when he sells stocks on margin to establish a short position. The minimum requirement of the New York Stock Exchange for maintenance-of-margin is 25% for the long position, but when a customer uses margin—as he must—for going short, the minimum is increased to 30%, or $5 a share, whichever is greater. (If the stock itself is selling below $5 a share, the minimum requirement is 100% of the market value or $2.50 a share, whichever is greater.)

That 30% maintenance-of-margin requirement on short sales means that the broker will call for more money whenever the amount of the margin that the short seller would have left if he bought the stock back and covered his short position would total only 30% of its current market price.

Suppose a man sells short 100 shares of a stock at 60. If the initial margin requirement was 50%, he would have to put up $3,000. Now, instead of declining to 50, suppose the price of the stock goes up to 70. If he were to cover at that point, he would owe $7,000, or $1,000 more than he sold the stock for originally. That means he would have only $2,000 margin left in his account ($3,000 minus $1,000), or a little less than 30% of the current value of the stock ($7,000 times .30 equals $2,100). At that point, unless he decided to take his loss and close out the transaction, he would receive a maintenance call to deposit at least $100 additional margin.

Sometimes a short sale can be prudently used to protect a profit in a stock at a time when the buyer doesn't want to sell it and take his capital gain. Suppose, for instance, you had bought 100 shares of a stock in August—a straight cash transaction—and that it ran up 20 points by December. If you were to sell before the year-end and take your $2,000 profit, you would have to pay a short-term capital-gains tax on that profit at the full tax rate applying to ordinary income. If you were in a 50% tax bracket, you would have to pay out $1,000 in taxes. So you want to hold on for just another month until your capital gain can be reported as income in another tax year when you expect you will be in a lower tax bracket.

But suppose the stock were to drop during that month waiting period and you were to lose a substantial part of your $2,000 profit? You don't want that to happen. And you're perfectly willing to forgo the prospect of further price appreciation, a bigger profit, just to protect yourself against the risk of loss. A short sale of 100 shares of the same stock offers you just that kind of insurance. When you are both long and short the same number of shares of the same stock, your position is stabilized. If the stock rises, you make money on your long position and lose an equal amount on your short position. If it goes down, you make money on the short side and lose an offsetting amount on the long side. Your capital gains and losses cancel each other.

When you stabilize this way, you don't change the tax status of your profit as it was when you went short;

you simply defer taking your gain and paying the tax on it until you enter a new tax year. All you lose is the additional commission, taxes, and interest you pay on the short sale. (It should be noted that under federal tax regulations a short sale of this kind cannot be used within a single tax year to convert a short-term into a long-term capital gain in order to reduce the tax. It can be used only when the carryover is from one year to the succeeding year.)

Another good thing about this kind of transaction, known as *selling short against the box,* is that the maintenance-of-margin requirement is reduced from 30% to 10%, because when the margin customer is long stock in his cash account in an amount that precisely offsets the number of shares he is short in his margin account, any chance of loss is eliminated, regardless of whether the market moves up or down.

While it is obvious that there is a legitimate place for short selling in a free and orderly securities market, it cannot be denied on the other hand that short selling has often been used for illegitimate purposes, and these abuses have frequently led to demands that short selling be outlawed. From the time three hundred fifty years ago when buyers and sellers first began to trade in the stock of the Dutch East India Company, the history of short selling has not been a pretty one. And it contributed some gaudy chapters to the history of the New York Stock Exchange, particularly in the nineteenth century, when short selling was a favorite tool of such famous market manipulators as Commodore Vanderbilt, Daniel Drew, Jay Gould, and Jim Fisk.

In many battles, these men tried to catch each other in market corners. A market *corner* is created when one man or group succeeds in getting such complete control of a particular stock that others who may have sold it short cannot cover their purchases by buying the stock back, as they eventually have to do, except on terms dictated by the controlling group.

One of the classic corners is that which involved the old Harlem Railroad, a predecessor of the New York Central. Vanderbilt got control of the Harlem and then proceeded to extend the road down Manhattan Island. Drew, who was also a stockholder in the road and had realized a handsome profit as the stock advanced in price, now saw an opportunity to make a much larger profit. He induced the New York City Council to repeal the franchise which had been granted for the extension of the road on the assumption that this bad news would depress the price of the stock. Simultaneously, he sold the stock short.

His maneuver did succeed in driving the price of the stock down, but as Drew sold, the Commodore bought. In the end, Drew and some of the members of the City Council who were associated with him in this notorious exploit found that they had sold short more stock than actually existed. They could not cover their short positions except on terms dictated by Vanderbilt—and the terms were ruinous. That is probably when the famous couplet, credited to Drew, came into our literature: *"He who sells what isn't his'n/Must buy it back or go to pris'n."*

Even when nothing so titanic as an attempted corner was involved, short selling proved an effective manipulative device for *pool* operators, who would join forces to bid the price of a stock up and then drive it back down again by the pressure of their short selling in order to make a big speculative profit.

Often such pool operators would risk very little of their own capital in the operation. They would stimulate public interest in a particular stock by adroit publicity and creation of considerable activity in the market for that stock. That activity was usually more apparent than real, because it would be generated by *wash sales*. A wash sale, now outlawed by the S.E.C., simply involved the simultaneous purchase and sale of large blocks, say, 1,000 or 10,000 shares. Such big volume would attract the public, which inevitably seems to buy whenever there is a lot of activity in a stock. As the public bought and as demand forced the price up, pool operators would wait for the strategic moment when they thought the stock was about as high as it could get, and then they would begin selling it short, hammering the price down to a level where they could buy it back at a handsome profit.

One of the most important reforms introduced by the Securities and Exchange Commission is the regulation that effectively prevents abuse of the right to sell short. The S.E.C. accomplished this objective in February 1938 by a simple regulation which essentially provides that a stock can be sold short only in a rising market, however temporary that rise may be.

The rule, generally referred to as the *"one-eighth rule,"* works this way: if a customer places an order to sell short, that order as it goes to the floor must be clearly marked as a short sale, and the floor broker is forbidden to execute that order except at what is, in effect, a higher price. Thus, if a stock were last sold at 50, the broker could not sell that stock short except at a price of 50⅛ or higher; in this case he would be selling on an up tick.

There is one exception to this: the broker may sell the stock at 50, the same price as prevailed on the last sale, provided that the *last previous* change in the price had been upward. In other words, there might have been one or two or six transactions that had taken place at the same price of 50, but a short sale could still be made at 50, provided the last *different* price had been 49⅞ or lower. This is called selling on an *even tick*.

With the debut of the *consolidated tape* and ticker systems in June 1975, the S.E.C. had some new problems to solve connected with short selling. The commission wanted to prohibit any short sale at a price that was lower than the last sale reported on the consolidated tape, regardless of where that sale was made. Further, the commission wanted to prohibit a short sale on an even tick and to impose short selling restrictions on all over-the-counter transactions in listed securities.

Such stringent regulations threatened to pose serious problems for the exchange specialists who are responsible for maintaining a fluid auction market in the stocks they handle. So the S.E.C. relaxed its rule to the extent of providing that short sales could be made by specialists regardless of the tick, as long as they were made at the last sale price reported on the consolidated tape. Still, the specialists were not satisfied. They argued that the consolidated tape might lag significantly behind the actual market that they were making in a given stock on the floor of the exchange, that a price change which might appear to be a down tick on the tape might actually be an up tick in their own market.

The S.E.C. then made another concession, which became effective on April 30, 1976. It gave the exchange the choice of basing short sales on prices that prevailed on the Big Board, or of using those that appeared on the consolidated tape. The N.Y.S.E., of course, adhered firmly to its own prices. But the situation was so confused that there even was "unofficial talk" that the S.E.C. might eventually rescind all curbs on short selling. No one was worried that such relaxation of the rules would permit the bears to raid the market again as they did in yesteryear, for the S.E.C. had many other ways to bring them to heel. So many, in fact, that the S.E.C. could afford to relax its short selling rules, in order to let free and open competition dictate the course of market action and, it was hoped, to produce the best and fairest prices for all— the bears as well as the bulls.

Most of the short selling that is done nowadays comes not from the public but from members of the exchange. Does this mean that brokers are up to their old tricks? Not at all.

The specialists account for 55% to 60% of all short selling on the New York Stock Exchange. They very often have to make these sales if they are to fulfill their obligations as specialists to maintain orderly and continuous markets in the stocks assigned to them. Thus, if a broker wants to execute a market buy order for a customer and there are no near offers to sell, except perhaps at a price that is wholly out of line—perhaps even as much as a full point higher—the specialist is expected to offer the stock at a better or lower price, even if he doesn't have that stock in his inventory and has to go short in order to complete the transaction.

Registered floor traders frequently engage in short selling for their personal accounts. When they do, it is not because they are trading on inside knowledge; often it's just because they are cynical about the public's perpetual bullishness. Then too, these traders customarily make fast and frequent trades on both sides of the market, first long and then short or vice versa, seeking to make a profit, even if it is only a fraction of a point, for they pay no brokerage commission by reason of their Big Board membership. However, such rapid-fire operations are much more closely scrutinized nowadays.

Short selling has been strictly regulated by the S.E.C., but it still remains an important trading tool. As evidence of that, the total number of shares sold short on the New York Stock Exchange, the so-called *short interest,* which is reported monthly by the exchange, continued to reach consecutive highs, month by month in the first half of 1975, when the market was headed up. In January 1976, it reached a record of more than 27 million shares. Obviously, there were many people who simply didn't believe that the market upsurge was justified by business conditions nor that it would be sustained. Some of them may have been selling short against the box, or otherwise trying to neutralize their positions by various "hedging" techniques. But there is no denying the fact that the stock market bears—the professional traders and perennial pessimists who just didn't believe that prosperity was just around the corner—were still making their weight felt in the market.

Paradoxical as it may seem, a big short interest is generally regarded as bullish. The argument is that as the short interest grows, so does the potential volume of buying orders; for ultimately every one of those short sellers is going to have to come back into the market and buy back the stock he previously sold short in order to make delivery of the shares. Hence, the short interest represents a cushion of buying orders that helps to sustain the market.

It is a truism that the public always wants the mar-

ket to go up and generally believes that it will. And so
most investors act accordingly. In the light of such
perpetual bullishness who could deny an old bear the
right to sell short on the assumption that the bulls
are wrong again?

CHAPTER 23

Options—"The Hottest Game in Town"

In addition to margin trading, pyramiding profits, and selling short, the speculator can execute still another market maneuver that has become increasingly popular in recent years, so popular in fact that traders, large and small, consider it "the hottest game in town."

If you think a certain stock is likely to increase in price over the next three months, for example, you can buy a *call* on that stock, which gives you the right to buy 100 shares of it at the price specified in the call contract at any time within the three-month period. Whether you exercise that option is wholly up to you; whether you do or don't depends on the market action of the stock. If its price advances and its increase is greater than the cost of the option which you bought, it can be of advantage to you to exercise your option and buy the 100 shares at the option price. Or you might decide to sell your option, which you can do at any time before the expiration date, and take your profit on it.

Thus, if Rod & Reel were selling at $50 a share on August 1, you might want to buy an October call on Rod & Reel at 50 which would entitle you to buy the stock at the same $50 price, at any time from August 1 until the last option trading day in October.

What would it cost you to buy such a call?

That depends on a variety of factors—what the outlook is for the market as a whole, how stable or volatile the price of Rod & Reel has been in the past, what its earnings prospects are, etc.; but, typically, a three-month option on 100 shares of a $50 stock —a round lot is the standard unit of trading—might cost you $500, plus a commission of about $25. At

$500, your option would obviously cost you $5 a share; that is the *premium* you pay. Unless Rod & Reel advances by the amount of the premium—from 50 to 55—within that three-month option period, you will lose money. Anything over 55 will represent a profit to you, because you have the right to claim 100 shares of Rod & Reel at 50. At 55, you break even; that's called parity. At 57, you would be $2 a share ahead of the game.

At that point you could sell your contract in the options market and net a profit of $200, minus commission on both the purchase and sale of your option contract, commissions that might total $50. But you would have made $150 on a $500 speculation, or 30% on your money.

Now suppose Rod & Reel never seems to be able to go higher than 53 and you conclude it never will before your option expires. In such a case you might decide to sell the contract even if it means losing $2 a share or $200, plus $50 in commissions—a total loss of $250.

The comforting thing about buying an option is that you can never lose more than the amount of your original cost. Maybe Rod & Reel goes up above your option price of 50. But maybe it goes down to 48 or 47 or even lower. Obviously, at such prices, nobody is going to be much interested in buying your call on the stock at 50, assuming that the contract is also about to expire. So your call is worthless, and you end up losing the $500, plus that $25 commission that you paid for the option. That's the most you can lose, no matter how low Rod & Reel sinks.

And therein lies the great attraction of options. If you buy one, you can't lose more than the contract cost you, but your profit potential is open-ended. You might make 40% or 100% or much more—and all on just a $500 speculation. In contrast, if you owned 100 shares of Rod & Reel outright at 50 a share and it moved from 50 to 57, you could sell them and make a profit of $700, or 14%. But if you had bought a $500 option at 50 and the price rose to 57 or two points beyond your break-even point, you would make a 40%

profit, and you would have put at risk only one-tenth as much of your capital. Of course, you did have to assume the risk that Rod & Reel would advance at least four points in order to make money, and that's a risk the man who owns the stock outright never has to take.

In all these examples, it is assumed that the value of your option moves up or down by exactly the same amount as the price of the stock. That isn't really the way options work. Obviously, the price at which an option is traded is always going to be influenced primarily by the price movement of the underlying stock. But, after all, options are traded in a separate market from that in which stocks are traded, and option traders may not have exactly the same idea about the future for any given stock as those who buy and sell the stock on the New York Stock Exchange. As a general rule, when options are selling below parity, the price at which purchases can break even, price swings are not apt to be as big as they are, either up or down, on the Big Board for the stock itself. But once an option reaches parity, its price is likely to move up or down by exactly the same amount as the stock itself.

If you have a profit in an option contract, you can sell it in the options market, take your profit, and get out. But an option contract gives you the right to buy that stock at a specified price, and this is a right you might decide to exercise, if you thought prospects were good for that stock. Thus, if you bought an option on Rod & Reel at 50 (plus $5 per share premium cost) and if Rod & Reel went to 58 during the life of your contract, you might decide to exercise your right to buy the stock outright at 50. In that case, your costs would add up like this: $500 for the option contract, plus $25 commission, plus $5,000 for 100 shares of Rod & Reel at 50, plus maybe $40 commission on that purchase—a total of $5,565 for stock then worth $5,800. So you come out $235 ahead.

Even if you couldn't show a profit on your option deal, you might, if you liked the stock, decide to exercise the option and cut your losses. Thus if you had paid $525 for the right to buy a round lot of Rod &

Reel at 50, you might decide to exercise the option when Rod & Reel was selling at 53. Your total cost would, of course, be the same, $5,565, but your stock would be worth only $5,300, resulting in a loss to you of $265. But a loss of $265 is better than a loss of $525, which is what you would be out of pocket if Rod & Reel dropped to 50 or below.

There is nothing new about buying calls. You could have bought a call on any number of popular stocks in the over-the-counter market for many years. Or you might have bought a *put* in the same market. A put is the opposite of a call and gives you the right to sell a stock at a specified price within a given time period on the assumption that the stock named in the contract will decline.

What has made trading in options so popular was the establishment in April 1973 of the *Chicago Board Options Exchange* for the sole purpose of providing an organized market for trading initially in calls. In 1975, the American Stock Exchange also initiated option trading, featuring a different list of Big Board stocks, as have the Philadelphia and Pacific Stock Exchanges. The exchanges have been doing a thriving business. Although option trading was restricted originally to calls, sooner or later, it seemed inevitable that they would begin trading in puts.

Meanwhile, in the old over-the-counter market, the old-line options dealers still offer a wide variety of puts and calls on assorted stocks, options of various durations that might expire on any one of the 250 trading days in the stock market year.

On the exchanges, order has been brought into that chaos. Options are offered there for three, six, or nine-month periods—just those and nothing else. Furthermore, option contracts expire on a set date, usually on the Saturday following the third Friday, but there are two different time cycles. Some operate on a January, April, July, and October cycle; some terminate in February, May, August, and November. Hence there are only eight terminal dates a year when contracts are closed out.

Finally, the prices at which options are offered have

been standardized. If a stock sells for under 50, prices are quoted in $5 steps, and those steps are closely related to the price at which the stock itself is selling. Thus, if Rod & Reel were selling at 30, you might at any given time be able to buy or sell Rod & Reel options at 25, 30, 35, and 40. No market would exist for option contracts that were farther away from the actual price of Rod & Reel. After all, no one would be interested in buying or selling a contract at 50 or 55, because it would not be realistic to expect Rod & Reel to trade in such a high price range. Option contracts on stocks selling from 50 to 200 are quoted in $10 steps, and those above 200 in $20 steps.

Options on stocks that have rapid price movements, either up or down, usually cost more than contracts on stocks whose price performance is more stable. Typically, on these more stable stocks you might have to pay 5% or 10% of the market price for an option, but on a real swinging stock, you might expect to pay as much as 15%.

One such "swinger" in the bull market of early 1976 was the stock of Company X*, which almost doubled in price in three months. Naturally, there were also wide swings in the price of Company X option contracts, but the very width of these swings makes it easier to understand how option prices are quoted and why they move the way they do. Here is the way option quotations of Company X appeared in the papers of February 7, 1976, reporting the previous day's trading:

	April		July		October		New York
Option & Price	Volume	Last Sale	Volume	Last Sale	Volume	Last Sale	Close
Company X 15	245	9	171	9⅛	129	9⅜	23⅞
Company X 20	805	4¾	532	5⅝	198	6⅛	23⅞
Company X 25	1804	2³⁄₁₆	874	3⅛	345	3¾	23⅞

Note, first of all, that Company X closed that day on the Big Board at 23⅞ (last column)—a price substantially above the option price that some people had bought earlier, permitting them to buy the stock at

*Company X refers to an actual stock, but in this edition the real name is omitted.

either $15 or $20 a share, whether those contracts were to terminate in April, July, or October (Last Sale columns). Contracts that offered buyers the right to purchase Company X at 25 attracted the greatest interest in all three time periods, as the volume figures for the number of round lots traded clearly and uniformly indicate. This is evidence of a strong bullish sentiment.

Characteristically, in all three contracts—15, 20, and 25—the premium that buyers were willing to pay shows a steady increase through the three time periods. The April 15 contract shows a premium of 9 resulting in a total price of 24, or ⅛ above the New York close (Close plus Last Sale). The premium on the July contract is 9⅛ and on October 9⅜. The longer the life of a contract, the higher the premium, as a general rule.

The same pattern is repeated in the Company X 20 contract. April buyers were willing to pay 4¾ (equivalent to a stock price of 24¾), and the July and October contracts carried premiums of 5⅝ (25⅝) and 6⅛ (26⅛). The Company X 25 contract underscores the optimism with premiums of 2 3/16 (27 3/16), 3⅛ (28⅛), and 3¾ (28¾). Company X closed that day at 23⅞, but buyers of the Company X 25 contract were willing to stake their money on the expectation that Company X would be worth 28¾ by October—more than 5 points above the February 6 close.

Now look at the Company X option quotations for the trading day of March 4, just four weeks later.

	April		*July*		*October*		
Option & Price	*Volume*	*Last Sale*	*Volume*	*Last Sale*	*Volume*	*Last Sale*	*New York Close*
Company X 15	135	15⅝	58	16⅛	14	16¼	30⅝
Company X 20	450	11	385	11⅜	129	11¾	30⅝
Company X 25	2047	6⅝	642	7⅞	229	9	30⅝
Company X 30	b.	b.	2092	5¼	302	6½	30⅝
Company X 35	b.	b.	2613	3⅛	630	4¼	30⅝

The most significant thing about this table is the addition of two new contracts for July and October closeouts—Company X 30 and 35. The *b.* for these contracts in April indicates that such contracts were not offered because the April closeout was only a month and a half away.

Essentially, these quotations show the same patterns as those of a month earlier, but the bullishness which they reflect is even more emphatic. It is climaxed by that premium of 4¼ for the Company X 35 contract in October. Buyers of this contract were estimating a price of 39¼ for Company X some seven months later, nearly 9 points, or 30%, above the March 4 close.

The value of the option as a speculative tool is clearly apparent. Anyone can take a flyer in the market by risking just a few hundred dollars. He doesn't have nearly so much money tied up in the operation as he would if he traded on margin, even when the margin was as low as 40% or 50%. With terminal dates on option contracts often forcing the buyer to take his losses, out-of-pocket costs may be higher operating on an option basis, rather than on margin. But if there is a significant price advance in the stock, his profit may make the cost look incidental.

The use of options for protection is not always so clear. But if you had a substantial profit in some stock and you wanted to be sure that that profit was protected against any possible loss for three, six, or nine months, you could buy a put on that stock at the then prevailing price. This would guarantee that you could make somebody else pay you the same price for the stock, no matter how much it had fallen.

For instance, suppose you had bought 100 shares of Rod & Reel at $20, and the price had risen to $40. You would have a paper profit of $2,000. Now let's assume that this was money you knew you were going to need a few months hence to help pay for your son's tuition at college. You don't want to sell Rod & Reel right then and take your $2,000 profit, because you think there's a good chance that Rod & Reel might run up to $50, maybe even higher. Nevertheless, you can't afford to lose that $2,000 profit you have in hand. To insure yourself against loss, you might buy a six-month put. The cost would depend upon the degree of volatility of Rod & Reel, its price at that time, where it was traded, and its previous history.

But then, if the market took a tumble and Rod & Reel declined to, say, $32 you could exercise your right before the option expired to "put" the stock to the seller of the option and force him to accept delivery at $40 a share. You would still be out the cost of the put, not counting commissions, but that's better than being out $800, as you would have been if you hadn't bought the contract. You would have achieved the same objective as would a margin trader, who sold short against the box.

Of course, if the market rose and Rod & Reel kept going up, perhaps to $47 or $48, you would have lost the cost of the put option, but you would be comforted by the $700 or $800 increase in the value of your holdings. In such cases, you might consider the cost of the put a cheap form of insurance.

Instead of buying a put, you could also protect yourself by selling your 100 shares of Rod & Reel at $40 and buying a call on it at $40. If Rod & Reel dropped, the most you could lose would be the cost of the call. But if it continued rising, you would be in exactly the same position as if you still owned the stock, except for the cost of the call.

A speculator who has sold Rod & Reel short could also use options to hedge his position, but he would use them in precisely the reverse fashion. Instead of buying a put to protect himself against a falling market, he would buy a call to protect against a rising market.

Of course, you could accomplish the same objective by placing a stop order to sell with your broker—the short seller would conversely place a stop order to buy —but many people dislike using stop orders to protect a profit because such orders have no elasticity, no "give" to them. For instance, suppose that you had bought Rod & Reel at $20 and it now stood at $40. Being willing to concede some of this twenty-point profit, you place a stop order to sell it at $37. Now suppose there was a brisk sell-off in the market on a given day because of some worrisome piece of news and Rod

& Reel suddenly dropped to $37. Your stop order would thereupon become a market order and you would be sold out immediately. Then, in a few days when the market has recovered from its temporary shock, Rod & Reel might bound back to $40. But you wouldn't own the stock any longer.

In addition to providing protection against loss, puts and calls can also be effectively used to convert a short-term capital gain into a long-term one, thus effecting a tax saving. Suppose you owned 500 shares of Rod & Reel and there had been a 5-point run-up in its price. You might be quite content to take a $2,500 profit and get out, but if you had only owned the stock for a few months—anything less than nine months in 1977 and twelve months thereafter—and if you were to sell then, you would have to pay the full tax rate applying to your income bracket on that capital gain. If you could only hold the stock for another few months, your capital gain would be taxed at the much lower long-term rate. But because Rod & Reel might decline during this waiting period, you wonder if you really shouldn't sell then, even if it did mean paying a higher tax.

Options offer you a way out. Instead of selling, you buy five long-term puts on the 500 shares of Rod & Reel at $40 and hang onto the shares you own, until the nine-month (1977) or twelve-month (1978) holding period is up. In the interim, if Rod & Reel might decline in those two months, you wonder if you really should sell then, even if it did mean paying a higher tax rate.

Options offer you a way out. Instead of selling, you buy five three-month puts on the 500 shares of Rod & Reel at $40 and hang onto the shares you own, until the six-month holding period is up. In the interim, if Rod & Reel does indeed decline, you exercise your puts, the right to sell 500 shares at $40. Your profit will amount to the difference between the price at which you bought the puts and the prices at which they were exercised, less contract costs and commissions. On the other hand, if Rod & Reel advances substantially your puts will be worthless, but you can satisfy yourself with the increased profit on the stock you own and the fact that you now can pay the gains tax on a long-term rather than a short-term basis.

In any situation where a fair-sized tax saving can be realized by holding stock a little longer than you might otherwise care to, the cost of the option may be considered not very important, in view of the protection it provides and the tax money you can save.

While many individuals buy options on one of the exchanges for trading purposes without exercising their right stipulated in the contract, the bulk of options that are sold, or "written," is derived from private individuals or large institutions that have substantial capital. Does this mean that these people who sell calls are primarily bearish on the market? Not at all. They are willing to assume the risk they take for several very good reasons: (1) they are well paid for that risk by the premium they receive for the options they write; (2) when they sell an option they have instant use of this money; (3) since they usually own the stock against which they write the option, they collect all dividends on that stock in the interim; and (4) the contracts they write often represent "hedge" insurance against wide price fluctuations in stocks held in their portfolios.

Since an active option writer deals in dozens of different stocks, he can count on the law of averages to absorb a good measure of his risk. Stocks simply do not move in identical price patterns; he will lose on some and win on others. Considering all these factors the trained and knowledgeable option writer does not carry as large a burden of risk as it might appear that he did on the surface. After all, sellers of calls always have that premium working for them. A stock has to advance by more than the amount of the premium before the seller loses any money.

Sometimes a trader will buy both a put and a call simultaneously on the same stock. This is called a *straddle*—a double stock option contract, each for 100 shares and each with identical exercise prices (both options are written at the same price), which entitles the holder to demand (call) or deliver (put) the stock named in the contract on or before a fixed date.

The trader's purpose in buying a straddle is usually to try to take advantage of anticipated large fluctuations in price of the underlying stock, without having to pinpoint either the time or direction of such fluctuations. Thus, a stock might rise sharply in price to a point where it became profitable for him to exercise his call and then drop drastically, enabling him to make a profit on the put.

Options are obviously very volatile with a high leverage factor—the chance to make a lot of money by putting only a comparatively small amount at stake—while the size of the loss is limited just to the size of your stake.

So popular has option trading become in just a few short years that options can now be bought on the exchanges on several hundred stocks. And they are substantial stocks, for the exchanges where options are traded have set certain requirements that a stock must meet before it becomes eligible for trading:

(1) There must be at least 10 million registered, outstanding shares, 80% of which must be publicly held.

(2) There must be at least 10,000 shareholders of record.

(3) Trading volume must have been at least 1 million shares during each of the two previous years on the principal exchange where the stock is listed. Options on over-the-counter stocks are not traded on the options exchanges, but lists of the stocks in which they do trade are available upon request.

(4) The price per share must be at least $10 at the time the stock is approved for option trading.

(5) The corporation that issues the stock must also meet certain requirements, quite similar to those that govern the original listing of the stock.

The central market system that the options exchanges have designed for options trading is a microcosm of the central market which the S.E.C has planned for securities. It includes a consolidated tape for reporting price and volume data, a consolidated quotation system for publicizing the prices at which competing brokers will deal in options, and a central clearing system for processing all trades. These and other time- and laborsaving innovations have reduced the many variables formerly associated with options trading to the one basic factor, the price of the option.

The computer, too, has been put vigorously to work in the option market. Programs have been created to estimate an option's value, based on its life span and the degree of risk in the underlying stock. The programs produce a value estimate, which is compared with the price at which the option sells in the marketplace, in order to determine if the option is overvalued or undervalued. Additional programs are then employed to establish buying and selling strategies.

The juggling of these various speculative devices— margin trading, short selling, puts and calls—weighing the risks and the costs of each against the other, makes the business of professional speculation a highly complicated one. This alone can explain why it is probably true that more people who speculate lose money than make money.

But an even more important reason lies in the inclination of many a speculator to act on the basis of a tip or hunch, his unwillingness to study thoroughly all the facts about a company before he buys or sells its stock. Bernard M. Baruch, probably America's most successful speculator, made it an inviolable rule never to become involved in a speculative venture until he had mastered all the facts about it. As he once explained, successful speculation demands not only courage, persistence, and a judgment unclouded by emotion, but above all things it requires an infinite capacity for taking pains—the pains to analyze all available facts.

CHAPTER 24

How to Tell What the Market Is Doing

WHEN most people buy securities for the first time, they are likely to do it for the wrong reasons. They will buy a stock because they've heard other people, their friends or business associates, talk about it.

It seems to be human nature to believe that the other fellow always knows a good thing, that he has reliable inside information on how a company is doing.

Is there such a thing as *inside information?*

Of course there is.

The officers and directors of a company know more about that firm and its prospects than anybody else could possibly know. And they have relatives and friends with whom they discuss their company's situation. In effect, these people do have what appears to be privileged information—the real "inside." And because they do, the S.E.C. has long kept close watch on the stock-trading operations of company executives and other insiders. The commission wants no recurrence of the pre-1929 situation when many company officials or directors considered the privilege of trading in their company's stock on the basis of their own inside information simply part of their compensation.

Today, any such insider is required to report to the S.E.C. every purchase or sale he makes of his own company's stock, and the list of such transactions is published monthly. He is never permitted to sell his own company's stock short. Further, if an insider realizes any profit from buying and selling his company's stock within a six-month period, that profit is recoverable by the company, whether or not it can be demonstrated that he had used inside information. And if it can be shown that he masked his transaction in the name of his wife or some other relative or friend, he is just as liable as if he had traded in his own name.

Inside information is, of course, no longer inside when it has been made public, but when can such information be said to have become public? This was the key question in a test case initiated by the S.E.C. in May 1966. The case involved a dozen directors and officials of the Texas Gulf Sulphur Company, which in 1963 discovered valuable deposits of lead, zinc, and copper on its property at Timmins, Ontario, in Canada. The company acquired adjacent properties and resumed drilling operations in March 1964. On April 16, 1964, Texas Gulf announced its discoveries at a press conference.

The S.E.C. in its suit alleged that various officials profited from their inside knowledge by buying stock in the company before the ore discoveries became public knowledge, and it even went so far as to charge one director with a violation, although his purchase of 3,000 shares was not made until an hour after news of the ore discovery was released at the press conference and published on a financial news service in virtually every major bank and brokerage office in the country. This particular charge was dismissed when the first verdict was returned in a federal district court, and all but two of the defendants were exonerated. But American industry was put on notice that the S.E.C. intended to be more vigilant than ever in supervising transactions by company officials and other insiders.

If there was any need for emphasis, the S.E.C. underlined its point in September 1968 when it brought an action against Merrill Lynch, Pierce, Fenner & Smith, charging that the firm had permitted a dozen of its large institutional customers to benefit from inside information which it had obtained in the course of working on a proposed underwriting for the Douglas Aircraft Company. Specifically, the firm was charged with passing along a report that Douglas earnings for the first six months of 1966 were actually going to be sharply lower than those reported just a little earlier for the first five months. On the basis of that information it was alleged that a dozen of its institutional customers had gone short an aggregate total of 190,000 shares of Douglas stock a day or two before the Douglas first-half earnings forecast was made public. Because the firm felt that there would be little profit to it in helping the S.E.C. define more precisely what did and didn't constitute inside information, it accepted the S.E.C.'s minimal penalities and did not contest the action, but some of its institutional customers who were also charged with violating the antifraud provisions of the Securities Exchange Act of 1934 persisted in fighting the case. All but one—the Dreyfus Fund—were convicted.

In 1974, a case was brought before a United States Court of Appeals which involved a dispute about whether a brokerage firm could function as investment banker for a company, while operating simultaneously as broker-dealer in that company's securities, without running afoul of insider trading regulations.

Shearson Hammill & Co., a large stock exchange member firm involved in the case, contended that it maintained a "Chinese Wall" between its retail sales and investment banking departments. The plaintiffs asserted that wall or no wall, the firm's investment department transmitted bullish information to its sales force on at least four occasions about Tidal Marine Co., despite the fact that it also had bearish information about the company, which was *not* released to salesmen or the public. However, Shearson maintained that its investment department did not possess this bearish information until several weeks after the plaintiffs had concluded their purchases of Tidal Marine.

Regardless of the ultimate outcome of the *Shearson "Chinese Wall" Case,* as it has come to be called, Wall Street houses that were confronted with the same problem took strenuous steps to sever all lines of communication between their investment banking departments and their retail salesmen, hoping thereby to avoid any charge of violating the S.E.C.'s rules on insider trading. However, the S.E.C. rather tartly suggested that a better way to avoid such problems would be for firms to prohibit their salesmen from recommending the securities of any of the companies with which that firm had an underwriting relationship.

On the basis of these cases, you may rightfully assume that there is, indeed, such a thing as inside information about a company; but you should also realize that the really important inside information is usually so closely guarded that neither you nor any other investor is likely to hear it until it becomes generally available to all investors.

All publicly owned companies are obligated to reveal promptly to the public any and all information that may influence the price of its stock or any investment decision about it. The news may be favorable or unfavorable—it still must be disseminated. The stock exchanges maintain strict and detailed policies about disclosure, particularly anything that might be considered inside information. Leaks of reliable information are rare indeed, and that's why anyone who invests his money on what he believes to be an inside tip is apt to be seriously misled.

How, then, should a man set about investing?

If he doesn't know anything at all about the market or the stocks of various companies, where can he turn for information?

Probably the first and most obvious answer to that is the newspaper—one of the big metropolitan daily newspapers that carries complete stock market quotations and has a well-rounded coverage of financial news, or one of the four regional editions of the *Wall Street Journal.*

If he is not already familiar with the *stock tables,* probably his first step should be to study them regularly for a period of time. If he reads a morning paper, he will find the stocks traded during the preceding day on the New York Stock Exchange, listed in alphabetical order. The late edition of the evening paper provides that information for the stocks traded that same day.

In their *consolidated stock tables,* some papers provide much more complete information than others, but if our Rod & Reel were sold on an exchange, or over-the-counter, and if your paper published complete consolidated stock tables, an entry for one day, with the appropriate column heads, might look like this:

Year to Date		Stock &	P-E	Sales in				Net
High	Low	Dividend	Ratio	100s	High	Low	Close	Change
42¼	38¾	Rod & Reel 2	12	17	40¼	39⅜	40¼	+¾

The column headings make much of the information self-explanatory. Obviously, the stock has been traded in a fairly narrow range, having fluctuated only between a low of 38¾ and a high of 42½ all year. A comparison of this price range with the range recorded by other stocks will give you some general idea of whether Rod & Reel might be classified as an investor-type stock or a speculation. As a very rough rule of thumb, the greater the price fluctuation, the lower the investment caliber of the stock.

The dividend figure immediately following the name of the stock gives you another clue to the quality of the stock. With an annual dividend rate of $2 and a current price of $40, Rod & Reel is yielding exactly 5%. Very often after the dividend figure there will appear a small letter which will refer to a footnote. These footnotes can be very important, because they may indicate that the dividend figure includes extra dividends, or that this was the dividend paid last year, or that it represents only the total paid so far this year for a stock not on a regular dividend basis.

The *P-E* ratio—*price-earnings ratio*—of the stock is computed by dividing the market price by its indicated or actual earnings per share. Thus, if Rod & Reel sells at 40¼ with estimated earnings of $3.50 per share, it has a price-earnings ratio of 11.5 ($40.25 divided by $3.50), which would be rounded out to 12 for reporting purposes.

The figure for the number of shares traded simply shows how Rod & Reel stacks up alongside others as far as market interest is concerned. Sales volume of a stock in which there is considerable speculative interest will very often exceed that of some of the better-grade market leaders.

The high, low, and close figures give you a bird's-

eye picture of how Rod & Reel moved during the trading day. On any given day, the pattern of price
movement will not be the same for all stocks, but this
profile on Rod & Reel will show you whether its market
performance is generally in line with that for other
stocks and for the market as a whole. If Rod & Reel
closed at its high for the day, as it did, and if the
market as a whole had declined that day, you could
conclude that because Rod & Reel ran counter to the
downward trend the stock had demonstrated strength.

On the consolidated tape, which covers all markets,
not just the New York Stock Exchange, the volume
figures and closing prices published in the newspaper
are those that prevailed at 5:30 P.M., E.S.T., for that
is when trading terminates on the West Coast market,
one and a half hours after the Big Board shuts down.

The *net change* figure (+¾) shows the difference
between the closing price for one day (40¼) and the
closing price of the *preceding day* (which thus had to
be 39½).

Occasionally you may notice that the price of a stock
is down from the preceding day, but the net change
figure doesn't show a corresponding drop. That's because the stock is being sold *ex-dividend*.

Suppose Rod & Reel pays its quarterly dividend of
50¢ to stockholders who are on its books as of the
close of business on Friday, September 15. Beginning
the previous Monday, September 11, and running
through Friday, the stock will be worth 50¢ less, because anyone who buys it during that period will not
be eligible for the dividend. This is so because five business days are allowed to make delivery of stock on a
sell order, and only those people who own the stock as
of the close of the markets on Friday, September 8,
will be on the company's records on Friday, September
15. On any day in which a stock is sold ex-dividend
(in this case Monday, September 11), its price is expected to decline by the amount of the dividend, and
if that is exactly what happens, the net change figure
will show no gain or loss. Sometimes, however, a stock
may show outstanding strength and "make up" the
amount of the dividend, thus closing with a net change

of $+\frac{1}{2}$, even though the price is exactly what it was before the stock went ex-dividend.

This five-day interval is also important when a stock goes *ex-rights*. Thus, a company with a new issue of additional stock might announce that stockholders as of Friday, September 15, would have the right to buy new stock in proportion to their present holdings at a price somewhat below the market. But obviously only those people who bought the stock on or before Friday, September 8, would appear on the company's records five business days or one week later, and anybody who bought the stock after that date wouldn't get the rights. Whenever a stock goes ex-rights, it usually sells at a price that is lower by an amount roughly equal to the value of the rights. During the time that the rights can be exercised, they are bought and sold separately and often quoted separately in the stock tables. They fluctuate up or down, generally reflecting strength or weakness of the parent stock.

Obviously, it would be a mistake to draw any positive conclusions about a stock on the basis of one day's trading pattern. But if you watch a stock over a period of time and compare it closely with a dozen or so others, particularly those in the same or a related field, you will begin to get an idea of how that stock is regarded by all the thousands of people whose transactions from day to day make the market.

Not all newspapers publish anything like complete quotations on Big Board stocks. Nor do many of them use the tables compiled from the consolidated tape. Some of them continue to cover just the transactions on the New York Stock Exchange, ignoring what might have taken place in the over-the-counter market or on regional exchanges and what might have happened to prices on the Pacific Coast after the Big Board closed. In smaller cities, the daily newspapers may list only 100 or so stocks with no detail on these except the closing price, plus usually the net change from the preceding day. In big cities, the former practice of publishing also the bid-and-asked quotations on listed stocks that did not trade during the day has been abandoned, primarily due to rising costs and the growth in number of listed issues.

The American Stock Exchange stocks don't get nearly as much play in the papers as those of the Big Board, and stocks listed on the regional exchanges are likely to get press notice only in the areas where the parent companies operate and where there is some public interest in their stocks. Much the same standard determines how many unlisted stocks are published from the national and regional quotations supplied by the National Association of Securities Dealers through NASDAQ, although big city newspapers usually publish the full N.A.S.D. national list.

Prices reported in the newspapers for bonds are apt to seem a little confusing. Although bonds are usually sold in $1,000 units, their prices are quoted as though they had a $100 denomination. Thus a quotation of 98 would indicate an actual price of $980, and one of 98⅜ would be $983.75.

Since government bonds sold on the open market are traded not in eighths or quarters but in thirty-seconds, a special price-reporting formula has been developed for them. Thus, a printed quotation of 99.16 actually means a price of $995. Here's how you arrive at that: the point in the quote isn't a decimal point; it is only a device for separating the round figure from the fraction. Hence the quotation really stands for 99$16\!\!/\!\!32$, or 99½, or $995. Sometimes Treasuries are sold on a price change of just $\frac{1}{64}$ rather than $\frac{1}{32}$. If a plus sign appears after the published quotation for a government bond, this means that $\frac{1}{64}$ should be added to the published price.

Almost every daily paper publishes, in addition to prices on individual security issues, some report on the average movement of New York Stock Exchange prices.

There are a number of these *averages* which are supposed to serve as barometers of the business. The best known of them is the *Dow Jones average*.

Actually, the Dow Jones average isn't one average but four—one for industrial stocks, one for transportation stocks, one for utilities, and a composite one which reflects the status of the other three. These averages are

computed constantly and are instantaneously available
on desk model quotation machines, but they are of-
ficially announced by Dow Jones only at half-hour intervals throughout the trading day.

The utility index is an average of prices for 15
utilities; the transportation index covers 20 railroads,
airlines, and trucking companies; the industrial average is based on the stocks of 30 leading manufacturers
and distributors; and the composite index includes all
65.

Over the years, these averages dating back to 1897
—except for the utilities index first computed in 1929
—have come to be accepted as the Bible of the business, partly because Dow Jones & Company, Inc., which
originated them, publishes the country's leading financial newspaper, the *Wall Street Journal,* and operates
the ticker news service, known as the *"broad tape,"*
which can be found in virtually every major bank and
brokerage office, often projected on a large electronic
screen.

But in recent years the suspicion has grown that
this Bible is not divinely inspired, that the Dow Jones
averages are not an infallible measure of the market.
This criticism has been aimed especially at the Dow
Jones industrial average, the most important of them
all, and it is based on two counts.

In the first place, it is argued that the 30 stocks
which make up the index are not truly representative
of all the industrials listed on the Big Board. Too
many of them classify as "blue chips"—stocks such as
General Motors, Exxon, du Pont, Procter & Gamble,
American Can, Eastman Kodak, General Electric,
General Foods, U.S. Steel, and Sears, Roebuck. Moreover, one of its components, American Telephone, is
really a utility and not an industrial stock.

In the second place, over the years many of these
stocks have been split several times, and with each split
the price of the stock has dropped proportionately.
Thus, if the split were two for one, the price of the
stock could be expected to decline about 50%; on a
four-for-one split it would decline about 75%.

In order to correct these occasional distortions and to maintain the continuity of the averages, Dow Jones introduced a new system of computation in 1928. Instead of dividing the total of the daily closing prices of stocks used in each average by the number of stocks in the average, the revised system is based upon an artificial divisor which remains unchanged until a stock is split, its price is reduced substantially by a stock dividend, or another stock is substituted. When any of these occur Dow Jones computes a new divisor which is intended to compensate for such change.

The inadequacy of the system, its lack of mathematical precision, is evident from the fact that it is possible for the Dow Jones industrial average to go up while the aggregate value of all the shares of the stocks that comprise the average goes down. For instance, on one particular day the Dow Jones average showed an increase of about ½ of 1%, but on that same day the actual value of all the shares of the 30 companies dropped from 26½ to 25½ billion dollars. The apparent gain in the average was all accounted for by a rise in the price of a comparatively few stocks that didn't have nearly as many shares outstanding as those companies whose stocks declined.

In recent years, the premier position of the Dow Jones industrial average has been seriously challenged by the 500-stock index of Standard & Poor's Corporation, the nation's largest securities research organization. For many years, Standard & Poor's had published other indexes—a 90-stock daily index and a 480-stock weekly index—but it wasn't until 1957, when high speed computers made more comprehensive indexes possible on an hourly basis, that Standard & Poor's decided really to lock horns with Dow Jones.

Its 500-stock index, covering stocks that account for 86% of the total value of all Big Board stocks, is unquestionably a more scientifically constructed index and provides a much more accurate picture of what is happening in the market. This is true because it is computed by multiplying the price of each stock by the number of shares outstanding, thus giving proper weight to the bigger and more influential companies like A.T.&T. and General Motors—and IBM, which isn't even in the Dow Jones average.

Despite the fact that the Dow Jones industrial average has statistical shortcomings and the 500-stock index is definitely more scientific, the two indexes do move together with surprisingly little disparity. It is unusual when one ends up showing a plus and the other a minus, a situation that can exist only on a day when the market has had no clear-cut movement in either direction. On major swings, they move pretty much together, although one or the other may boast that its index gave the first indication of such a move. On balance, the Dow Jones is apt to be more sensitive to short-term movements, and the 500-stock index provides a more reliable long-term perspective.

Although Standard & Poor's is proud of the fact that its index is used by the Federal Reserve Board and the Department of Commerce, as well as many other federal officials and business economists, Dow Jones—by virtue of its age and its popularity with financial editors of press, radio, and TV—continues to have an ironbound grip on the public mind, particularly that public which frequents brokerage offices.

There is one significant difference between the two indexes, and that lies in the magnitude of the numbers they use. When the Dow Jones industrial stands at 975, as it did in January 1976, the 500-stock index stands at about 100, and that relationship holds pretty true right up and down the line: the Dow figure is about ten times greater than the Standard & Poor's. This results from the calculated effort by Standard & Poor's in 1957 to devise a computation process that would yield an index figure more nearly comparable to the average dollar price of all stocks traded on the New York Stock Exchange than the inflated Dow figures are.

For years the New York Stock Exchange attempted to persuade Dow Jones to divide its index by 10 or devise another formula that would yield an index figure only a fraction of the present level. But Dow Jones, which regards its averages as sacrosanct, despite the many changes brought about by substituting one company for another over the years, has turned a deaf ear to all such suggestions.

The reason why the exchange would like to see the Dow Jones average fractioned is perfectly obvious: the exchange worries about the effect on the public of front-page headlines or news announcements that proclaim the stock market dropped 15 points, 20 points, or even 25 points, as it has often been known to do in a single day. It isn't much happier when the headlines say that the market went up 15 points, 20 points, or 25 points. The big figures, up or down, give the public an entirely wrong impression of the volatility of the market.

No matter how you attempt to explain the situation, people will go on confusing Dow Jones points with actual dollars, and there is no relationship between the two. On a day when the Dow might move 15 points—say from 900 to 915—the aggregate dollar value of all stocks listed on the exchange would increase only about 2%.

Dissatisfaction with the Dow Jones average was certainly one of the key reasons why the New York Stock Exchange decided in 1966 to begin publishing its own official composite index, as well as four group indexes —industrial, transportation, utility, and financial. The composite index covers all 1,532 common stocks on the exchange, and is computed continuously and publicly announced on the exchange ticker every half hour. No one was surprised to learn that the computation process used in this "official" index yielded a starting figure close to the $50 average price of all shares then on the exchange. To be sure that the exchange is never embarrassed by its own index, if in the future it ever should reach a level significantly above the median price of its listed shares, the exchange plans to bring the index back into line either by splitting it or by changing the base period.

Another new index made its debut in 1966: the first index of American Stock Exchange securities. But this so-called Price Change Index was replaced in 1973

by the index currently in use—Market Value Index
—which aligns the American Stock Exchange more
closely with other market value indicators in the industry.

CHAPTER 25

How to Read the Financial News

ONCE a man starts following stock prices and averages, it isn't long until he is reading the rest of the *financial section* of his newspaper.

Here, obviously, he will find much important information both about business in general and about individual companies—their plans for expansion, their new products, their sales and earnings records. Some of these news stories dealing with individual companies may be a little on the optimistic side, since they are often based on publicity releases furnished by the companies themselves, but every responsible newspaper today makes an effort to be as objective as possible in the handling of such news.

A standard feature of the financial section in every big-city newspaper is the daily column in which the action of the stock market is reported and often analyzed in terms of various technical factors—the primary trend, the secondary movement, the resistance levels, and so on.

While there are *technical factors* in the market that may indicate its direction over short periods of time —the volume of short sales, the ratio of odd-lot transactions to round lots, whether odd-lot customers buy or sell on balance, the number of stocks hitting new highs and the number falling to new lows, etc.—these are factors that are apt to be of far greater importance to the professional trader or speculator than to the average investor, especially the newcomer who may be understandably confused by some reference to a "double top" or "head and shoulders," chart configurations that are so dear to the heart of point-and-figure and bar-and-line technicians.

Nevertheless, the market columns can make interesting reading after one gets used to the jargon, and soon even the neophyte finds himself acquiring some familiarity with such phrases as *"technically strong"* or *"technically weak,"* the "short interest" and the *"Dow Theory."*

The phrases technically strong and technically weak have fairly precise meanings. Suppose stock prices have been moving more or less steadily upward over a long period of time. Inevitably, in such a bull market movement, there are price advances and price reactions, ups and downs in the market. If the volume of sales is heavy when stocks go up and light when they go down during a bull movement, the market can be described as technically strong. Conversely, if volume is heavy on the down side and light on the rallies, the market is technically weak. This interpretation is based on the theory that volume usually identifies the dominant trend.

The term short interest refers, of course, to the total number of shares of Big Board stocks that all the sellers are short; they have sold these various stocks, but must buy them back at some future date to cover their positions. Many stock market commentators are fascinated by the short interest and take it to be an index of the technical strength or weakness of the market. Its fluctuations, often very sharp, are interpreted to be bullish or bearish signals by many technicians. But it is worth remembering that even when the short interest rose to a record high above 27 million shares in January 1976, that figure still represented only about two-tenths of 1% of all shares listed on the Big Board. You might well ask if so small a tail can really wag so big a dog. On the other hand, it's the big operators who account for the short interest, and they are the people who are supposed to be most knowledgeable about the market.

The Dow Theory is at once the most celebrated, complicated, and least understood interpretation of market action, probably because neither Charles Dow, who founded Dow Jones & Company, nor any of his various disciples, has ever adequately defined the theory.

In essence, the Dow theorists hold that three movements of the Dow Jones averages are simultaneously under way: The primary movement—broad upward or downward trends, which may last for several years (the great bull or bear markets); the secondary movement —a significant decline in a primary bull market, or a strong recovery in a primary bear market, generally lasting from three weeks to three months; and, finally, the tertiary movement—day-to-day price fluctuations, which usually are relatively unimportant.

The main crux of the theory is that reliable conclusions cannot be drawn about the trend of the stock market until it has been ascertained that the industrial average, consisting of thirty stocks, and the transportation average, consisting of twenty stocks (known as the "rail average" until January 1970, when nine airline and trucking company stocks were substituted for nine railroad issues), are moving upward or downward "in gear." When that happens, the averages are said to be "confirming" one another.

Opinions based on the movement of one average, if unconfirmed by the other, are generally wrong—according to the theorists. When successive rallies by both averages exceed previous high levels and when ensuing declines hold above preceding low levels, the inference is bullish. The averages are then said to be charting a pattern of "higher highs." Conversely, when rallies fail to carry above the old highs and subsequent declines penetrate the previous lows, the implication is bearish—a pattern of "lower lows."

Dow theorists contend that by their somewhat occult formula they have been able to forecast almost every significant movement in the market for many years. Other analysts, looking at the same set of facts, dispute the Dow Theory's record. They say it can be made to look good only when the forecasting has become history. Nevertheless, many financial editors continue to expound the Dow Theory, and various Dow disciples appear in the advertising columns from time to time, offering a letter service to explain the market action in terms of their interpretation of the Dow Theory and the Dow averages.

Very often in reading his newspaper the new investor will encounter what appears to be a striking contradiction between the news and the market reaction to that news. For example, a company may announce some good news, such as an increase in its dividend—and its stock drops in price. A prime example of this occurred on January 10, 1962, when Ford Motor stock opened 1½ points lower and then closed down four points on the day, after a two-for-one split and an increase in the dividend were declared—announcements that one would expect might have given the stock a sizable boost. Again, news may break that Congress expects to enact a new tax bill lightening the tax burden on business—and that day stocks sell off right across the board.

There is one simple explanation for these paradoxes: the stock market has "discounted" the news. The big traders, the people supposedly in the know, were sure that a dividend increase was coming on Ford, because profits had been increasing spectacularly. And as for the tax legislation favorable to business, they would have been surprised if Congress hadn't moved to enact it. They had already bought or sold in expectation of these developments, and when the actual news breaks attracted public interest in the market, the professionals seized their opportunity to realize profits—to sell when others bought on the basis of the published news.

Some people consider the market an infallible barometer of general business. They say that you can tell what's going to happen to business by the way the stock market acts over a period of time. Even government economists classify stock market action as a key economic indicator.

Actually, the stock market is far from being an infallible business barometer. Consider just a few of the most glaring exceptions.

For instance, business conditions began to look a little less than rosy in the late spring of 1929, but it was not until late October of that year that the market hit the big slide, with some popular stocks slumping 100 points or more in four successive trading sessions.

More recently the stock market has performed very little better as a guide to our economic health; since the end of World War II, it has missed the boat on several important turns in business.

Thus, in 1945, business was retarded by the necessity of reconverting from war to peace, but the stock market generally continued its upward course until mid-1946, then declined 21% in five months when business had already begun to improve. The economy continued steadily on the upgrade for several years, but the market didn't catch up with this postwar boom until early 1949.

The market did turn down before general business in late 1948, early 1953, and mid-1957, but it gave an utterly fallacious signal in the first six months of 1962 when stocks sold off 25%, while business generally continued to boom merrily along, unperturbed by the Wall Street Cassandras. Again in 1966, the market missed the boat; it declined 25% from February to October, but business continued on its steady course with only an insignificant drop of 2% in production.

As for the big stock-slaughter period of 1973–1974, the market did perform rather creditably as a forecaster of coming events. The market began its toboggan slide in January 1973 while the business climate was still quite favorable. However, it could be argued that it wasn't so much the condition of business that triggered the decline, as it was the Watergate affair, the tightening of credit by the Federal Reserve Board, soaring interest rates, and heavy speculation in gold, which went steadily up in price and which, in turn, badly undermined the dollar's value.

In fact, overall business actually held up quite well despite these bearish influences, until about the middle of 1974 when the stock market—already down some 27% from its 1973 high—began to take the final plunge that would carry it from that level down another 27% to an ultimate low in December—46.6% below its 1973 intraday high. Paradoxically, as soon as the market reached its bottom and began to recover, business itself was still in a tailspin. Unemployment soared; dividends were cut or passed entirely; various leading economic indicators just dropped, dropped, dropped.

It wasn't until the stock market had already recovered more than 40% from its 1974 low in the spring of 1975 that business first showed indications of having also reached a bottom, and although business and the market were both up in early 1976, the economic improvement didn't begin to compare with the spectacular bull market in stocks.

However, like the perennial question "Which comes first, the chicken or the egg?," the question of whether the stock market leads business, or business leads the stock market, is one that probably can never have an unequivocal answer.

But if the stock market doesn't faithfully anticipate business, it must sooner or later fall into step with the basic business trends, because in the end stock values are determined by our economic health. That's why the investor is well advised to keep his eye on some of the more basic indexes of business such as the Federal Reserve index of industrial production and various series on employment, steel output, electric power production, construction, carloadings, retail sales, unfilled orders and prices, both for farm goods and industrial raw materials, as well as data on credit, bank deposits, and interest rates. These will tell him how much America is producing, how rapidly this output is moving into the channels of distribution, what kind of consumer demand there is for it, and the availability and cost of money and credit. In the long run, these are the vital factors that will determine the real values of the stock that you own in any company—how much the company is likely to earn and what kind of dividend it can pay.

If he reads the financial pages of his newspaper, obviously the investor will gain something of an insight into what's happening to business. But he is likely to get a much more objective and detailed view of the business scene if he subscribes to some specialized publication, such as the Dow Jones daily *Wall Street Journal* ($42 a year) or *Business Week* ($17). Over the years, the *Wall Street Journal* with its four regional editions has won the unqualified respect of investors for its comprehensive coverage of business and the financial markets. That's why you see so many people in brokerage offices watching the Dow Jones news ticker; the broad tape provides them with brief digests of many of the news developments that will make headlines in the next day's *Journal*. These investors want today's news today—and they are getting it not only from the broad tape but from the business and financial news ticker supplied by the Reuters News Service and from specialized news services operated by investment firms.

Because political developments are increasingly important in the conduct of business affairs, the *Kiplinger Washington Letter* ($28) and the *Whaley-Eaton American Letter* ($50) are also widely read by investors.

Still others look to Washington for another reason: various government publications provide the most authoritative data about business conditions, however dully, at the lowest cost. Most noteworthy of these are the Council of Economic Advisors' *Economic Indicators,* a monthly compilation of more than 200 basic economic measures (including charts), and the Commerce Department's *Survey of Current Business,* which costs $48.30 a year, including a weekly statistical supplement, and provides a monthly collection of several thousand statistical series originating both in government and in business. An even sharper focus on key indicators that often point the way in which our economic cycle is moving is provided by *Business Conditions Digest*. Issued monthly by the Commerce Department, this valuable publication ($55.28 a year) covers about 90 principal statistical series with about 250 components. The Federal Reserve Board's monthly *Bulletin* ($20 a year) is another important and reliable source of information about our economic health.

In addition to general business publications there are, of course, the financial periodicals—*Barron's* ($25), *Financial World* ($33), and *Forbes* ($12)—that undertake to appraise the business situation primarily in terms of stock market values.

Perhaps as helpful a publication as any in this business and financial field is the *Exchange,* which is published monthly by the New York Stock Exchange and costs subscribers $8 a year. And for the investor with an interest in companies listed on the American Stock Exchange, that exchange makes available its very readable *American Investor* at a nominal price of $6 a year for ten issues.

But all of these publications and services, in the final analysis, leave the investor to work out his own destiny. They give him basic information, but they can't tell him precisely what he should do about it.

CHAPTER 26

Financial Advice – At a Price

Do you want help with your investment problem—information, advice, recommendations?

You can get it—at a price. Whether it's worth the price you pay is something else again.

Maybe you want something more than advice. Maybe you don't want to worry about your investment problem at all. If that's the case—and if you have at least $100,000 to invest, preferably a good deal more—you can turn the whole matter over to some *investment counselor* whose sole business is that of guiding the investment destiny of his clients—making all the buying and selling decisions for them and seeing that they are properly executed by a brokerage firm. In New York City alone there are well over a hundred of these counseling firms that spend their full time investing other people's money—for a sizable fee, of course, which is tax deductible—and there are many others in all the major cities, from coast to coast.

In the main, these investment counselors do a sound job for their clients, which include many institutions, but their services are obviously beyond the reach of the average investor.

Many big-city banks will be glad to take your investment problem off your hands—but again, only at a price that most investors can't afford. One kind of service these banks offer is the *investment advisory account* for which they charge an annual management fee, usually ½ of 1%. That may not sound like much, but they expect a minimum annual fee of at least $500, often much more. So again, unless you have at least $100,000 to invest such service is not for you, unless some unusual circumstance, such as a long-term absence from the country justifies payment of the bank's supervision fee.

Under another type of bank service the depositor agrees to let the bank withdraw a fixed amount of money from his checking account each month to buy as many shares or fractional shares as possible of stock in a company, or companies, selected from a list prepared by the bank. The bank then combines the funds allocated for specific stocks and makes bulk purchases, thus saving something on commission costs.

For about thirty years the banks had not been permitted to operate as brokers or securities dealers by the terms of both the Securities Exchange Act and the *Glass-Steagall Banking Act*. However, in 1966 the S.E.C. did approve the First National City Bank's idea for a wholly new investment vehicle, called a *commingled investment account*. Under this plan, the funds of all participants would have been pooled and invested by the bank for a management fee of ½ of 1%. Each participant would share in the fund's investment results in proportion to the amount of money he put into it, with $10,000 being the minimum participation.

The National Association of Securities Dealers challenged this plan, even before it became operative, and in 1971 the U.S. Supreme Court held that the plan did indeed violate the Glass-Steagall Act. Since then, both the S.E.C. and the Treasury Department have been investigating the role of banks in the securities business. And in October 1975 a Senate subcommittee began a major study to determine if important changes were needed in the Glass-Steagall Act.

Apart from investment counselors and banks, where else might the average investor look for help?

The answer is that there are dozens and dozens of *investment advisory services,* all of them only too willing to help him, regardless of how competent they are. They offer the investor a bewildering array of publications and services. Some are simply compilations of statistical information. Some undertake to review business conditions as they affect the investment outlook. Some provide recommendations about hundreds of different securities—what to buy, what to sell, what to hold.

Some are perennially bearish, but the majority are usually bullish. Some, believing that good investment advice can't be turned out on a mass-production basis, undertake to provide a kind of tailor-made service; they offer to answer inquiries and to permit occasional consultation with their experts. And some even offer a reasonably well-rounded counseling service available at a negotiated fee to the smaller investor, perhaps the man with only $25,000 to invest.

Some of the financial advisory organizations have for sale many of these different kinds of services, while others offer only one kind or another.

Most controversial of all the services are those that undertake to give advice about the "market," usually in a weekly letter sold on a subscription basis. Many of these publications offer the subscriber their own rating service covering hundreds of different stocks that tell the subscriber whether to buy or sell, and most of them maintain *supervised lists* of those investments that they consider particularly attractive. In effect, these supervised lists are supposed to represent model investment programs.

Many of these services are more concerned about the short-term outlook—what the market is likely to do in the next couple of months—than they are with the problem of long-term investment. A few of them even limit themselves almost exclusively to a discussion of technical factors affecting the market.

Regardless of their different approaches to the investment problem, they generally share one common characteristic: they will all tell you how successful they've been in calling the turns in the market and in recommending good buys and good sells at just the strategic moment.

The S.E.C. has the authority to compel investment advisers to conform with strict and detailed standards of advertising; failure to meet these standards is considered fraudulent conduct in violation of the antifraud provisions of the *Investment Advisers Act of 1940*. But there are those who feel this is an area in which the S.E.C. has not yet done the policing job it might.

In trying to bring these services to heel, the commission has been admittedly handicapped by not having an industry organization like the New York Stock Exchange with which to share the regulatory responsibility. It has tried to induce the advisory services to form some kind of an organization, but the services, realizing how much easier it would then be for the S.E.C. to bring pressure to bear on them, have turned a deaf ear. Then too, such highly ethical and responsible organizations as Standard & Poor's and Moody's Investors Service have an understandable reluctance to be associated on any basis whatsoever with the obvious quacks in the business.

In the absence of an industry organization that could pursue a program of self-regulation, the S.E.C. has accomplished most of its housecleaning job on a piecemeal basis by bringing legal action against palpable offenders. This course has been time-consuming and expensive, but the commission has won some landmark decisions in the courts, and has brought a number of the services sharply to heel.

The first and most important action was that brought against the Capital Gains Research Bureau. The S.E.C. charged that officers of this advisory service were guilty of price manipulation by buying stock, touting it in their service, then selling out when the price advanced. The U.S. Supreme Court held that such *scalping* practices were a "fraud and deceit upon any client or prospective client," and it said that the commission could enforce compliance with the Investment Advisers Act by obtaining an injunction to halt such practices.

Under this act, designed "to protect the public and investors against malpractices by persons paid for advising others about securities," all investment advisers who receive compensation in any form for their service must register with the S.E.C. They must state the name and form of the organization, names and addresses of the principal officers, their education and business affiliations for the past ten years, the exact nature of the business, the form of compensation for their services, etc.

In addition, the services must keep accounts, correspondence, memorandums, papers, books, and other records and furnish copies of them to their clients or to the S.E.C. at any time upon request. Banks, lawyers, accountants, engineers, teachers, and newspapers and magazines are exempt from registration—an exemption not entirely satisfactory to the S.E.C.

Brokers are also exempt, as their advisory service is presumed to be incidental to their execution of orders for which they receive only commissions. Brokers who do perform an advisory service for which they are paid by clients are not exempt.

It is the S.E.C.'s responsibility to see that there is no conflict of interest in the service that investment advisers offer the public. In other words, an adviser cannot offer advice about a stock if there is any possibility of personal gain to himself from what he reports without revealing that fact.

Significantly, it is *not* the S.E.C.'s responsibility under the Investment Advisers Act to guarantee the competence of the adviser or the quality of his service. Of course, the original Securities Exchange Act does prohibit "any person" from distributing information which is false or misleading, but it's not as easy for the S.E.C. to prove a case against an investment adviser under this broad but somewhat nebulous grant of power as it is to establish a case of fraud or deceit.

The S.E.C. has proposed legislation that would increase sharply its authority over investment advisers and make them subject to the type of professional and responsibility standards that apply to brokers and dealers.

The S.E.C. has been so shorthanded and the field it must supervise has become so vast that many publishers of market letters have been plying their trade with little interference from regulatory authorities. However, in 1972 the S.E.C. established an Advisory Committee on Enforcement Policy and Practices, which recommended that the S.E.C. double the size of its staff by 1977. The S.E.C. accordingly was granted about $45 million more in 1975 in order to augment its staff by some 385 people in the succeeding three years.

Actually, how good is the advice that investment services generally provide?

There's no answer to that, because there is no way to compute and compare their batting averages. Some make flat-footed recommendations, and some hedge their suggestions with all kinds of qualifications. However, one stock market analyst who did keep check on sixteen services for a period of years found that if an investor had followed all their 7,500 different recommendations, he would have ended up just 1.43% worse than the market averages.

Here are some of the most reputable companies whose investment services are in no wise to be compared to the many market letters with their "get-rich-quick" recommendations:

Companies rendering a comprehensive research and advisory service

The biggest firms in the financial research business are:

STANDARD & POOR'S CORPORATION,
345 Hudson Street,
New York, New York 10014

MOODY'S INVESTORS SERVICE, 99 Church Street,
New York, New York 10007

Known primarily as publishers of financial data, these two firms supply the entire investment business, including all the other advisory services, with the basic facts and figures on all securities sold in the public market and on the companies that issue them. Many of their publications, such as those dealing exclusively with bonds, are too specialized to be of significance to the average investor, but both he and his broker would be utterly lost if it were not for the complete and detailed information which these organizations supply on stocks, both listed and unlisted.

Much of the research material supplied by one firm is also supplied by the other, but they use different methods of organizing and publishing the material.

Most fundamental of all the reference books are

Standard & Poor's *Corporation Records* and Moody's *Manuals*. In these massive volumes, running into tens of thousands of pages, you'll find a brief history of virtually every publicly owned company in the United States and full financial data running from the present back over a period of years—the figures on assets, income, earnings, dividends, and stock prices.

Standard & Poor's Corporation Records consist of six looseleaf volumes in which reports on nearly 7,500 individual companies are arranged in alphabetical order. These reports, providing all the basic financial data, are revised whenever new reports are issued or other important developments alter the outlook for a company; supplements are issued every two months summarizing news bulletins on a company-by-company basis. Standard & Poor's also has a special service reviewing conditions industry by industry, called *Industry Surveys*. It is supplemented by a monthly *Trends and Projections Bulletin,* which covers developments in 36 industries and more than 1,400 different companies. The reports on individual industries are updated four times a year.

Moody's presents its financial information on publicly owned securities in six twice-weekly publications covering municipal bonds, banks and finance, industrials, public utilities, and transportation. It also publishes weekly news reports on over-the-counter industrial stocks. Subscribers to each of the publications receive an annual bound volume containing basic descriptions of these companies and investment situations at no extra cost. Moody's is also the publisher of the authoritative twice-weekly *Dividend Record.*

Standard & Poor's subsidiary, *Investors Management Sciences,* provides a broad spectrum of computerized financial and corporate data relied upon by security analysts, researchers, and corporate financial executives.

These services, keeping abreast of all corporate facts and figures, are far too costly for most individuals. Nor is it necessary for a man to spend several hundred dollars a year on them, since he can usually refer to them in a public library or in his broker's office, or his registered representative can get for him the information he wants on any company.

Even more condensed information is provided in the *Stock Guide,* a pocket-size manual published by Standard & Poor's. Here, in tabular form, the investor can find the high-and-low prices over the past few years, current data on assets, earnings, and dividends, figures on institutional holdings, and Standard & Poor's own quality ratings for 4,800 common and preferred stocks, listed and unlisted. A new edition of the Stock Guide, complete with lists of stocks recommended for different objectives, is issued monthly, and the service is priced at $35 a year.

For the individual investor, both Standard & Poor's and Moody's have special services and letters that comment on business developments as they affect the outlook for individual stocks and industries. Standard & Poor's has its weekly *Outlook,* a twelve-page market letter ($99.50 a year); an *Investment Advisory Survey* ($99.50), which consists of an eight-page confidential bulletin featuring a supervised list of recommended investments; and a *Watching Service* ($49), which offers periodically revised reports on up to 25 stocks, plus either the Outlook or Investment Advisory Survey.

Moody's Stock Survey, a weekly letter of eight to twenty-two pages, reviews market conditions and analyzes various investment opportunities. Subscribers also receive a quarterly handbook of common stocks, containing charts and data on hundreds of different companies.

Chart and Statistical Services

M. C. HORSEY & CO., INC., 120 South Blvd.,
Salisbury, Maryland 21801

Horsey's *The Stock Picture,* issued bimonthly, provides price charts on more than 1,700 stocks for periods of time ranging from 5 to 15 years. The cost of an annual subscription is $70; the price of a single copy is $17. Both prices include first class postage.

Charts show earnings, dividends, and present capitalization. The company will make a chart on any New York or American exchange stock, covering up to a ten-year period if possible, for $5 and it offers a group of 188 old charts, covering the period from 1926 to 1950, at a price of $25. Sample pages are sent upon request.

TRENDLINE, 345 Hudson Street,
New York, New York 10014

Trendline, which is owned by Standard & Poor's, publishes three major stock market services. *Daily Basis Stock Charts,* covering 744 companies and 14 market indicators, is published weekly. Each company chart shows the daily high, low, close, and volume and the 200-day moving average (for the previous seven months), as well as the yearly range for 10 years. Earnings figures, with comparisons for eight quarters, dividends, and capitalization data, are also provided. The cost is $260 a year plus postage, or $5 a copy. *Current Market Perspectives,* published monthly, includes charts of 972 individual companies showing the weekly high, low, close, and volume for the last four years, along with historical price-earnings ratios. The cost is $72 a year plus postage, or $10 a copy. Trendline also publishes the bimonthly *OTC Chart Manual,* which includes charts of 840 leading over-the-counter stocks. Each chart includes weekly high, low, and closing bid prices, and volume for up to three years, annual price ranges for eight years, and an earnings-dividend record for six years. The cost is $75 plus postage for 6 issues, or $15 a copy.

AMERICAN INSTITUTE FOR ECONOMIC
RESEARCH, Great Barrington, Massachusetts 01230

AIER is an independent scientific and educational organization conducting economic research and publishing the results of that research whenever it considers that the public interest would thus be served.

AIER publishes a weekly bulletin entitled *Research Reports.* The issues analyze current economic developments. Important factors such as industrial activity,

prices, and money-credit trends are depicted in an unusual series of charts.

It also publishes monthly *Economic Education Bulletins* which are studies of such basic topics as property problems, financial relationships, insurance, investment trusts, taxes, estate problems, business cycles,
commercial banking, and the role of gold. These cost
$1 to $3.

Its publications are sent free to all sustaining members who contribute a minimum of $9 a quarter or
$35 a year.

In order to retain its tax exemption, in 1963 AIER
transferred its investment advisory activities to *American Institute Counselors, Incorporated,* which contrib-
utes all of its income after taxes to AIER. This service publishes a semimonthly report entitled *Investment
Bulletin,* which covers business and monetary developments and analyzes their significance for investors.

The bulletins do not advise on margin trading and
do not attempt to forecast short swings, or technical
movements of the stock market. They are intended primarily to assist those who wish to follow long-term investment programs. The cost is $15 a year.

AMERICAN INVESTORS SERVICE,
88 Field Point Road,
Greenwich, Connecticut 06830

On the assumption that most market moves are first
made apparent by conditions within the market itself
rather than by economic factors, the *Industry Group
Data, Stocks Ranked by Percentage-Strength,* and *Stock
Selection Guide* of this service focus primarily on matters of timing and selection as influenced by complex
technical considerations. The service also publishes its
Group Action Charts covering 70 industry groups
and the principal market averages on a weekly basis,
which are helpful to investors making their own stock
selection and market timing decisions. The price is
$190 a year for the complete service.

An investment counseling subsidiary also makes
available personal management services under which
an account manager assumes complete responsibility

for the management of the assets in a client's portfolio. Accounts are billed $325 per quarter plus ¼ of 1% of the portfolio's value. On a yearly basis this service costs $1,300 plus 1% of the portfolio's value.

BABSON'S REPORTS, INC., Wellesley Hills, Massachusetts 02181

The Babson organization, founded in 1904 by Roger W. Babson, offers investors three different advisory services—a consultation service at $204 a year, a quarterly appraisal and review service of the client's portfolio at $420 a year, and a complete investment management service at $1,200 a year. The three rates refer to these three services. No additional charges are made based on portfolio value or income. The company's *Investment and Barometer Letter* is supplied as a supplement to all three services.

FORBES SPECIAL SITUATION SURVEY, 60 Fifth Avenue, New York, New York 10011

Published by a subsidiary of the company that publishes *Forbes* magazine, *Forbes Special Situation Survey* is for the more sophisticated investor interested in "high potential" situations and willing to assume the risk. The subscriber receives twelve recommendations a year for a fee of $250. Each recommendation covers a stock which the service believes has a potential to perform substantially better than the market in a period of roughly one to two years. Subscribers are kept informed by periodic reviews and, where necessary, suggestions are made about when to get out of stocks previously recommended.

UNITED BUSINESS AND INVESTMENT SERVICE, 120 Newbury Street, Boston, Massachusetts 02116

Each issue of its comprehensive *Weekly Report* contains a review of the business outlook, a report on Washington developments, a forecast of commodity prices, an appraisal of the stock market, and specific recommendations for buying or selling different stocks. Regular reports are made on all stocks that are kept on supervised lists. Periodic features include analysis of individual stocks and groups of stocks, a report on bonds, various statistical indexes of business and a summary of opinions and recommendations of other leading advisory services. The total cost is $98 a year, $55 for six months; a subscription also includes a personal consultation.

CHARTCRAFT, INC., 1 West Avenue, Larchmont,
New York 10538

Publisher of the *Chartcraft Weekly Service* ($150 per year), *Chartcraft Option Service* ($96), *Chartcraft Commodity Service* ($150), *Chartcraft Technical Indicator Review* ($60), and the *Chartcraft Monthly Point and Figure Chart Book* ($180), this organization offers services devoted to point-and-figure charting and analysis. The Weekly Service and the Monthly Chart Book (combination $300 yearly) cover every stock on the New York and American Stock Exchanges. The Technical Indicator Review deals with point-and-figure analysis of market trends.

DOW THEORY FORECASTS, INC.,
7412 Calumet Avenue, Hammond, Indiana 46325

General market projections are based upon the Dow Theory, which this service has undertaken to interpret and apply since 1946. The Dow Theory does not deal with the selection of individual stocks, but seeks to determine and project overall market trends. However, this service does provide monthly buy-sell-hold advice on more than 800 issues. Clients may call at any time for specific advice on their individual problems; unlimited consultation privileges are provided. Published weekly, 52 times a year; annual subscription rate: $98.

CHAPTER 27

How Your Broker Can Help You

IN the last analysis, the best answer that any investor can find to the problem of what stocks to buy is likely to be the answer that he works out for himself through study and investigation.

But where, you ask, can the average man who is willing to do his own investigating turn for the facts and the information he needs? The answer to that is—his broker, preferably a member firm of the New York Stock Exchange.

Perhaps you think this is dubious advice. After all, isn't a broker interested in selling securities? Yes, a broker is a salesman. But that doesn't mean that your interests and his are completely opposed. Quite the contrary. Any salesman of any product wants his customer to be satisfied, because that's the best way of building his own business. That's especially true of the broker.

Then, too, there's an important difference between him and other salesmen. The automobile salesman wants to sell you a particular car. The insurance salesman wants to sell you a policy in his company. The salesman for a financial advisory service wants to sell you that service and nothing else.

As far as his own commission is concerned, the broker, as a general rule, doesn't care which stocks you buy. He has essentially no ax to grind, at least as far as listed securities are concerned, because he stands to make about the same commission on the same total investment. When it comes to over-the-counter stocks, admittedly, he could have an ax to grind as far as any particular stock is concerned if his firm makes a market in that stock, but most securities dealers realize that such a self-seeking policy can prove to be bad business in the long run.

All this is not intended to imply that the brokerage business is wholly without sin. Any business has a certain number of sinners in it, and if that business happens to involve the handling of money, large sums of money, as the brokerage business certainly does, it is likely to have an even greater-than-average number of sinners, do what you will to exorcise them.

Over the years, the brokerage business has done an unparalleled job of policing itself, of trying to rid itself of any unprincipled and unscrupulous element, and in recent years it has redoubled its efforts. That increased effort can be traced directly to the publication in 1963 of the S.E.C.'s final report to Congress on its study of the securities business, which led to the enactment of the 1964 Amendment Acts, and to the even more sweeping revisions and regulations imposed by the Securities Reform Act of 1975.

The S.E.C. has made it unmistakably clear with each passing year that it intends to supervise strictly and thoroughly all member firms all over the country and every man in every office. Furthermore, the commission has made it equally clear that unless the New York Stock Exchange, which it always has accused of treating disciplinary matters too tenderly, did a more competent policing job, it would hold the exchange and the member firms responsible.

The result has been that the exchange has increased the efficiency of its own police force which schedules surprise calls on branch offices of member firms all across the country, checking customer trading records and the character and performance of the registered representatives. And the member firms have followed suit; some initiated policing of their own offices as early as 1965 to forestall trouble with the S.E.C. and customer lawsuits.

What are these policemen—or *compliance officers,* as they are euphemistically called—looking for? In general, they are looking for any abuses of public confidence.

In particular, they are looking for evidence of *churn-*

ing, the overstimulation of customer's trading in order to build commission revenues.

They are looking for high-pressure salesmanship—telephone calls at night, undue persuasion of widows, attempts to prey on the unsophisticated and the unsuspecting.

They are looking for misrepresentation. "The stock is bound to go up . . . you can't miss."

They are looking for abuses of the *discretionary* authority that a customer gives his broker to manage his account, to buy or sell whatever and whenever he thinks best.

They are looking for margin trading by customers who plainly lack the resources to undertake the risks involved.

They are looking for the flagrant incompetence or the willful malfeasance that could result in the recommendation of a clearly unsuitable investment—a highly speculative penny stock for a retired couple to whom safety of capital is paramount.

They are looking for situations in which securities firms, or even individual partners or salesmen, seek to further their own undisclosed interest in a stock by promoting its sale in order to enhance the value of their own holdings.

In summary, they are looking for any abuse of what is known in Wall Street as the S.E.C. *"shingle theory"* —the theory that when a broker hangs out his shingle he guarantees to the world that he will deal fairly and honestly with his customers.

The S.E.C. holds the home office executives of member firms wholly responsible for supervising their branch offices. If there ever was any doubt about this, it vanished quickly in the mid-sixties, when the S.E.C. and the N.A.S.D. emphasized their intent by instituting action against several leading firms. Those actions resulted not only in the expulsion of individual employees and branch office managers, but in fines and suspensions levied against the firms' top officials in Wall Street.

The public furor stirred up by these headlined cases was actually disproportionate to the problem involved.

Admittedly, there were some sharp operators, utterly lacking in moral scruples, among the 25,000 registered representatives then employed. Admittedly, top management among the member firms had been lax in exercising supervisory responsibility. And, admittedly, the exchange had been less than stern in its disciplinary actions.

Still the fact remains that the business as a whole adheres to a standard of ethics and a concern for the public good that few other businesses can match.

And still the fact also remains that the vast, vast majority of registered representatives are honest, are scrupulous, are trustworthy, and are sincerely concerned about the welfare of their customers.

But even if the reliability of your broker can be taken for granted, what about his ability? How competent is he likely to be when it comes to giving you sound advice about your money and how to invest it?

Obviously, that's a question to which there is no absolute answer. Nobody could possibly contend that all the thousands of men in the business are preeminently well qualified to give investment help. Some are and some aren't. But thanks to the training programs that many leading brokerage firms have been operating for years—some since World War II ended, when Wall Street began to recognize that it had to attract young men into the business—the standards of professional ability have been steadily raised. Most of these programs are of six months' duration, and with half that time spent in the classroom, eight hours a day, the graduates can be considered to be pretty knowledgeable about the investment business, even before they start to work in it.

Certainly this much can be said: as a general rule, there isn't anybody to whom you can go who is apt to be nearly as well qualified to advise you about your investments as your broker—not your banker, not your lawyer, and certainly not just a business associate or the fellow in the club car.

After all, the registered representative works at the job of investing at least eight hours a day, five days a week, and he has been doing it for years. He has facts, figures, and information at his fingertips that nobody else can lay hold of easily. He has easy access to the basic reference works—Standard & Poor's Corporation Records or Moody's Manuals—and he can get detailed data on almost any publicly owned company in the United States.

"Investigate before you invest" is still one of the soundest pieces of advice anyone can give you. And you might start your investigating by thumbing through either Standard & Poor's monthly *Stock Summary* or the *Monthly Stock Digest,* published by Data Digests, Inc. Either of these two publications will at least give you an idea of the kind of information you should have about any stock before buying it.

The *Stock Summary* is a condensation of Standard & Poor's *Stock Guide,* providing key data on all New York State Exchange stocks, 170 stocks listed on the American Stock Exchange, and more than 220 over-the-counter stocks. The *Stock Digest* covers an even greater number of stocks and provides even more detailed data on the trend of earnings and dividends over the preceding few years, plus data on working capital, the capital structure of the company, and thumbnail charts to show the nine-month price trend of each stock.

If your preliminary investigation leads you to develop an interest in several specific stocks, most brokers can supply you—within reason, of course—with free reports on these companies, reports that they buy from accepted research services or reports that are prepared by their own *research departments* and often made available to customers without charge.

In the brokerage business today, research has become vitally important, for it is the one service that can give a firm a genuine competitive advantage. No member firm can buy a listed stock for you any cheaper than another firm. They all pay the same price for it on the exchange at any given moment. But not all firms can give you the same well-qualified advice about how good a particular listed stock—or an unlisted stock, for that matter—may be for you in your particular circumstances and with your particular investment objective.

This, plus variable commission rates and service charges, makes a decision about which brokerage firm to use almost as important as deciding which stock to buy. How can you form an opinion about which broker might best be able to help you? Well, you might visit three or four different ones and ask them about the same stock. That would give you some idea of how well-informed each one was, what kind of research service each one provided and the cost, if any.

If brokers do charge for research advice they'll tell you, and you can decide whether you want to pay the fee or not. On the basis of their replies, you can make a reasonably informed judgment about the quality of their research—provided, of course, that you have leveled with them and given them detailed information about how much money you have to invest, what your financial situation is, and what you want most out of your investments—safety of capital, dividend income, near-term price appreciation, or long-term growth. The more complete the information you provide about your circumstances, the more pertinent the broker's recommendations are apt to be.

And you need not feel that you are imposing on a broker for this service. After all, that's part of the job for which he and his firm get paid by you. Many of them widely advertise their willingness to set up a program for the new investor or to review the holdings of present shareowners and make suggestions about what to buy or what to sell—and why.

A good research department is staffed with *analysts* who spend their full time following developments in certain assigned industries. Through business and industrial publications and some of the more reliable financial advisory services, an analyst keeps up with the published information on his industries, including, of course, the reports of competing brokers. He tries to establish and maintain contact with key officials in all the major companies in the fields he covers, and visits them as often as possible. This is one way in which he determines the quality of a company's management, the key factor, after all is said and done, in determining a company's success.

Over the years, such officials have come to respect the qualified securities analysts. However, as opposed to bull market days in the mid-sixties, when corporate officials would level freely with analysts about new products or services, development plans, dividend policy, and, especially, earnings, today they are far more likely to maintain strict silence about anything that could possibly be construed as inside information.

Publicly owned companies are obligated to reveal promptly to the public any and all information that may influence the price of their stock; indeed, anything that might prompt a person to buy it or to sell it. The news may be favorable or unfavorable; it still must be disseminated. But definitely *not* through the medium of a securities analyst who happens to telephone an executive or visit him at his office and inquires if an earnings estimate of so much per share is "in the ball park." Casting around for information in this manner has become generally outmoded anyway; not only by much tighter and more rigidly enforced disclosure regulations, but by the increasing unwillingness of executives to cooperate. As a result, many analysts depend more upon what is known as the *"mosaic theory"* when trying to estimate earnings.

By his intimate knowledge of a company's past record and balance sheet and the performance of its stock, an analyst can come pretty close to a reliable earnings estimate by piecing carefully together the myriad parts of a corporate puzzle—factors such as size of inventories, labor conditions, plant cost and capacity, new product development, order backlog, quality of management, and other related data.

Yet the analyst at any given time may still lack just one vital piece of information—perhaps the status of a labor contract or facts about inventory—that would probably complete his puzzle, or mosaic. If he could obtain that, he would be much more confident about his earnings projection. In such circumstances, he has absolutely no qualms about calling his closest contact in the corporation and asking for the information. And the official normally doesn't have to worry about answering the question, since it doesn't really constitute inside information.

In addition to contacting the company itself, an analyst can usually pick up valuable information to complete his mosaic by checking that company's principal competitors. Very often he might even get from the competitor an earnings estimate with which he can compare his own.

It is the analyst's responsibility at all times to see that his firm's registered representatives are fully informed about all important developments affecting the companies he follows, and periodically he prepares reports on these companies for distribution to the firm's customers and the public. Many firms also prepare "tailor-made" reports that are much longer and more detailed for their institutional clients.

These research reports are a far cry from the old *"broker's letter,"* a catch-as-catch-can commentary on the stock market, liberally interspersed with tips on what to buy or what to sell. Today, the typical research report on a company, prepared and distributed by a member firm, is a substantial piece of work, factual and honest. So that the customer may allow for any possible bias, many firms go so far as to disclose in such reports any special interest which the firm or its owners might have in the stock as a result of their own substantial holdings, representation on the company's board of directors, or a long-standing underwriting relationship.

In recent years securities analysts have found a valuable new tool to aid them in their complicated studies. That tool is the high-speed computer, including all the paraphernalia that goes with a complete electronic data-processing system. Since the early sixties, major brokerage firms have been equipped with sophisticated computers—their number increases steadily—and since that time Standard & Poor's Corporation has made available to them, as well as to banks, mutual funds, and other big financial institutions, its *Compustat* service, which consists of reels of magnetic tape on which are recorded virtually all the essential accounting data that an analyst needs. These Compustat tapes include millions of figures from the financial reports of some two thousand corporations listed on the major exchanges plus another thousand companies whose stock is sold over-the-counter. On each company, the tapes provide annual data back twenty years on sixty different items that can be vital in measuring a company's health, and quarterly data for the past years are available on forty of these item. Even brokers who cannot afford the tremendous expense involved in installing their own data processing systems can have access to vital data such as that provided by the Compustat tapes through time-sharing, a mechanism that permits them to submit their problems to a central computer and get an answer back—all by telephone or teletype.

As a consequence, securities analysts no longer have to work endless hours digging the figures they need out of old corporate reports and performing calculations of their own to arrive at a reliable statistical analysis of a company's performance as compared with its competitors. The computer does much of their work for them and does it instantly once the proper programs are prepared to query the computer's memory bank.

Although computer-oriented research can be regarded more or less in its infancy, brokerage firms have found data processing machines particularly useful in several areas—information retrieval, security screening and selection, and basic research into the nature of securities prices and price movements.

It is in the field of portfolio management and evaluation that computers have made their most significant contribution in recent years. This development was spurred by the enactment on Labor Day 1974 of the *Employee Retirement Income Security Act,* one of whose primary requirements is that pension fund trustees evaluate the performance of their fund managers. Several major brokerage firms have created highly sophisticated computerized techniques for the diagnostic evaluation of fund performance. These programs not only calculate the rates of return earned on the assets under management; they also determine the amount of risk taken, the degree of diversification, and the impact of the fund manager's attempts at stock selection and timing.

Finally, each pension fund that is evaluated is compared with hundreds of other professionally managed portfolios, so that the relative performance of the fund manager can also be gauged. Today, several thousand pension funds are evaluated by these computer-based performance measurement systems and a continuing record of their investment results is stored in the computer's memory. Other computer programs verify that custodians of securities have paid required interest and dividends into the appropriate account and determine whether each trade occurred between the high and low prices for the day.

Several large firms have computer systems whereby branch office representatives can have direct wire access to the computer and retrieve instantly from its vast "memory" the latest opinion of the firm's research department on several thousand different stocks. The individual registered representative could not be expected to have valid information and opinions on anything like that many stocks to satisfy a customer who wants to know what he thinks about this company or that one. Now, if he works for a firm with a computer-operated retrieval system, all he has to do is punch a few keys and instantly, no matter how far away he is —even Europe—he gets by teletype wire a printed summary of the analyst's latest thinking about the stock, complete with his projections for earnings, dividends, and future price range. It is, of course, the responsibility of the research department at headquarters to see that the information file in the computer is kept constantly up to date.

In the area of security selection, the vast capacity of the computer makes it possible to screen rapidly an almost unlimited number of securities in order to find those that will match some predetermined set of standards—stocks that have shown consistent growth of earnings over some specified period, or stocks whose price performance has exceeded some established yardstick by a significant margin, or stocks that match some particular standard for dividend-payout in relation to earnings. In using computers in this fashion, the analyst establishes the criteria and lets the machine survey the field to find those that meet his standards. The ultimate objective of this kind of computer research is to find stocks that are undervalued or overvalued in relation to the market as a whole or any specified segment of it.

Portfolio management by computer is really only a further development of the techniques used in stock selection, although infinitely more complicated because the computer must be asked to deal with a variety of criteria. Stocks must be chosen not only to satisfy the individual investor's circumstances—cash available for investment, income requirements, tax considerations, and the like—but also to keep the degree of risk which the investor assumes in reasonable relationship to his investment objective. Here, thanks to the computer, new analytical methods seek to differentiate between that element of risk in a given portfolio that can be attributed to general market action and that portion that is inherent in the specific securities included in the portfolio. Certain it is that in tailoring a portfolio to an individual investor's needs the computer is used to review a vast number of alternative investments—a far greater number than an individual analyst could review in months or years—and because of the computer's high speed, the job can be done in a matter of minutes.

The technical market analyst who is interested in trying to predict long- or short-term swings in the market on the basis of such factors as the volume of short selling, the ratio of odd-lot to round-lot transactions, cyclical and random variations in price movements, and other esoteric data finds in the computer the answer to an infinity of mathematical problems he has wrestled with for years. In addition, with the improvements in data communication and the development of electronic screens, a technical analyst can command the computer to create instantly at his desk a wide variety of charts —trend lines, moving averages, volume data, and high-low-close figures—to help him in his predictions of the outlook for the market as a whole or for individual stocks.

The computer has had one interesting effect on the analyst himself. Accustomed over the years to generalizations about the probable price action of a stock—"although short-term prospects are not promising, there is appreciable potential for long-term growth"—the analyst now finds it necessary to express his opinion in specific figures if his projections are to be used in any kind of a computer program. He must say, for instance, that over the next three months he expects no more than a 1% increase in the price of a given stock, while over a five-year period he anticipates a 12% price appreciation. The necessity of replacing qualitative judgments with quantitative predictions has had the salutary effect of sharpening his evaluations and even improving his accuracy.

How much you lean on your broker for help is up to you. You can in special circumstances open a discretionary account and give him a power of attorney to make all buying and selling decisions for you, but most brokers are loath to accept such complete responsibility for an account because losses, no matter how small or infrequent, breed trouble and discontent. They prefer to act on your specific instructions. That's why some brokers won't even accept discretionary accounts. One thing you can be sure of: lacking such instructions, no reputable broker, no member firm of the New York Stock Exchange, is going to "put you into" some stock or "sell you out" of it. As a general rule, the registered representative today wants you to assume responsibility for managing your own investments—with his help.

He'll be glad to get you the facts and figures you need and to help you to interpret them, but he prefers that the decisions about what to buy and what to sell be wholly your own. For one thing, you'll be less inclined to blame him for whatever might go wrong if you determine your own investment course. More important, he knows that in the long run you are going to be a better and more successful investor. You'll have a greater interest in the problem, and you'll be more willing to work at the job of investing.

Many investors have already learned the ropes in this investment business on a cooperative basis through the medium of an *investment club*. Typically, an investment club will be composed of a dozen or more neighbors, business associates, fellow commuters, or brother lodge members who meet together once a month, put $10 or $20 apiece into a common pool, and spend an hour or two discussing the best possible investment for their money. These are serious sessions in which the pros and cons of various stocks are ardently debated.

The rise of the investment club was little short of meteoric, especially in the "go-go" years of the late sixties. However, from a peak of about 56,000 in 1970, the number of clubs declined to around 30,000 in the middle of the decade. The demise of so many is attributable mainly to various stock market slumps during the period, but at least part of the trouble is due to the rise in broker's commissions for small transactions and to the differing investment philosophies of club members.

Despite the bookkeeping problems and occasionally the legal complications which such club business creates, broker's representatives are more than willing as a rule to provide the clubs with company reports and meet with them to answer questions and guide the discussions. The commission return for the time and work involved is negligible, but the opportunity for valuable missionary work, for educating club members in the techniques of investing, is tremendous. And many a worthwhile individual account has been generated by participation in an investment club.

Information on how to start an investment club is available in the form of a manual costing $5 from the National Association of Investment Clubs (1515 East Eleven Mile Road, Royal Oak, Michigan 48067). The manual has a membership application form, which gives the purchaser a $5 credit on his club's first year dues.

One thing is sure: investment club members get a

good grounding in the investment facts of life. They learn, as every investor must, that it's a difference of opinion that makes the market.

If you as an investor can arrive at buying or selling decisions that are better grounded in fact than the other fellow's, you are going to be right more often than he is. It's just that simple—and that complex.

CHAPTER 28

Can You "Beat the Market"?

Isn't there any system to "beat the market," any system that will protect you against price fluctuations and virtually guarantee you a profit over the long pull?

Yes, there are such systems, and some of them work pretty well. They are far from foolproof, but at least they do point out some important lessons about successful investing. They are called dollar cost averaging and formula investing.

Dollar cost averaging simply involves putting the same fixed amount of money—$200, $500, $1,000 —into the same stock, regardless of its price movement, at regular intervals—say, every month or every six months or so—over a long period of time. The Monthly Investment Plan is built on precisely this basis.

Following a system of investing a fixed sum of money in the same stock at regular intervals, you could have made a profit on probably 90% of the stocks listed on the New York Stock Exchange over almost any period of four or five years you might want to pick in the last quarter century.

Dollar cost averaging works most times simply because you buy more shares of a stock with your fixed amount of money when the stock is low in price than you do when it is comparatively high, and when the stock rises again, you make a profit on the greater number of shares you got at low cost.

Suppose you bought $500 worth of a particular stock when it was selling at $10 a share, another $500 worth three months later when it was $9, another $500 worth at $8, and so on, while the stock fell to

$5, then rose to $15, and settled back to $10. If you then sold out, you would be able to show a profit of about 10%, ignoring both dividends and commission

Price per Share	Number of Shares Purchased	Cost of Shares	Number of Shares Owned	Cumulative Cost of Shares	Total Value of Shares
$10	50	$500	50	$500	$500
9	56	504	106	1004	954
8	63	504	169	1508	1352
7	71	497	240	2005	1680
6	83	498	323	2503	1938
5	100	500	423	3003	2115
6	83	498	506	3501	3036
7	71	497	577	3998	4039
8	63	504	640	4502	5120
9	56	504	696	5006	6264
10	50	500	746	5506	7460
11	45	495	791	6006	8701
12	42	504	833	6505	9996
13	38	494	871	6999	11323
14	36	504	907	7503	12698
15	33	495	940	7998	14100
14	36	504	976	8502	13664
13	38	494	1014	8996	13182
12	42	504	1056	9500	12672
11	45	495	1101	9995	12111
10	50	500	1151	10495	11510

costs, despite the fact that you had paid an average price of $10 and sold out at exactly that same price. You don't believe it?

Don't bother to figure it out, because the proof is in the table above. To avoid the complication of fractional shares of stock, it is assumed that at every different price level the buyer would purchase whatever number of shares would yield a total cost nearest $500.

All told, you paid $10,495, and your holdings would be worth $11,510, a gain of $1,015, or almost 10%. Exactly the same results—again exclusive of all dividends and purchase costs—would be achieved if the stock first rose steadily from $10 to $15, then dropped to $5, then came back to $10. Here are the figures on that:

Price per Share	Number of Shares Purchased	Cost of Shares	Number of Shares Owned	Cumulative Cost of Shares	Total Value of Shares
$10	50	$500	50	$500	$500
11	45	495	95	995	1045
12	42	504	137	1499	1644
13	38	494	175	1993	2275
14	36	504	211	2497	2954
15	33	495	244	2992	3660
14	36	504	280	3496	3920
13	38	494	318	3990	4134
12	42	504	360	4494	4320
11	45	495	405	4989	4455
10	50	500	455	5489	4550
9	56	504	511	5993	4599
8	63	504	574	6497	4592
7	71	497	645	6994	4515
6	83	498	728	7492	4368
5	100	500	828	7992	4140
6	83	498	911	8490	5466
7	71	497	982	8987	6874
8	63	504	1045	9491	8360
9	56	504	1101	9995	9909
10	50	500	1151	10495	11510

There's only one significant difference between the two tables. Note that you are considerably better off all the way along the line until the very end if your stock drops first and then comes back. Thus, in the first table, after the stock had fallen to $5 and recovered to $10, you could have sold out and made a profit of $1,954, or about 35%, on your money.

So if the stock you buy drops in price and you have the confidence to believe that it will come back, as stocks in general always have, you would do well to continue buying it as it slides on down. This is called "averaging down," and it's a concept which the investor who is worried about the decline in the price of some stock he owns might well keep in mind.

While no stock is likely ever to follow the precise pattern set in the tables, the examples do serve to demonstrate the validity of the dollar cost averaging principle.

There's only one big catch to this system of beating the market. You've got to have the cash—yes, and the courage, too—to buy the same dollar amount of the stock at whatever interval of time you've fixed on, be it every month or three months or a year.

And if it drops, you've got to keep right on buying, in order to pick up the low-cost shares on which you can later make your profit. Unfortunately, when the stock market is down, the average man's bank account is likely to be down too, and so he often can't afford to buy at just the time he should. If instead of buying he should have to sell at such a time, he might have to take a loss. This will always be true if a person has to sell at a price lower than the average cost of the shares he owns. In such circumstances, the dollar cost averaging technique will have provided no protection. Most times, it works over the long pull because the long-term trend of the stock market has been upward.

If an investor beginning in 1946 had followed a dollar averaging plan through the postwar years and applied $1,000 a year to the stocks in Standard & Poor's 500-stock index, reinvesting dividends all along the line, by the end of 1974 he would have realized a return about four times the out-of-pocket cost of his investment. He would have achieved this result despite the fact that the bear market reached a twelve-year low in December 1974. The closing low for the Dow Jones industrials was 577.60 and that low was recorded on December 6. At this point, the average had fallen 45% from the then all-time closing high of 1,051.70 which it had attained less than two years before on January 11, 1973. Had our hypothetical investor sold at that point, he would have realized a return of about seven times his out-of-pocket cost.

The stock of the RCA Corporation offers a dramatic example of the way dollar cost averaging works most of the time to the advantage of the investor, but occasionally to his disadvantage. Let's assume that back at the beginning of 1929 you had a lump sum of $23,000 and you decided to invest it all in RCA stock. RCA was a popular stock then, highly regarded for its growth possibilities, and it was selling early in 1929 in the price range of $375 to $380 per share. So for your

$23,000 you would have been able to buy 61 shares. Over the years, thanks to splits in the stock, those shares would have increased to 1,087 and you would have received a total of over $16,700 in dividend payments. But 46 years later at the end of 1974 when we will assume you had to sell, your stock would have been worth only $11,685 because of the 72% drop in price that RCA sustained during the bear market of 1973–1974. This means that, together with your dividends, you would have had a net gain of only $5,400 on your $23,000 investment after 46 years.

That's pretty bad, especially considering the fact that if you had sold only two years earlier at the end of 1972 you would have had a net gain of $33,800 on your $23,000, counting both dividends and price appreciation.

Now consider how much more you would have made if you had followed the dollar cost averaging plan and put that same $23,000 into RCA stock at the rate of about $500 a year over the same 46 years. Here it is assumed that the number of shares purchased (at the opening of the market each year) would have been that number which you could have bought for an amount closest to $500—sometimes a fraction of a share less, sometimes a fraction more.

At the end of 1974 you would have owned 5,476 shares of RCA, and you would have had a net gain, after payment of all brokerage commissions on your purchases, of more than $121,000—this despite selling out at the end of 1974. Of this sum, the $85,000 you would have collected in dividends would have been more than three and a half times the total cost of your investment. This is an impressive record, and it could have been achieved only because of the opportunity you would have had to pick up RCA shares at bargain levels during the half-dozen severe market slumps that occurred in that 46-year period.

However, we would have an entirely different story to tell if we had taken 1933 as our starting date instead of 1929; then it would have been decidedly more advantageous for you to have made a big lump-sum purchase of RCA than for you to have acquired RCA stock in units of $500 a year over the 41-year period, 1933 to 1974.

If you had put $20,500 into RCA at the beginning of 1933 (the equivalent of $500 a year for 41 years) your investment would have been worth almost $372,000 at the end of 1974, counting both price appreciation and dividends, whereas if you had bought the stock at the rate of $500 a year throughout that 41-year period, you would have realized just a little more than 36% of that figure—a bit over $136,000.

Because few people have large sums that they can put into a stock at one time, and because most stocks do fluctuate quite widely from time to time, it is generally more prudent and more profitable for an investor to follow the dollar cost averaging plan, which can make it possible for him to capitalize on price fluctuations, rather than to take one big plunge.

The table (page 265) shows how you would have made out by June 1975 if, beginning in 1929, you had put roughly $500 a year into RCA and 19 other stocks that also proved especially popular with M.I.P. investors in the first few years after that plan, which seeks to capitalize on the dollar cost averaging principle, was initiated in 1954.

Of course, this is history, and no one can guarantee it is the kind of history that will repeat itself. But it does provide a convincing demonstration of the value of accumulating shares on a dollar cost averaging basis over a period of time, and this is one of the most persuasive features of the Monthly Investment Plan, which makes it possible for the small investor to follow precisely this course in buying most of the stocks listed on the New York Stock Exchange.

Formula investing is not so much a system for beating the market as it is a mechanical means for enforcing prudence and caution. There are many different formula plans—almost every expert has his own—but stripped of their technicalities all of them can be reduced to the basic premise that an investment fund should be balanced between stocks and bonds, and that the ratio of one kind of security to the other should be changed as the market rises and falls. You buy bonds

$500-A-Year Investment Program
January 1929–December 1975

	Total Cost of Shares Purchased	Shares Owned	Market Value	Total Dividends Received	Total Dividends Plus Market Value of Stock	Net Gain
Aluminum Co. of America	$23,689	2,283	$ 88,181	$55,975	$144,156	$120,467
American Tel. and Tel.	23,552	744	37,851	40,877	78,728	55,176
Caterpillar Tractor	23,780	9,263	646,094	199,244	845,338	821,558
Consolidated Edison	23,793	1,283	19,245	43,410	62,655	38,862
Dow Chemical	23,951	8,386	768,367	141,317	909,684	885,733
du Pont (E.I.) de Nemours*	23,981	453	89,805	97,645	187,450	163,469
Eastman Kodak	23,757	5,858	621,680	133,729	755,409	731,652
Exxon Corp.	23,533	1,706	151,407	126,504	277,911	254,373
General Electric	23,569	2,384	109,962	71,075	181,037	157,468
General Motors	23,613	1,897	109,315	154,775	264,090	240,477
Goodyear Tire & Rubber	23,856	12,590	273,833	190,628	464,461	440,605
Gulf Oil	23,672	6,152	126,116	137,561	263,677	240,005
Nabisco Inc.	23,916	1,208	46,508	47,338	93,846	69,930
Pacific Gas & Electric	23,706	1,683	34,922	53,065	87,987	64,281
Phillips Petroleum	23,600	4,547	246,675	127,612	374,287	350,687
RCA Corp.	23,532	5,523	105,627	90,682	196,309	172,777
Sears, Roebuck	23,863	4,738	305,601	128,614	434,215	410,352
Union Carbide	23,817	1,263	77,201	61,151	138,352	114,535
United States Steel	23,629	1,404	91,260	81,690	172,950	149,321
Westinghouse Electric	23,235	2,985	39,924	56,353	96,277	73,042

*Results for du Pont include the market value of General Motors shares distributed to holders of du Pont stock, as well as the dividends subsequently paid on those shares.

and sell stocks when the stock market gets high—on the assumption that the stock market becomes increasingly vulnerable as prices advance—and you reverse the procedure when the market drops.

Even if it is granted that the premise is basically sound, the theory is one that the average investor can't apply very effectively, since his investment fund is rarely large enough for a formula plan to operate without distortion. This is so because all formula plans assume that that portion of the fund which is invested in stocks will perform generally as the market average does. Obviously, the fewer stocks you can afford to own, the less likely are they to perform in line with the general market; they may do significantly better or they may do significantly worse. Again, the only bonds that a small investor can generally afford are government E bonds, and he can't expect to achieve the same interest return on these bonds as he might earn on other government or corporate bonds, particularly since the return on E bonds is measurably less in the early years. Savings bank deposits can, of course, be substituted for bonds.

Basically, there are three kinds of formula plans— the constant dollar plan, the constant ratio plan, and the variable ratio plan. The *constant dollar plan* assumes that a fixed dollar amount of stocks will be held at all times. Thus, if you had $20,000, you might decide to keep $10,000—no more or no less—invested in stocks. If the dollar value of your stock portfolio rose—say, to $11,000—you would sell $1,000 of stocks and put the proceeds into bonds. If your stocks declined $1,000, you would sell $1,000 of bonds and buy stocks. One objection to the plan is that over any long period of years stock prices are likely to advance —at least they have historically—and if your stock investments are frozen at any specified level, you won't keep up with the parade.

The *constant ratio plan* works like the constant dollar plan except that you determine to keep 50% of your investment fund in stocks at all times and 50% in bonds. You don't use fixed dollar amounts. The constant ratio plan is obviously more flexible, can be adopted more readily to the shifting cycles of the stock market, and assures you of at least partial participation in the long-term growth of common-stock values.

The *variable ratio plan* operates like the constant ratio plan, except that you decide to vary the ratio invested in common stocks as the market rises or falls. Thus, you might start out on a 50-50 basis, but decide to keep only 40% of your funds in common stocks whenever the market, as measured by one of the accepted averages, moved up 25%. When the market advanced 50% you would cut back your common stock holdings to 30% of your total funds, and if it went up 75%, you would have only 20% invested in stocks. If the market fell, you would reverse the operation, buying stocks at the designated market levels and selling bonds. There are dozens and dozens of variations in the variable ratio theme, many of them involving complicated mathematical formulas and using a variety of economic indexes as well as the market averages. They are designed to permit the investor to take maximum advantage of interim fluctuations in the market while simultaneously protecting his long-term position.

But they don't always work that way. Thus, anyone investing on a formula plan which called for reducing his commitments in common stocks as the market advanced would have lost out on the big bull market that began in 1950 and continued with only short-lived slumps in 1957, 1962, 1966, 1969, and 1973–1974. That's why even many big, conservative institutions have either abandoned or modified extensively the formula plans that they initiated 20 or 30 years ago. Of course, a shift into bonds, such as these formula plans would have dictated at bull market peaks, would have paid off handsomely during the subsequent corrective phases.

While the average investor may not be able to apply any neatly devised mathematical formula to his own situation, he can profit by paying heed to the one basic precept of all these formulas: keep an eye on those market averages, and as they rise, let them act as a brake on your buying enthusiasm. Remember, no bull market movement lasts forever. And neither, for that matter, does a bear market, although it wasn't until 1954, a quarter of a century later, that the Dow industrial average and Standard & Poor's 500-stock price index surpassed their 1929 highs of 381.17 and 31.92, respectively.

CHAPTER 29

Should You Buy a Mutual Fund?

THINKING is always hard work. Thinking about an investment problem is doubly hard because it frequently involves dealing with words and ideas that are somewhat strange.

In a situation like that, it's understandable why you might want to let somebody else do your thinking for you.

And that's just what thousands and thousands of new investors have done in recent years. They have turned to the *investment trust*—especially the *mutual fund*—as the answer to their investment problems.

There's no special magic about an investment trust —nor anything mysterious about its operation. Suppose you and some of your friends—twenty of you, all told—each have $1,000 to spare. Instead of each of you investing his own money, you might decide to pool it. Then instead of forming an investment club and arriving at collective investment decisions, you turn the whole sum over to one individual, or manager, to invest for you.

In that situation, the twenty of you would constitute an investment trust or *investment company* in miniature.

Now let's assume you're lucky and that at the end of the first year the manager of your little trust is able to report that he has made money for you. The value of the stocks which the trust owns has risen from $20,000 to $22,000. Each of your shares in that trust is now worth $1,100 ($22,000 divided by 20).

You've been so successful, as a matter of fact, that some of your other friends would like to join your little trust. The twenty of you must now make one of two decisions.

You can decide that you're going to restrict the trust to just the original members and their original capital. If that's what you decide, you will, in effect, have converted your organization into a *closed-end trust*. There will be no new members or shareholders in your company, unless, of course, one of the original twenty wants to sell his share to somebody else for whatever he can get for it. That's a right all of you always have.

The alternative plan would involve a decision to expand your trust and take in new members. Since your own shares are now worth $1,100 apiece, you decide to allow them to buy in on that basis—$1,100 a share. That $1,100 would represent the *net asset value per share* at that time—a figure determined by taking the current market value of all the shares held in your trust or fund and dividing it by the number of shares outstanding. Net asset value per share is a constantly changing figure for two reasons: (1) the total value of your fund's holdings fluctuates as the prices of the stocks that it owns change in the stock market; (2) the number of shares outstanding changes too, as additional shares are sold to new or present participants in the fund and as the fund redeems shares for those who want to sell.

If you decide that your fund should be operated in this manner, you will have transformed your company into an *open-end* trust, or what is known more popularly as a mutual fund.

This, in theory, is the essential difference between the closed-end and open-end trusts. In actuality, there are other differences.

Closed-end trusts are stock companies whose shares are bought and sold just like other stocks. The business of these trusts is investing, instead of manufacturing or merchandising, but they are operated just like any other company by officers and directors responsible to the shareholders, who stand to make or lose money as the value of the stocks owned by the trust goes up or down and as the dividend paid on those shares increases or decreases.

Some of these companies, like Lehman Corporation and Tri-Continental Corporation, are listed on the New York Stock Exchange. Anything from one share to hundreds of shares of their stock can be purchased through a member firm, at the commission rate that firm charges. The stocks of some closed-end trusts are sold over-the-counter, but these are usually smaller, less well-known companies.

Sometimes the stock of a closed-end investment trust will sell at a premium price, a price greater than its net asset value per share, and sometimes it will sell at a discount or below that value figure, as during a bear market. Closed-end trusts usually compute and publish this net asset value per share just once a quarter.

In contrast, shares of an open-end trust or mutual fund are always bought and sold on the basis of their exact net asset value. Mutual funds usually compute and announce the net asset value of their shares every day, and this determines the price dealers will charge a buyer, or what the owner will get if he sells.

Mutual funds pay dividends, if earned, and these are taxed at regular income tax rates. They also distribute long-term capital gains when they are realized on the sale of their holdings. Since these distributions of capital gains constitute a return of capital, the individual owner of mutual shares pays a tax on such distributions in accordance with his own individual tax situation, just as he would on any other long-term capital gain. Fund shareholders can generally elect to have dividends and capital distributions reinvested if they wish.

The two kinds of trusts do much the same type of business, but the difference in their setup makes for a difference in their operation. A closed-end trust cannot at will increase its original capital; an open-end trust not only can but usually wants to. The more shares that are sold the more the trust grows, and the more its salesmen and investment advisers stand to profit.

There were more than 600 mutual funds in existence

at the end of 1974, and it is the mutual fund, not the almost-forgotten closed-end trust, that has been getting all the play in recent years.

Their growth has been little short of phenomenal—from a half-billion dollars in 1941 to nearly $60 billion in 1972, although in the bear market years of 1973–1974, net assets did decline to $36 billion. The half-dozen market slumps since 1941 have naturally been rough on the mutual funds. In these periods their net asset value declined to about the same extent as stock prices generally, but over the long haul they have managed to maintain a fairly steady and impressive growth record. Some funds have grown to gigantic size. Just before the 1973–1974 market collapse, there were 5 funds with assets of more than a billion dollars each, 18 topped the half-billion figure, and 84 funds could boast assets exceeding $100 million.

This growth has meant that a lot of new shareholders have been created by the mutual funds, people who never had previously ventured into the stock market. As a matter of fact, mutual funds *must* attract a lot of new business, a lot of new shareholders every year to offset those who sell their shares. In bad years, they are often called upon to redeem more than they sell. The same situation prevails sometimes even in good years. In March 1976, although the stock market continued to rise, total net redemptions of fund shares were at a record high.

Who are the owners of these mutual funds? According to a survey by the Investment Company Institute in 1970, they are individuals of reasonably substantial means, in their mid-forties, with some college education, and with incomes that average about $14,000 a year.

In recent years, however, many large institutional investors have turned to mutual funds because the funds relieve institutional managers of responsibility for managing the institution's investment portfolio. These big investors in 1974 held about 25% of the total assets of all mutual funds, and they accounted for a major portion of the big-unit sales. Sales to employee pension funds and to corporation treasurers, who must employ a company's idle funds, are also fast-growing areas of the mutual fund business.

Why have mutual funds enjoyed such spectacular growth? One answer is that the mutual fund has obvious appeal to the man who sees in the fund a ready-made answer to his investment problem. It is easier to trust another man's judgment about the market, especially one who is supposed to be an expert, than it is to make up your own mind about whether to buy stock X or stock Y, whether to sell A or B.

But there is another reason for the fantastic success of the funds, and you can label it "sales incentive." Mutual fund salesmen get big commissions, and to earn that commission they don't mind resorting to some pretty high-pressure tactics on occasion.

It was the big commission that attracted a lot of "moonlighters" into the business years ago—part-time shoe salesmen, gas station operators, and a lot of retired people who found in the mutual fund a way to make an extra buck. But in recent years, as the business became more professional, these moonlighters have been driven out of it to be replaced by the registered representatives of member firms, salesmen for over-the-counter houses, and to some extent by a mutual fund's own trained sales force. But to all these salesmen the commission is still the main attraction of the mutual fund.

Any individual buying a mutual fund in 1975 typically paid a commission or, as it is more commonly known in the fund business, a *loading charge* of around 8½% of the price of the fund. The rates are set by the funds themselves, and some charge 7½% and some 9%, the maximum permitted by law.

To realize just how great a sales incentive the loading charge is, look at the situation from the point of view of a brokerage firm which is a member of the New York Stock Exchange. Suppose one of its sales representatives sells a $5,000 investment in a mutual fund. An 8½% loading charge on such a sale would amount to $425. (Since the loading charge is deducted first, that means that only $4,575 of the $5,000 would actually be invested in the fund's shares. Thus, as far as the purchaser is concerned, he is really being charged a sales commission of 9.3%—not 8½%—on the amount of money actually invested.) Of the $425 loading charge which the brokerage firm collected, it would typically be permitted to keep 75%, or $317, with the balance going to the fund itself to cover operating costs.

But if the same sales representative of the brokerage firm were to sell his customer $5,000 worth of a stock listed on the New York Stock Exchange, the commission the firm would realize would be a whole lot less. How much less would depend, of course, on that firm's rate schedule. But before Mayday 1975, when rates were fixed, the commission on 100 shares of a $50 stock would have been just $71.50.

Mutual funds, as a general rule, make no charge when the customer redeems or sells his shares, and so the broker doesn't stand to make anything more than his original $317 on the mutual fund transaction. In contrast, the customer who buys the listed stock may sell it someday, and the broker will have a chance to make a second commission. Still, even the commission on a *round-trip* trade—the purchase and the sale—would be distinctly less than the loading charge. And anyway, a commission in hand is worth two in the bush.

While the average investor might pay 8½% on a $5,000 order, big orders get big concessions. Thus, on orders of $100,000 the rate might be only 1% and on a million share order, the loading charge might be as little as ½ of 1%. But then, the big institutions also pay much lower commission rates on their big volume orders on the exchange than does the small investor.

During the sixties, the most aggressively promoted and rapidly growing mutual funds were the *front-end load funds*. The buyer of such a fund agrees to make uniform periodic payments to the fund, usually over a 10–15 year period, and in exchange acquires whatever number of fund shares such payments will cover. When a salesman sells such a front-end load fund he collects 50% of everything the purchaser puts into the fund the first year. Thus, if the customer signed up for a $50-a-month plan and paid in $600 that first year, $300 would be paid out immediately as a commission to the salesman, and only $300 of the customer's payment would actually be invested for him. With a sales incentive like that is it any wonder that sales of front-end load funds zoomed in the sixties, while the funds themselves grew in number from about 10 to more than 70?

Over the life of a front-end contract, the sales cost may average out to an 8½% loading charge, but the big advantage to the salesman is that he gets the lion's share of the total commission due over the whole life of the contract in the first year, and he doesn't have to worry about his commissions in case the buyer cancels his contract in a couple of years, because he has already collected the lion's share of his commission.

If the buyer of a front-end load fund wanted to cancel his contract and redeem his shares, he couldn't normally expect to recover the sales cost and break even until he had been in the plan for about three years, not unless there had been a spectacular increase in the value of the fund's shares. And if the stock market wasn't robust, it might be five or six years before he could break even—maybe never. Meanwhile, the salesman had his take, all tidily sewed up.

In contrast, the buyer of a noncontractual or *level load* mutual fund plan might put the same amount of money into the fund and pay the same 8½% commission —say, $50 a month, plus $4.25 commission—but he would never be in the hole, assuming the value of his fund shares didn't decline; he wouldn't have to keep on buying in order to recover a whopping big commission paid in advance. He could quit when he wanted to.

In 1966, the S.E.C. asked Congress for legislation to curb many mutual fund selling practices. Specifically, it wanted an outright ban on front-end load contracts. In defense of such contracts the funds argued that investors needed some form of compulsion—such as the threat of loss if they backed out of a contract in its early years—to keep them saving and investing regularly. But the S.E.C. pointed to its studies which showed that 20% of all those who bought front-end contracts were forced to sell at a loss, because they couldn't keep up payments. And, in general, these were the investors, buying plans at $10 or $20 a month, who could least afford such loss.

When Congress finally passed the *Investment Company Amendments Act of 1970,* the industry heaved a sigh of relief. The front-end contractual plan had survived, even if subjected to new restrictions. Under the 1970 law such funds may still pay a sales commission equal to 50% of the buyer's first-year payments, but the law stipulates that in such a case the buyer can cancel his contract any time in the first 45 days and get back the full commission he paid, and further, that at any time in the first 18 months, he can cancel the contract and get back 85% of the commission—plus, of course, the value of his shares at that time.

The law further provides that the buyer shall receive a statement at the time of his purchase setting forth the commissions that will be deducted from his purchase and informing him of his right to withdraw from the fund and obtain a refund. And if the buyer misses three payments in the first fifteen months or one payment from the fifteenth to the eighteenth month, the fund is obligated to notify him again of his right to withdraw and the terms of the withdrawal.

If a front-load fund wants to escape these specific provisions governing the purchaser's right to withdraw, it can do so only by limiting its sales commission to a maximum of 20% in any one year and 64% in the aggregate for the first four years.

Apart from the commission, mutual funds offer brokers still another incentive to push fund sales. As the funds grow, they are constantly buying additional stock, big blocks of stock. Furthermore, they keep changing their portfolios, selling 5,000 or 10,000 shares of this stock and buying 5,000 or 10,000 shares of that one. The funds obviously tend to give this highly lucrative block business to those brokers who do the best job of selling their shares.

All through the sixties and very early seventies the in-and-out trading activity of the funds grew apace, as competition forced them to become increasingly "performance-oriented." Sometimes, in striving for speculative gains in a rising market, a fund would turn over half of its entire portfolio in a year or less.

Since the funds themselves are not permitted to be members of the big exchanges, they execute their orders for listed stocks through established member firms, and in the halcyon days of the bull market before the 1973–1974 slump, when the funds were setting a feverish trading pace, member firms competed vigorously for this big-ticket business. Occasionally, some broker who rendered valuable service to a fund, such as providing research information or handling block business with minimum impact on the market, might get a fund order to buy or sell a block, but generally *reciprocity* reigned. "You scratch my back, and I'll scratch yours" was the order of the day, and brokers and dealers intensified their fund-selling efforts in order to get more of the fund's commission business.

With the abandonment of fixed commission rates in 1975, reciprocity faded measurably. What became all-important to the funds was not what a broker's record was on fund sales, but how much he would cut the commission to get the fund's block business.

So abrupt was the change, that the National Association of Securities Dealers could pretty much forget the tough *Antireciprocal Rule* that it had been thinking of imposing on the business. And the Antitrust Division, which had warned that all reciprocal deals were clearly illegal, could also relax its vigilance.

While it may be true that mutual funds are aggressively sold, that does not mean that they are not good things to buy. Quite the contrary. One great investment virtue that all investment trusts, closed-end and open-end alike, have to offer is the protection afforded the investor by virtue of their diversified holdings in many different companies and usually many different industries. There is obviously less risk (but less hope of making a killing, too) in owning an interest in 50 or 150 different companies than in owning stock in just one company.

This is the argument, the protection provided by diversification, which mutual fund salesmen stress, and it's an argument of significant merit. However, the importance of diversification as a protective device is minimized or magnified, depending upon which kind of mutual fund you buy. And there are many different kinds of funds.

The most popular type of fund is the *common stock fund,* a fund whose assets are wholly invested in a diversified list of common stocks. Such funds are not permitted to invest more than 5% of their assets in the stock of a given company and generally they put no more than 10% of their assets in a given industry, but even so, there is a wide diversity of investment policy among them. Some accent income; some aim at the twin objectives of growth and income; and some, probably the greatest number, emphasize growth or long-term capital growth.

Still other common stock funds take an opposite tack. They invest all their assets in the securities of companies that operate in a single industry—chemicals, drugs, electronics, etc. During the 1973–1974 recession, when the price of gold was soaring and the dollar was declining, there were even funds that invested exclusively in gold stocks, and they had a vogue till the price of gold fell. Some of these *special purpose funds* concentrate their investments in specific geographical areas, and still others seek to cater to a particular class or type of investor, such as farmers, airline pilots, even cemetery owners.

Then there are the *"go-go" funds,* whose assets are totally invested in aggressive growth situations, with the objective of racking up big capital gains, and the *hedge funds* that operate still further out in a speculative orbit all their own.

Originally, a hedge fund consisted of a group of wealthy men who operated the fund as a private partnership, but as speculative fever rose and the market boiled to its peak in 1973, many of these privately owned and privately operated hedge funds were offered to the general public. If you wanted to become a partner in such a fund, it didn't matter whether you could afford to speculate or not. And hedge funds are the rankest kind of speculation. They buy on margin and sell short—trading techniques forbidden to regular mutual funds; they deal in warrants and options; and they put money into "special situations," even buying the stocks of companies so small or so new that their stock does not enjoy a public market.

Just as the S.E.C. began turning its attention to the "go-go" and hedge funds, the market applied its own corrective. With the 45% decline in the Dow Jones industrial average during 1973–1974, the speculative fever died and these hot-shot funds virtually vanished from the scene. But with another strong bull market, they may well reappear in full force.

In addition to the all-common-stock fund, there are the *balanced* funds, funds whose assets are divided among common stocks, preferreds, and bonds. Most of these highly conservative funds operate on some kind of a formula investing plan. As common stocks rise into high ground, more and more of the assets of such funds are shifted into preferred stocks and bonds to protect against a break in the stock market. In a falling stock market, they sell bonds and begin buying stocks in anticipation of an upturn.

In addition to these various types of mutual funds, there is one wholly different species—the *no-load fund*. There are some fifty no-load funds—Scudder, Stevens & Clark and Loomis-Sayles are probably the best known—and these funds employ no salesmen, charge no commission. And that is the reason why you might find it difficult to buy a no-load fund. Your broker is not apt to be interested in arranging for you to buy such a fund direct from the management company of the fund, because he doesn't make a penny on the deal. He'd prefer to sell you a fund that yields him a good commission.

All mutual funds employ the services of a professional management firm to direct and guide their investment policy, and one of the proudest boasts of fund salesmen is that such management can invest your money for you better than you can yourself. That's the way mutual funds justify the *management fee*, usually ½ of 1%, that they uniformly charge the buyer.

Very often the men who comprise the management company are the same men who guide its sales destiny, and since they wear two hats they collect two incomes —often very substantial incomes. The law does provide, with some exceptions, that no more than 60% of a mutual fund's directors can be connected with its advisory or management company, but there are still quite a few mutual fund executives who take a double dip out of a fund's earnings.

If professional management is worthwhile, if it's worth ½ of 1% a year, it might seem logical to assume that mutual funds would show a performance record over the years superior to that measured by one of the accepted indexes that reflect the average action of the market.

Have the funds beaten the averages?

Perhaps there can be no clear-cut, categorical answer to that question, because the answer depends on what period of time you are measuring and what kind of fund you are talking about out of the many different types that exist.

Nevertheless, after a definitive study of mutual funds and their performance over a period of almost six years the Wharton School of Finance and Commerce reported as follows to the Securities and Exchange Commission: "Performance records vary considerably, both within and among types of funds, but on the average conformed rather closely to the behavior of the securities market as a whole. . . . The average performance by the funds did not differ appreciably from what would have been achieved by an unmanaged portfolio with the same division among asset types (i.e. common stocks, preferred, bonds, governments, etc.). About half the funds performed better, half worse, than such an unmanaged portfolio." In a follow-up study of 136 of the most widely held funds covering a period from 1960 through mid-1968, Professor Irwin Friend of the Wharton School reported that the funds had not performed quite as well as the average for all stocks listed on the New York Stock Exchange.

Every year *Forbes* magazine reports on the performance of virtually all of the widely held funds and contrasts their records with one of the accepted stock market indexes. In the twelve-month period from June 30, 1973, to June 30, 1974, *Forbes*'s index of common stock funds fell 17.2%, compared with a 17.5% drop by Standard & Poor's 500-stock average. On the whole, *Forbes* found the performance of mutual funds so mediocre during this period that it could not find even one fund which it considered worth naming to its annual honor roll.

In general, mutual fund studies seem to bear out the Wharton School's conclusion that professional fund management doesn't yield superior results, that the funds perform about as the averages do. And the larger the fund, the more likely it is to perform as the market does, for their portfolios are necessarily so diversified that their holdings inevitably represent a cross section of the whole market.

Smaller, more aggressive funds that are fortunate enough to have bought good growth stocks at an early point in their development are apt to have more spectacular records, but no fund can make the spectacular showing that the Dreyfus Fund did with Polaroid stock some years ago, because today funds are prohibited from investing more than 5% of their assets in any one corporation, or owning more than 10% of any corporation's voting stock.

From year to year, mutual funds are likely to turn in surprisingly inconsistent results. This was demonstrated by Professor Eugene Fama of the University of Chicago's Graduate School of Business in a study which showed that not one of the 39 major funds he studied appeared in the top half of the group consistently each year for the ten years from 1951 through 1960.

It is this record of mutual funds over the years, their failure to achieve outstanding investment results and the year-to-year inconsistency in those results, that has caused the S.E.C. to question whether the average buyer of a mutual fund gets full value for the loading charges and management fees that he pays.

The S.E.C.'s concern about mutual fund performance has a certain irony about it, for in a sense the whole meteoric growth of the mutual fund industry can be traced to an inadvertent mistake the S.E.C. itself made when the original Investment Company Act of 1940 was passed. At that time mutual funds were almost unknown, and in approaching Congress with a request for legislation in the investment company field, the S.E.C. primarily had in mind a law that would enable it to regulate the closed-end investment trusts and outlaw the many practices that had permitted those trusts to enjoy an ill-starred boom as the market roared to its 1929 high.

In those days many of the trusts played fast and loose with the investor's money. Trust fund managers paid themselves large fees and bonuses for their somewhat questionable services. They split commissions with accountants and legal counsel to line their own pockets. Enjoying almost complete freedom to invest trust funds as they saw fit, the managers placed themselves too willingly at the service of investment bankers anxious to market new and dubious stock issues. They resorted to all kinds of speculative practices. They bought on margin. They pyramided paper profits. And they used the trusts to obtain control of whole industrial empires, often with only a paltry outlay of actual cash—cash furnished, of course, by investors in the fund. When the crash came in 1929, 700 trusts collapsed with virtually no show of assets.

The 1940 law may have been drafted to prohibit such practices, require full and open disclosure, and drive the manipulators from the business, but it was nonetheless that act which sanctioned, however unintentionally, all the selling practices that permitted the mutual funds to prosper. Specifically, the act approved loading charges, front-end load contracts, and management fees.

There was only one thing the funds would have liked to have and didn't get in 1940 and that was freedom to advertise. Since mutual funds are constantly issuing new stock, they necessarily fall under the prospectus provisions of the 1933 act which applies to all new stock issues. This means that a mutual fund advertisement must consist of the full offering prospectus or be limited to a "tombstone" announcement, consisting of the name of the fund, the offer of a prospectus, and a descriptive sentence or two about its objectives. Although these restrictions have been somewhat relaxed in recent years, mutual funds still regard them as a thorn in the flesh.

When the S.E.C. went to Congress in 1966 to ask for legislation that would restrict many mutual fund selling practices, it wanted an outright ban on front-end contractual plans, a 5% ceiling on loading charges, and a drastic reduction in the standard ½ of 1% management fee, which, as the S.E.C. pointed out, was considerably more than banks charged for their investment advisory services.

What the S.E.C. got from Congress four years later was distinctly less than half a loaf. Front-end load contracts were not disallowed but simply altered to permit buyers to withdraw from such a plan without losing all the money they paid down as a commission. The maximum loading charge was fixed at 9%, not 5%, although the N.A.S.D. was empowered to see that loading charges were "reasonable." Finally, the management fee went unchanged, subject only to the provision that the S.E.C., or any fund shareholder, could bring suit against a fund charging that the management fee was so excessive that it represented a breach of "fiduciary duty."

Back of all the demands for reform of the mutual fund business was a concern that even the Securities and Exchange Commission was reluctant to express: what might happen if the market went into a real tailspin—a prolonged downturn? That's the time when people who owned shares in a mutual fund would be most tempted to cash them in, for that is when they, as individuals of generally modest means, would be most likely to need their savings. And yet that is precisely the time when it would be most difficult for a mutual fund to redeem its shares, because to raise cash it would probably have to sell stocks.

Funds, of course, always have a substantial cash reserve to meet redemptions, but if there should be a persistent demand for redemptions a fund would have to sell off sizable blocks of stock to raise cash and swallow whatever loss it sustained in these forced sales. Additionally, those very sales might further depress the market and make it even more awkward for the trust to meet the next round of redemptions as prices fell further.

Although fund selling was blamed in some quarters for deepening and protracting the 1969–1970 and 1973–1974 market slumps, the funds as a whole suffered through those difficult periods about as individual shareholders did. Despite sharp declines in total assets, the funds have always met the redemption bill.

Many of the changes in the mutual fund industry that the Securities and Exchange Commission has wanted may, in the years ahead, be achieved not by legislative enactment but by the abrasive effect of new competition.

Most notable among the new competitors are the insurance companies. For years the insurance industry took the position that there could be no substitute for the guarantee of a fixed-dollar payment to survivors, regardless of how the market might perform or of how inflation might depreciate the purchasing power of those dollars. The first crack in the wall came when the Prudential Insurance Company offered *variable annuity* insurance policies, on a group basis. These policies provided that premiums would be invested, principally in diversified common stocks, and that the ultimate payoff, either on death or at retirement, would be determined by the value of the investment at that time.

Since then, more than 150 life insurance companies, including all of the biggest ones, have either offered variable annuities, formed mutual funds of their own, or made some arrangement for the sale of existing funds by their agents.

Many old-timers worried that the venture into the investment field would result in the reduced sale of life insurance or in the substitution of the cheaper term insurance for ordinary life policies—and these fears may yet prove to be well-grounded—but the lure of profits was so great that nothing could stop the stampede of insurance companies into the mutual fund field.

Still other organizations are encroaching on the sales potential for mutual funds by making their appeal on a class or professional basis. Thus, for years the College Equities Retirement Fund has pretty well usurped the market among professors, and the giant American Farm Bureau Federation signed up Scudder, Stevens & Clark to manage a no-load fund for farmers. Labor unions have made similar incursions into the mutual fund field.

And as the mutual fund concept catches the fancy of the mass market, the existing funds can anticipate competition from the big retail chains. Allstate Enterprise Management Co., a wholly owned subsidiary of Allstate Enterprises, itself wholly owned by Sears, Roebuck & Co., offers fund shares to the public at a maximum sales charge of 7%, which declines to a minimum of ¼% as the size of the investment increases.

Still another form of competition—although the mutual funds certainly do not recognize it as such—is that represented by the *conglomerates*—corporations like Litton Industries, the Ogden Corporation, International Telephone & Telegraph, and a number of others, which undertook to bring under one corporate management dozens of companies in totally unrelated fields, usually by stock-swapping or the issuance of convertible securities.

A smooth-talking securities salesman might tell you that by buying stock in a conglomerate with subsidiaries in a dozen or more different fields you could obtain all the diversification you needed. He might make much of the theory that if sales and income were down in one field, there would be an offsetting success in some other field, pointing out, too, that all the subsidiaries benefited from sharing the parent company's dynamic management and expensive equipment like data processing systems.

Unfortunately, the promise of the conglomerates was greater than their performance. In the 1973–1974 recession, the conglomerates, burdened with heavy overhead expense, suffered more than most companies. As a consequence, while the Dow Jones industrial average declined 45%, the stocks of conglomerates experienced a far more precipitous decline, with Litton Industries, for example, plummeting from a high of 120% in 1967 to a low around 3 in 1974, while Ogden Corporation plunged more than 85% from its 1968 high of 52.

However, that's not to say that the conglomerates, once they have put their house in order, may not rise again and retrieve some of their lost popularity among the less sophisticated investors. Indeed, such conglomerates as Litton, Textron, I. T. & T., Teledyne, and Gulf & Western were among the star performers in the 1976 market revival.

All things considered, if you want the protection of diversification on a relatively small investment, if you want somebody else to assume the responsibility of making investments for you at a modest fee, and if you are content to settle for average market performance—or something near it—buy a mutual fund, but be sure it's a good one and be sure it's right for you. Study how well it has succeeded—the performance record is available if you ask—in meeting your objective, be it growth, income, or reasonable safety of capital. There are hundreds and hundreds of different funds, and it can be as difficult to pick the right one for you as it is to select one right stock out of all those listed on the New York Stock Exchange.

Above all things, don't just say yes to the first mutual fund salesman who calls on you.

CHAPTER 30

Why You Should Invest—If You Can

WHY should a man who has extra money invest it in stocks?

Here is the answer to that in one chart and one table.

Chart I (page 288) shows the movement of stock prices from 1925–1975, as measured by Standard & Poor's long-term index for 425 industrial stocks.

The table below shows the average annual yield on the stocks included in Standard & Poor's industrial index back to 1926, which is as far back as this series of statistics goes:

1926	4.86	1939	3.87	1952	5.88	1965	2.94
1927	4.73	1940	5.51	1953	5.86	1966	3.32
1928	3.93	1941	6.62	1954	4.92	1967	3.07
1929	3.61	1942	7.04	1955	3.97	1968	2.91
1930	4.84	1943	4.76	1956	3.95	1969	3.07
1931	6.40	1944	4.69	1957	4.18	1970	3.62
1932	7.74	1945	4.13	1958	3.87	1971	2.94
1933	4.06	1946	3.81	1959	3.11	1972	2.61
1934	3.37	1947	4.90	1960	3.36	1973	2.79
1935	3.52	1948	5.47	1961	2.90	1974	4.13
1936	3.39	1949	6.63	1962	3.32	1975	3.96
1937	4.83	1950	6.69	1963	3.12		
1938	4.96	1951	6.17	1964	2.96		

In a period like 1973–1974, it was hard for investors to be enthusiastic about investing. After all, the Dow Jones industrial average had dropped 45%, and investors had lost more than $300 billion in that slump. But that's a good reason for looking at the stock market in the long historical perspective—and noting, incidentally, that in the past quarter century there have been a half-dozen slumps which seemed just as disastrous at the time they occurred.

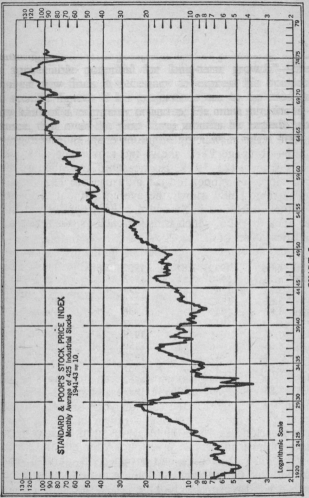

STANDARD & POOR'S STOCK PRICE INDEX
Monthly Average of 425 Industrial Stocks
1941-43 = 10.

Logarithmic Scale

CHART I

The historical record demonstrates the solid fact that the market has always come back and that in the long run common stocks have proved to be good things to own.

But, you might ask, what about that almost steady downtrend in the average return on stocks (table, page 287) over the past twenty-five years? Isn't that a cause for concern?

No, it isn't, because those returns are percentage figures arrived at by dividing dollar dividends by dollar prices for the stocks included in the index. Hence, any decline in the average return could be the result either of an actual decrease in the dollar dividends paid—or an increase in the price of the stocks. The latter explanation is clearly the right one as far as the last two and a half decades are concerned. The average return may have dropped from 6.69% for the year 1950 to 3.96% in 1975, but during this same period, as Chart I shows, per-share prices rose from an average index number of about 20 to over 130, and as a result of that great price appreciation dividends, as a percentage of price, inevitably dropped. But the decline was relative, not absolute.

To illustrate, suppose you had bought a stock at $20 a share in 1950 and received the average dividend of 6.7% on it that year. On this basis, you would have received a dividend of $1.33. If that stock behaved like the average of all others, it would have been selling at about $100 a share at the end of 1975 and yielding a return of 3.96%, which would mean that your actual dollar dividend would have increased to $3.96. Furthermore, it would mean that on your original investment you would be earning a return of 19.8%, since you would be getting a dividend of $3.96 on your $20 original investment.

The return that an investor realizes from a stock is not affected in any way by changes in its price *after* he buys it; it is affected only by a change in the dividend. Thus, if you pay $100 for a stock paying a $5 dividend, you realize 5% on your money, regardless of whether the stock drops to $80 or goes up to $120, as long as the $5 dividend is paid. If the dividend is in-

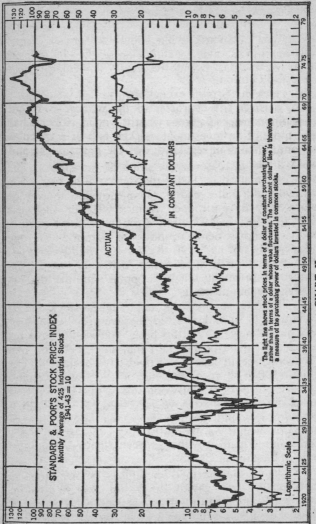

STANDARD & POOR'S STOCK PRICE INDEX
Monthly Average of 425 Industrial Stocks
1941-43 = 10

ACTUAL

IN CONSTANT DOLLARS

The light line shows stock prices in terms of a dollar of constant purchasing power, rather than in terms of a dollar whose value fluctuates. The "constant dollar" line is therefore a measure of the purchasing power of dollars invested in common stocks.

Logarithmic Scale

CHART II

creased to $6, you make 6%, and if it is reduced to $4, you make 4%—regardless of what happens to the price of the stock.

Now let's take another look at the chart. It shows that stock prices have moved generally upward for the past 50 years in a fairly well-defined path. One notable exception is that precipitous drop from the 1929 peak to the 1932 bottom.

Isn't that an alarming exception?

No, it isn't. The character of the market in recent years differs markedly from what it was in 1929. It has been more of an investment market, less of a speculative one. Thanks to regulations of the government and the exchange, there has been little or none of the speculative orgy which produced the big crash. Certainly, from time to time, glamour stocks like data processing or drug stocks have had a big play, but there has been no overextension of credit, no pyramiding, and, most important, little or no manipulation of the market.

Why have people been investing? Why have stock prices been going generally up over the years?

Because American business has grown steadily, and there is every reason to believe it will continue to grow—continue to develop new products, new industries, new markets, and continue to expand all along the line, despite recessions from time to time.

Figures compiled by the U.S. Department of Commerce on our *gross national product*—the total value of all goods and services produced in this country—tell the story of growth better than any others. In 1929, the first year for which such figures were compiled, gross national product was valued at $103 billion. In the Great Depression, it fell to a low of $56 billion in 1933. Since then, growth has been steady—and little short of phenomenal. In 1960 gross national product was valued at $504 billion; by 1965 it had advanced to $685; by the last quarter of 1970 it was moving at the rate of about a trillion dollars a year; and by the end of 1975, it approximated $1.5 trillion—apparently on its way to the two trillion a year level that forecasters have predicted for 1980.

That's one good reason for investing—for owning a

share in American business—but there's a second equally persuasive reason.

Take a look at Chart II (page 290). Something new has been added—a second line showing stock prices in terms of a dollar whose value, or purchasing power, does not fluctuate from year to year. This line is, in effect, a measure of the purchasing power of common stocks, since it shows how much stocks were worth at any given time in terms of a dollar whose value has been adjusted to reflect changes in the *cost of living,* as measured by the Bureau of Labor Statistics.

When the cost of living goes up and the country is in a period of inflation, prices tend to rise. When the dollar declines in value, it obviously takes more dollars to buy the same amount of food, clothing, other goods —virtually everything, including common stocks, because they represent the ownership of companies that produce these goods.

Thus, in periods of inflation, money that is invested in common stocks or other property is generally not as likely to lose its purchasing power as money which is simply set aside in a savings bank or invested in bonds that have a fixed dollar value. No one can argue that common stocks provide a guaranteed protection against inflation. That was all too evident in 1973–1974 when the country experienced for almost the first time in its history simultaneous recession and inflation with business and stock prices both declining, while prices of consumer goods soared. But most times, it is hard to find a better hedge against inflation than common stocks.

Certainly for the average man stocks offer better protection against inflation than real estate, for instance. Real estate prices usually rise, too, in a period of inflation, but it is not as easy to be a good judge of real estate as it is to be a good judge of stock values; the element of risk is much greater. Furthermore, stocks are a liquid asset; they can always be sold, and it is never so easy to dispose of real estate if you suddenly need to raise cash. Finally, with real estate you have to contend with a great many other problems, like taxes, maintenance, zoning changes, and special assessments, whether or not the property produces income for you or simply remains vacant.

For all these reasons—for income, for a chance to see your capital grow, for the protection of its purchasing power—you may decide you want to invest in stocks.

But wait a minute. Maybe you shouldn't. Are you sure that those dollars you plan to put into the stock market are really extra dollars? Remember, there is an inescapable factor of risk in owning stocks, even the best of them. Not only does the market go down from time to time, but even if stocks generally go up, your stocks may go down. That can be a risk worth taking for the man who isn't going to be seriously hurt in case he loses some of those dollars. But it's not a risk that a man should take if he's likely to need those dollars to meet some emergency.

What if there were a serious and expensive illness in the family? Are your savings adequate to meet that situation? What about the other expenses you may have to meet, such as the cost of a new car, house repairs, furniture, college expenses for your children? What about insurance? Have you got enough so that you are sure your family would be able to maintain a decent living standard if you were to die?

If you can answer yes to all these questions, you can and you probably should consider putting your extra dollars into common stocks.

CHAPTER 31

How Good Are Common Stocks?

PROBABLY the most convincing evidence of the value of investing in common stocks is that supplied by several studies measuring the rate of return—dividends plus price appreciation—provided by common stocks listed on the New York Stock Exchange, which were conducted by the Center for Research in Security Prices at the Graduate School of Business of the University of Chicago. The center, under the direction of Professor James H. Lorie and his associate Professor Lawrence Fisher, has been sponsored since its inception by Merrill Lynch, Pierce, Fenner & Smith, and the studies that have been published on rates of return constitute the most definitive measurement of the stock market that has ever been made.

Basically, the question to which the center addressed itself originally in 1958 was this: just how good are common stocks as investments? What average rate of return might an investor expect to realize if he simply selected a stock at random—without any professional guidance or research information—from those listed on the New York Stock Exchange, and what would be his average risk of loss?

Obviously, such a question could be answered only in terms of the historical record, and this the center set about compiling. It took five years and $250,000 to put all the essential data on computer tape because of the high standards of accuracy which were established.

First, the center insisted on going back to January 1926, so that it could not be accused of ignoring the 1929 bull market or the consequent crash. It also insisted on covering all the 1,856 stocks that had been listed at any time since 1926 on the exchange—not just a cross section or sample but all the stocks—good, bad, and indifferent—including those that had been delisted. (By the end of 1975, what with new listings and delistings, this meant a total of 2,603 different stocks.)

Finally, the center wasn't satisfied to work with an annual or semiannual price but insisted on recording the price at each month's end for each listed stock, and since those prices had to be comparable throughout the whole period, it meant that the prices had to be adjusted to take account of every stock dividend, stock split, spinoff, merger, or other change in a company's financial structure. (All told, through 1974 about 50,000 such adjustments had to be made in the price data.) In addition, information on about 150,000 dividend payments was put on the tapes.

The center's file of price and dividend data is unquestionably the most authoritative record that exists, guaranteed to be 99.44% accurate, despite Ivory Soap's prior claim to that purity figure.

Because the compiling and recording took almost five years, the first study on rates of return was not published until 1963, and it told the story of the market only through 1960; but once the data were put on tape and the computer programs written, it has become a comparatively simple matter for the center to keep its study up to date. Now it is possible to tell the rate of return on listed common stocks for any period of time from January, 1926 right up to the present.

The key table from this study is the one reproduced on pages 296–299. A few words of explanation are in order. The table shows the percentage gain or loss that an investor would have realized over any given period of time if he had invested equal amounts of money in each of the Big Board stocks and had reinvested all dividends that he received.

While it does take account of the varying commissions that the investor would have had to pay in acquiring the stocks over the years, it does not take account of the commission he would have had to pay in selling out his holdings at the end of the period. Nor does it take account of the taxes that the investor would

TO	FROM 12//25	12//26	12//27	12//28	12//29	12//30	12//31	12//32	12//33	12//34	12//35	12//36
12/26	0.7											
12/27	15.8	30.0										
12/28	23.6	37.6	44.8									
12/29	8.2	9.9	0.6	−29.2								
12/30	−2.1	−3.4	−12.7	−31.4	−37.7							
12/31	−11.2	−13.3	−21.3	−36.1	−40.9	−48.1						
12/32	−10.8	−12.6	−18.8	−30.0	−32.0	−30.7	−9.7					
12/33	−2.7	−3.2	−7.5	−15.5	−11.9	−1.4	37.1	106.0				
12/34	−1.0	−1.4	−5.0	−11.1	−7.0	2.3	28.3	54.4	15.2			
12/35	2.3	2.1	−0.7	−5.6	−0.6	9.2	33.1	53.4	32.1	50.7		
12/36	4.7	4.8	2.4	−1.6	3.8	13.9	35.6	52.3	37.2	50.6	46.8	
12/37	0.7	0.3	−2.3	−6.1	−2.9	3.0	16.2	23.0	8.1	6.0	−11.7	−46.1
12/38	2.9	2.6	0.5	−2.9	0.8	6.7	18.7	25.0	13.0	12.1	0.6	−16.2
12/39	2.7	2.4	0.4	−2.6	0.8	5.7	15.6	20.3	10.3	8.8	0.0	−11.2
12/40	2.1	1.7	−0.1	−2.9	0.1	4.5	13.0	16.8	8.0	6.2	−1.3	−9.8
12/41	1.5	1.0	−0.7	−3.2	−0.6	3.3	10.8	13.7	5.9	4.1	−2.2	−9.2
12/42	2.2	1.9	0.4	−1.9	0.8	4.6	11.5	14.1	7.2	5.8	0.6	−4.9
12/43	3.5	3.5	2.2	0.1	2.9	6.9	13.7	16.3	10.2	9.5	5.2	0.8
12/44	4.6	4.6	3.5	1.6	4.5	8.5	15.1	17.8	12.3	11.5	8.2	4.5
12/45	6.2	6.4	5.4	3.8	6.9	11.1	17.5	20.3	15.4	15.4	12.3	9.3
12/46	5.4	5.6	4.6	3.1	5.9	9.7	15.5	17.9	13.3	12.9	10.1	7.2
12/47	5.3	5.5	4.5	3.1	5.7	9.2	14.6	16.8	12.4	12.0	9.3	6.7
12/48	5.1	5.1	4.2	2.7	5.1	8.4	13.5	15.4	11.3	10.8	8.2	5.7
12/49	5.7	5.8	4.9	3.6	5.9	9.0	13.8	15.7	11.8	11.4	9.0	6.8
12/50	6.5	6.6	5.8	4.5	6.9	10.2	15.0	16.7	12.9	12.8	10.5	8.5
12/51	6.9	7.1	6.3	5.1	7.4	10.5	15.1	16.7	13.2	13.0	10.9	9.0
12/52	7.0	7.2	6.4	5.2	7.5	10.4	14.8	16.4	13.0	12.9	10.8	9.1
12/53	6.7	6.8	6.1	4.9	7.0	9.7	13.9	15.4	12.2	12.1	10.1	8.4
12/54	8.0	8.2	7.5	6.4	8.6	11.3	15.6	17.1	14.0	14.0	12.1	10.6
12/55	8.4	8.6	8.0	6.9	9.2	11.9	16.1	17.5	14.6	14.6	12.7	11.2
12/56	8.5	8.7	8.1	7.1	9.3	11.9	15.9	17.3	14.5	14.5	12.6	11.2
12/57	7.8	8.0	7.4	6.4	8.4	10.8	14.5	15.7	13.0	13.0	11.2	9.9
12/58	8.9	9.1	8.4	7.5	9.6	12.0	15.7	16.9	14.4	14.4	12.7	11.5
12/59	9.0	9.2	8.5	7.7	9.7	12.2	15.8	16.9	14.5	14.5	12.9	11.7
12/60	8.8	9.0	8.3	7.5	9.4	11.7	15.1	16.2	14.0	14.0	12.4	11.2
12/61	9.4	9.6	9.0	8.1	10.0	12.3	15.6	16.7	14.5	14.6	13.1	11.9
12/62	8.7	8.8	8.2	7.3	9.2	11.3	14.4	15.5	13.3	13.3	11.9	10.8
12/63	9.0	9.1	8.5	7.7	9.5	11.6	14.7	15.7	13.6	13.6	12.2	11.1
12/64	9.1	9.3	8.8	7.9	9.7	11.7	14.7	15.7	13.7	13.7	12.4	11.3
12/65	9.4	9.5	9.0	8.2	10.0	12.1	15.0	16.0	14.0	14.0	12.7	11.7
12/66	8.9	9.1	8.6	7.8	9.5	11.4	14.2	15.0	13.2	13.2	11.9	10.9
12/67	9.6	9.7	9.2	8.5	10.2	12.1	14.9	15.7	13.9	14.0	12.7	11.8
12/68	9.8	10.0	9.5	8.8	10.5	12.3	15.0	15.8	14.1	14.1	12.9	12.0
12/69	9.2	9.4	8.8	8.2	9.7	11.4	13.8	14.7	13.0	13.0	11.9	11.0
12/70	9.0	9.1	8.6	8.0	9.4	11.0	13.4	14.2	12.5	12.5	11.4	10.5
12/71	9.1	9.2	8.7	8.1	9.6	11.1	13.5	14.2	12.6	12.6	11.5	10.7
12/72	9.3	9.4	9.0	8.4	9.9	11.3	13.6	14.3	12.8	12.7	11.7	10.9
12/73	8.7	8.8	8.4	7.8	9.1	10.4	12.6	13.2	11.7	11.7	10.7	9.8
12/74	8.0	8.1	7.7	7.1	8.3	9.5	11.6	12.2	10.7	10.6	9.7	8.9
12/75	8.5	8.6	8.2	7.7	9.0	10.3	12.3	12.9	11.5	11.4	10.5	9.7
	12//25	12//26	12//27	12//28	12//29	12//30	12//31	12//32	12//33	12//34	12//35	12//36

RATES OF RETURN ON INVESTMENT IN COMMON STOCKS
LISTED ON THE NEW YORK STOCK EXCHANGE
WITH REINVESTMENT OF DIVIDENDS
(*Percent per Annum Compounded Annually*)

12/37	12/38	12/39	12/40	12/41	12/42	12/43	12/44	12/45	12/46	12/47	12/48	12/49
30.6												
13.0	-8.1											
6.3	-4.9	-9.9										
2.6	-5.5	-9.0	-9.9									
6.2	0.7	1.0	7.5	30.7								
12.3	9.3	12.0	22.2	46.7	57.0							
15.7	13.7	17.1	26.8	45.5	49.5	38.9						
20.4	19.4	23.7	33.7	51.4	55.6	50.5	60.7					
16.3	15.0	17.8	24.2	34.7	34.6	26.1	20.4	-9.5				
14.7	13.6	15.5	20.3	27.6	26.5	19.1	13.3	-4.2	0.0			
12.7	11.7	13.3	17.0	22.5	20.9	14.3	9.2	-3.4	-0.8	-3.1		
13.3	12.4	13.9	17.3	22.4	21.0	15.3	11.6	2.0	5.7	8.3	19.7	
14.8	14.1	15.6	19.1	23.6	22.6	18.1	15.1	7.9	12.6	16.7	27.2	35.8
14.9	14.2	15.7	18.7	22.8	21.8	17.9	15.4	9.5	13.5	16.5	23.4	25.3
14.6	13.8	15.2	18.0	21.7	20.6	17.0	14.7	9.6	13.0	15.3	19.9	19.8
13.4	12.5	13.8	16.2	19.5	18.3	14.9	12.7	8.0	10.6	12.1	15.2	13.7
15.6	14.9	16.3	18.8	22.1	21.2	18.4	16.5	12.6	15.7	17.8	21.5	21.6
16.0	15.4	16.7	19.0	22.1	21.5	19.0	17.3	13.6	16.4	18.4	21.6	21.9
15.8	15.3	16.4	18.4	21.2	20.6	18.3	16.7	13.5	15.9	17.4	20.0	20.2
14.1	13.4	14.4	16.2	18.6	17.8	15.5	13.9	10.8	12.6	13.7	15.6	15.0
15.7	15.1	16.1	18.0	20.5	19.8	17.6	16.2	13.5	15.5	16.8	18.9	18.8
15.7	15.2	16.2	17.9	20.2	19.5	17.4	16.1	13.6	15.5	16.8	18.8	18.8
14.9	14.3	15.2	16.8	19.0	18.2	16.1	14.9	12.5	14.2	15.4	17.0	16.7
15.6	15.1	16.0	17.6	19.6	18.9	16.9	15.8	13.5	15.2	16.3	17.8	17.6
14.2	13.6	14.4	15.8	17.6	16.9	14.9	13.8	11.6	13.0	13.9	15.1	14.7
14.4	13.9	14.7	16.0	17.7	17.0	15.2	14.2	12.0	13.5	14.2	15.4	15.1
14.5	14.1	14.8	16.1	17.7	17.1	15.4	14.4	12.4	13.7	14.4	15.6	15.3
14.8	14.4	15.1	16.3	17.9	17.4	15.7	14.8	12.9	14.4	15.1	16.2	16.0
13.9	13.4	14.1	15.2	16.7	16.2	14.6	13.7	11.8	13.1	13.8	14.7	14.5
14.8	14.4	15.0	16.1	17.6	17.2	15.6	14.7	12.9	14.2	14.9	15.9	15.7
14.9	14.5	15.1	16.3	17.7	17.3	15.8	14.9	13.2	14.5	15.2	16.2	16.0
13.7	13.3	13.8	14.8	16.1	15.6	14.1	13.3	11.7	12.7	13.3	14.2	13.9
13.1	12.9	13.2	14.2	15.3	14.8	13.3	12.6	11.0	12.0	12.5	13.2	13.0
13.3	13.0	13.3	14.2	15.4	14.8	13.5	12.7	11.2	12.2	12.7	13.5	13.2
13.3	12.9	13.3	14.2	15.3	14.8	13.5	12.8	11.4	12.4	12.8	13.6	13.3
12.1	11.7	12.1	12.9	13.9	13.3	12.1	11.5	10.1	11.0	11.3	11.9	11.7
11.1	10.8	11.0	11.8	12.6	12.1	10.8	10.2	8.9	9.6	9.8	10.4	10.0
11.9	11.7	11.8	12.6	13.5	13.0	11.8	11.2	9.8	10.6	10.8	11.4	11.2

TO	FROM 12//50	12//51	12//52	12//53	12//54	12//55	12//56	12//57	12//58	12//59	12//60	12//61
12/51	14.8											
12/52	12.4	8.9										
12/53	7.6	3.6	-3.1									
12/54	17.9	18.6	22.8	55.1								
12/55	18.6	19.3	22.5	37.9	20.1							
12/56	17.1	17.2	18.9	27.2	13.9	6.6						
12/57	12.2	11.4	11.5	15.0	3.9	-3.6	-13.6					
12/58	16.7	16.7	17.8	22.3	14.9	13.1	16.8	57.9				
12/59	16.8	16.8	17.8	21.5	15.4	14.0	17.1	36.0	14.4			
12/60	15.0	15.0	15.6	18.1	12.8	11.2	12.7	21.9	6.4	-1.9		
12/61	16.2	16.2	16.9	19.3	14.9	14.1	15.9	23.7	13.7	12.9	27.5	
12/62	13.2	13.0	13.2	14.9	10.8	9.5	10.3	15.2	6.4	3.8	5.9	-13.4
12/63	13.7	13.4	13.7	15.3	11.6	10.5	11.4	15.8	8.8	7.4	10.4	2.0
12/64	13.9	13.8	14.1	15.7	12.3	11.3	12.2	16.3	10.5	9.7	12.8	7.7
12/65	14.6	14.6	14.9	16.6	13.5	12.6	13.5	17.7	12.7	12.5	15.9	12.9
12/66	13.2	12.9	13.2	14.6	11.6	10.7	11.3	14.8	10.2	9.6	12.0	9.0
12/67	14.5	14.4	14.8	16.4	13.7	12.8	13.6	17.2	13.3	13.3	16.0	14.1
12/68	14.9	14.9	15.3	15.8	14.3	13.7	14.5	17.9	14.4	14.6	17.3	15.7
12/69	12.8	12.7	13.0	14.1	11.6	10.9	11.5	14.0	10.7	10.4	12.0	10.1
12/70	12.0	11.8	11.9	13.0	10.7	10.0	10.3	12.5	9.4	9.0	10.2	8.2
12/71	12.2	12.1	12.3	13.3	11.1	10.5	10.9	12.9	10.1	9.8	11.0	9.3
12/72	12.4	12.2	12.4	13.3	11.3	10.6	11.0	13.0	10.3	10.1	11.2	9.7
12/73	10.6	10.4	10.5	11.3	9.3	8.5	8.7	10.3	7.7	7.4	8.2	6.7
12/74	9.0	8.7	8.7	9.4	7.4	6.6	6.7	7.9	5.4	5.0	5.6	4.0
12/75	10.2	10.0	10.1	10.8	8.9	8.3	8.4	9.8	7.5	7.2	7.9	6.5
	12//50	12//51	12//52	12//53	12//54	12//55	12//56	12//57	12//58	12//59	12//60	12//61

RATES OF RETURN ON INVESTMENT IN COMMON STOCKS
LISTED ON THE NEW YORK STOCK EXCHANGE
WITH REINVESTMENT OF DIVIDENDS
(Percent per Annum Compounded Annually)

12/62	12/63	12/64	12/65	12/66	12/67	12/68	12/69	12/70	12/71	12/72	12/73	12/74
17.6												
18.6	16.6											
22.7	23.7	28.5										
14.9	13.0	10.1	-8.2									
20.7	21.3	22.4	17.6	51.1								
21.3	22.0	23.1	20.9	40.1	28.5							
13.9	13.3	12.7	9.0	15.8	1.5	-20.1						
11.2	10.2	9.0	5.7	10.1	-0.2	-12.0	-4.5					
12.1	11.3	10.4	7.6	11.7	4.1	-2.8	6.6	16.8				
12.3	11.5	10.8	8.3	11.7	5.6	0.8	7.9	13.3	6.6			
8.6	7.6	6.3	3.7	5.6	0.3	-4.3	-0.6	-1.2	-9.9	-28.1		
5.4	4.2	2.8	0.2	1.3	-3.6	-7.9	-5.6	-7.4	-14.6	-26.0	-27.3	
8.1	7.2	6.2	4.1	5.6	1.4	-1.7	1.5	1.7	-2.1	-6.5	6.3	53.7

have paid on dividends as received or on any ultimate capital gain he might have realized. In other words, this is the story of how a tax-exempt individual would have made out in the market over the years.

The resultant figures can be compared directly to the compound interest rates paid by banks on savings in the various periods and to the published yields on most other kinds of investment, since these result figures never take account of taxes either.

It is not difficult to read the table. If you want to see how a hypothetical investor would have made out over any given period, select any starting year you like from the columns labeled FROM and read down the column till you reach the figure for whatever terminal year you select in the column at the left labeled TO. That figure, expressed as a compound interest return, shows the rate of return that an investor would have realized had he bought all the stocks on the Big Board at the beginning date and reinvested all his dividends until the terminal date. Since his investment covered *all* the listed stocks, the rate of return can be taken to represent the average of what he might have realized on any one stock. On some stocks, the rate of return might have been infinitely higher, while on others there would have been a 100% loss.

Actually, the center computed results in dollars, not in percents, and these results show how the invested dollar would have increased or decreased (by thousandths of one cent) during each of the 1,275 time periods shown in the table. The dollar difference between any starting date and any terminal date is simply expressed here in terms of its compounded interest equivalent, either minus or plus.

Probably the most significant figure in the table is that 8.5% at the bottom of the first column. That figure means that an investment of an equal amount of dollars in each of all the Big Board stocks on December 31, 1925, would by December 31, 1975, with the reinvestment of dividends, have yielded a return equal to 8.5% interest per annum compounded annually. That in turn means that $1.00 invested in December 1925 would have grown to $61.84 over that half century. Of course, as the table also shows, had such an investment been terminated at the end of 1972, when the market was near its peak before the collapse of 1973–1974, the return would have equaled 9.3% compounded interest; at this rate an invested dollar would have grown to $66.85 by the end of 1972.

Other significant findings, as demonstrated by the table, are these:

(1) In all the 1,275 year-to-year time periods, January 1926 to December 1975, there are only 91 periods with negative rates of return—in other words, losses; in the other 1,184 time periods you would have had a profit. The longest span of years showing losses is the fourteen-year period from 1928 to 1942. The only other periods when you would have had to hold on for as long as six years in order to show a profit were the periods from 1929 through 1935 and from 1936 through 1942. Because of the market declines of 1968–1969 and 1973–1974, you would have been able to show a profit in only 25 of the 45 year-to-year time periods from 1966 through 1975.

(2) The longest period of time in which the rate of return was less than 5% was 1928 through 1950. If you ignore the 1929–1932 crash, the longest period of time in which the return was less than 5% was 1936 through 1944.

(3) In the last 25 years, there has been only one period (1968–1975) of more than three consecutive years in which the rate of return was consistently less than 5%. Furthermore, in this 25-year span there has never been a 10-year period in which you could not at some point have realized a return of at least 10%.

(4) If you had bought in 1932, there was never a year in which you would not have realized a profit of at least 10%—usually much more—until 1974.

The Lorie-Fisher study also reports the results that would have been obtained if dividends had simply been accumulated and not reinvested and if dividends were completely ignored. Obviously, the rates of return were considerably lower in both cases.

A second study conducted at the Center for Research in Security Prices by Professor Fisher answers the questions of how often and how much an investor might have gained or lost on each of the stocks listed on the exchange from 1926 to 1960. While this study has not been updated, there is no reason to believe results would be materially different.

To arrive at its conclusions, Professor Fisher computed results for every possible combination of month-end purchase and sales dates for every stock throughout the 35-year period from January 1926 to December 1960. For any one stock, this would have represented 87,900 monthly combinations, and for all exchange stocks it meant tabulating results on more than 56 million such possible transactions.

Here is the key finding of this study: if one had picked a stock *at random* from the Big Board list, if he had then picked a purchase date *at random* between January 1926 and December 1960, and if he had picked *at random* any later sales date within those some 35 years, he would have made money 78% of the time, and the median return, assuming reinvestment of all dividends and payment of brokerage commissions on purchase and sale, would have been 9.8% per annum compounded annually. At that rate of interest, money doubles in about seven years, and the study showed that the investor would have had a better than 50-50 chance of doing exactly that—doubling his money—with purely random selection. His risk of losing as much as 20% a year on his investment was only one in thirteen whereas his expectation of making as much as 20% per annum compounded annually was one in five.

The study demonstrated two other points of vital significance to any investor:

(1) If the investor had picked three or four stocks at random instead of just one, the risk of loss would have been considerably reduced and the probability of a larger profit considerably improved.
(2) If the investor had not been forced to sell during a period of economic recession—if he had been able

to hold on for a year or two—his chance of making a profit and the amount of profit would have both been significantly increased.

The value of long-term investing, the value of being able to hold on through a period of weakness in the market, is convincingly demonstrated by the table on pages 304–305. It may look complicated, but it's well worth five minutes of study.

The table shows by economic periods from 1926 through 1960 how you would have made out if you had bought a stock at random from those traded on the New York Stock Exchange, reinvested your dividends, and sold that stock in the same period or in any later period. The boldface decimal figures show you what percentage of the time you would have made money—thus, .46 means you would have made money 46% of the time—and the lightface italic figures on each line immediately below show you the median rate of return (percent per year compounded annually) you might have expected to realize. The periods themselves are all of different lengths, but each one corresponds to a recognized upswing or downswing in business as defined by the National Bureau of Economic Research. The U identifies an upswing, and the D a downswing. The periods listed vertically are for purchases; those listed horizontally are for sales.

Here's how to read the table: let's assume that you made your random purchase in the first period be-between January 1926 and September 1926 and then sold out in that same period. Your chance of making a profit would have been only 46%, and your average profit or loss would have been minus 4.2%. However, if you had made your purchase in that first period and did not sell until the last period, between May and December 1960 (the last figure in the first line of the table), your chance of making a profit would have been 90%, and your median profit would have been equal to 7.3% compounded interest for 35 years.

To see how the table proves the value of long-term investing, look at the boldface figures diagonally down

PROFIT PROBABILITIES ON COMMON STOCKS LISTED ON THE NEW YORK STOCK EXCHANGE, 1926–1960

Sale Period

Purchase Period		Jan. 26 Sept. 26 U	Oct. 26 Oct. 27 D	Nov. 27 July 29 U	Aug. 29 Feb. 33 D	Mar. 33 Apr. 37 U	May 37 May 38 D	June 38 Jan. 45 U
Jan. 26–Sept. 26	U	.46 −4.2%	.60 8.3%	.77 18.2%	.37 −8.0%	.38 −4.6%	.44 −1.9%	.48 −0.5%
Oct. 26–Oct. 27	D		10.0%	.59 21.0%	.32 −11.9%	.33 −6.7%	.40 −3.0%	.45 −1.5%
Nov. 27–July 29	U		.58	.75 10.0%	.15 −29.7%	.21 −13.0%	.27 −7.4%	.35 −1.0%
Aug. 29–Feb. 33	D				.13 −45.6%	.56 4.3%	.59 3.9%	.62 3.9%
Mar. 33–Apr. 37	U					.69 21.0%	.49 −0.8%	.55 1.7%
May 37–May 38	D						.13 −59.6%	.55 2.3%
June 38–Jan. 45	U							.66 9.1%
Feb. 45–Sept. 45	D							
Oct. 45–Oct. 48	U							
Nov. 48–Sept. 49	D							
Oct. 49–June 53	U							
July 53–July 54	D							
Aug. 54–June 57	U							
July 57–Mar. 58	D							
Apr. 58–Apr. 60	U							
May 60–Dec. 60	D							

Feb. 45 Sept. 45	Oct. 45 Oct. 48	Nov. 48 Sept. 49	Oct. 49 June 53	July 53 July 54	Aug. 54 June 57	July 57 Mar. 58	Apr. 58 Apr. 60	May 60 Dec. 60
D	U	D	U	D	U	D	U	D
.72 4.1%	.77 4.7%	.71 3.9%	.82 5.4%	.84 5.8%	.83 7.0%	.89 6.6%	.91 7.5%	.90 7.3%
.70 3.7%	.75 4.4%	.69 3.5%	.79 5.1%	.82 5.4%	.87 6.7%	.88 6.3%	.91 7.2%	.90 7.1%
.62 1.9%	.67 2.8%	.62 2.1%	.73 3.9%	.77 4.3%	.84 5.7%	.85 5.3%	.90 6.3%	.89 6.2%
.84 8.6%	.86 8.9%	.83 7.3%	.89 8.8%	.90 8.8%	.94 10.0%	.93 9.4%	.95 10.3%	.95 10.0%
.90 9.0%	.92 9.4%	.86 6.4%	.93 9.7%	.94 9.4%	.96 10.9%	.95 10.0%	.97 11.0%	.96 10.6%
.93 11.6%	.95 11.4%	.90 8.5%	.95 10.7%	.96 10.5%	.98 12.0%	.97 10.9%	.98 11.9%	.98 11.4%
.98 24.0%	.97 18.6%	.92 11.5%	.97 14.1%	.97 13.1%	.99 14.9%	.98 13.1%	.99 14.1%	.99 13.4%
.65 16.6%	.74 11.1%	.60 2.8%	.83 9.4%	.85 9.5%	.93 12.3%	.92 10.7%	.95 12.2%	.94 11.6%
	.38 −7.0%	.36 −5.2%	.78 9.1%	.83 9.3%	.92 12.8%	.90 10.7%	.95 12.4%	.94 11.5%
		.48 −1.8%	.93 21.7%	.92 15.1%	.96 18.2%	.94 14.3%	.98 15.9%	.96 14.4%
			.73 11.9%	.68 7.3%	.91 15.8%	.88 11.4%	.95 14.0%	.92 12.5%
				.70 18.8%	.94 24.8%	.88 12.3%	.95 15.6%	.93 13.2%
					.64 7.6%	.48 −0.9%	.79 10.5%	.77 8.6%
						.37 −17.3%	.88 25.6%	.82 13.9%
							.64 11.8%	.50 0.2%
								.40 −11.0%

the table from upper left to lower right. These figures show your average chance of making money if you had bought and sold within the same time period. Now contrast the irregularity of these figures with the bold-face ones in the last column to the right, reading straight down from top to bottom. These show your expectation of profit if you had held your stock and not sold it until the last period covered by this study. Down to 1954, all but one are over 90%.

The table on page 307 shows how the figures look when set down right together.

Certainly these figures demonstrate emphatically the value of long-term investing.

None of these studies guarantees anything about future investment success, but if you are willing to assume that the past is any kind of a guide to the future, their meaning is clear and unmistakable.

One of the most recent studies conducted by the center throws significant light on the question of how large a portfolio has to be in order to achieve essentially the same rates of return as an investor would get if he owned all the stocks on the New York Stock Exchange. The study calculated results for portfolios, selected at random, that consisted of 2, 8, 16, 32, and 128 stocks and that were held for each of the 40 single years from 1926 to 1965, for the eight 5-year periods, four 10-year periods, and two 20-year periods. The study shows that with 8 stocks in the portfolio you would have achieved between 89% and 92% of what the market as a whole did, and with 16 stocks performance was raised to a range of 94% to 96%. At 128, the figure was a straight 99% for all time periods. One inference that might be drawn from this study is that if you think you can pick stocks that will perform better than an equal number picked purely at random you have pretty good assurance of beating the performance record of the stock market as a whole.

Since these studies cover all the stocks listed on the New York Stock Exchange, the results they show are the results you might have expected on the average to achieve with the random selection of any one stock, and for this reason they exemplify what is called the

PROFIT PROBABILITIES ON COMMON STOCK

Buy and sell in same period			Buy and hold till last period	
Period	Chance of Profit	Purchase Period	Sale Period	Chance of Profit
Jan. '26–Sept. '26	46%	Jan. '26–Sept. '26	to May '60–Dec. '60	90%
Oct. '26–Oct. '27	58%	Oct. '26–Oct. '27	to May '60–Dec. '60	90%
Nov. '27–July '29	59%	Nov. '26–July '29	to May '60–Dec. '60	89%
Aug. '29–Feb. '33	13%	Aug. '29–Feb. '33	to May '60–Dec. '60	95%
Mar. '33–Apr. '37	69%	Mar. '33–Apr. '37	to May '60–Dec. '60	96%
May '37–May '38	13%	May '37–May '38	to May '60–Dec. '60	98%
June '38–Jan. '45	66%	June '38–Jan. '45	to May '60–Dec. '60	99%
Feb. '45–Sept. '45	65%	Feb. '45–Sept. '45	to May '60–Dec. '60	94%
Oct. '45–Oct. 48	38%	Oct. '45–Oct. 48	to May '60–Dec. '60	94%
Nov. '48–Sept. '49	48%	Nov. '48–Sept. '49	to May '60–Dec. '60	96%
Oct. '49–June '53	73%	Oct. '49–June '53	to May '60–Dec. '60	92%
July '53–July '54	70%	July '53–July '54	to May '60–Dec. '60	93%
Aug. '54–June '57	64%	Aug. '54–June '57	to May '60–Dec. '60	77%
July '57–Mar. '58	37%	July '57–Mar. '58	to May '60–Dec. '60	82%
Apr, '58–Apr. '60	64%	Apr. '58–Apr. '60	to May '60–Dec. '60	50%
May '60–Dec. '60	40%	May '60–Dec. '60	to same	40%

random walk hypothesis. They have been accepted today in financial and academic circles as establishing the
standard yardsticks against which anyone who has a
technical theory of his own must measure performance
if he wants to prove that he is better than average.

The entry of scholars into the field of stock market
research may not guarantee that someday the touch-
stone to investment success will be found, but it should
go a long way toward disabusing the public of its misplaced confidence in those who regularly advertise its
easy availability in the financial pages of our newspapers.

In this connection, the following observations of
Professor Lorie are highly pertinent:

> Many people have been beguiled by the possibility of
> buying wealth, believing that it is possible to buy infor-
> mation or formulas which will permit extraordinary high
> rates of return on capital. As evidence for my statement,
> one need only look at any issue of the numerous periodi-
> cals dealing with the stock market; they are thickly
> strewn with offers to sell for a few dollars the secret of
> getting rich. It should be clear that one cannot buy
> wealth for a few dollars, but this is not the same as
> saying that research on the stock market is without value
> or that it cannot provide the basis for the more prudent
> management of funds.
>
> For many years, it was probably true that formal and
> quantitative research was not very useful either because
> of its lack of comprehensiveness or its lack of rigor. It
> was very difficult to do comprehensive financial research
> before the availability of high-speed computers. Rigor
> was frequently or even typically lacking because research
> was usually the product of persons familiar with the
> financial markets under investigation but not the canons
> of scientific inquiry. . . .
>
> As an example of the lack of rigor which formerly
> characterized much research, I cite the Dow Theory of
> stock price movements. This theory is based on crude
> measurements, and in its typical formulation is so am-
> biguous as to require interpreters, and they often dis-
> agree.
>
> It is clear that much of the work done so far [at the
> center] has had the effect of discrediting beliefs—and

even some relatively sophisticated ones—about the behavior of security prices. . . .

For the businessman and investor, it is true that an awareness of ignorance is better than an erroneous belief, if only because it tends to eliminate buying the services of charlatans and attending to the insignificant.

CHAPTER 32

How You Should Invest—If You Can

THE stock you'd like to buy, of course, is the one that just doesn't exist. You'd like a stock that is completely safe, one that pays a liberal dividend, and one that's bound to go up.

There are a lot of good stocks that will probably satisfy you on any one of these counts, but none that will accomplish all three objectives.

If you want safety in a stock, you'll have to give up the hope that it will increase sensationally in value.

If you'd like to see your money grow, you have to be prepared to take a considerably greater measure of risk.

Sometimes it's possible to find either a fairly safe stock or one that seems likely to appreciate in price that will also yield you a better-than-average dividend. But even here, as a general rule, you can't have your cake and eat it too. If you get a liberal dividend, it will probably be at the expense of one of the other two factors.

Hence, the first step in solving your investment problem is to decide on the one objective you most want to attain by your investments. Is it safety of capital? Or liberal dividends? Or price appreciation?

When you start thinking about stocks that might best match any of these objectives, you should first take a look at various industries and their future prospects. Remember, the carriage industry was a thriving business at the turn of the century.

To see how these various factors might influence your own investment selections, consider how seven different people in widely varying circumstances might approach their investment problem.

Mr. Adams is twenty-four years old, unmarried, and, as far as he can see, likely to pursue his course of single blessedness for some time to come. Having received his college degree, he now has a trainee's job as a chemist with a large food-manufacturing company. His income is $15,000 a year, and thanks to the fact that he still lives with his parents, he can save at the rate of $3,500 a year. With a $10,000 ordinary life insurance policy and a $25,000 group policy issued by his company, he has made a start toward building an estate for himself.

With the savings which he accumulated while he was in the army, he now has about $6,000, very little of which has to be earmarked for emergencies as long as his responsibilities are as light as they are. Then too, if he really got in a serious jam, he knows he could count on his folks to help him out.

He wants to see his capital grow, and so he wants to invest in stocks that have good growth possibilities, even though such stocks may yield only a scant return in dividends now.

Such a young man can afford to take a considerable measure of risk, but before he starts eyeing some of the more speculative stocks, he probably ought to put out an anchor to windward. Marriage has a way of creeping up on a man when he least expects it.

He can probably afford to invest $5,000 of his nest egg, and of this at least $1,000 ought to go into a savings account or Series E government savings bonds so that he can have funds of known amount instantly available to him if he should need them. Another $2,000 might be divided between two solid common stocks—stocks that might be described as defensive in character because they have weathered many an economic storm in the past with comparatively little loss in value and with an unbroken record of dividend payments.

One of these might be a public utility like Pacific Gas & Electric or Tampa Electric, utilities that stand to benefit from the rapid growth of the areas they serve. And the other one might be a stock like General Electric. Such a stock may fluctuate a little more when business expands or retracts, but it is still essentially stable because the company makes so many different products for so many different markets.

Mr. Adams might then very properly put his remaining $2,000 into stocks of a more speculative nature—stocks with good growth possibilities. Maybe one of the drug stocks that seem likely to benefit from the Medicare program available to the increased number of older people in our population. Maybe something in computers or electronics. But probably first of all a chemical stock—a field in which he should know firsthand something about new and promising developments.

Whatever he buys for long-term growth, it may pay him to comb the list for some "sleepers" rather than simply to fall for some of the well-known glamour stocks that usually sell at very high price-earnings multiples. There are many good solid companies with growth records and further growth potential that can match the glamour stocks, but that are available at lower price-earnings ratios. Finding these overlooked stocks can be worth a good deal of study and effort. Don't forget that most of today's glamour stocks were once in the overlooked category themselves.

As for his future savings—that $3,000 he expects to accumulate each year—that money too can go largely into growth stocks as long as his present situation remains unchanged. But he probably ought to start a systematic investment plan with his broker, or he won't have those funds for investment.

Mr. Adams can accomplish that in one of two ways. He can open a Monthly Investment Plan account, or invest in a similar accumulation plan, such as many large banks and most big brokerage firms have available, and apply his monthly savings toward the regular purchase of some stock. Or he can save his money, and when a sufficient sum has accumulated, he can buy additional shares on an odd-lot basis.

Consider now the case of Ms. Baxter, a capable young woman of thirty. As an executive secretary in a large company, where she has worked for ten years, she now makes $275 a week, about as much as Mr. Adams. She lives alone in a small studio apartment, responsible only to herself. She has no family to worry about, and she doesn't expect her mother and father, who live in a little town out West, ever to have to worry about her. She stands on her own feet.

A thrifty person, she has managed over the years to put a little away every month. Now and again she has supplemented these savings with a special bonus check. Currently, she finds she is able to bank about $125 a month out of her salary. All told, she has about $4,000, a large part of it in E bonds, which yield 5%.

Now Ms. Baxter has decided she wants to invest in stocks. Why? Because every time she cashes a bond, the $100 she gets for it buys less than it did the last time—usually not even as much as she could have bought a few years ago with the $75 she put into the bond. She wants to put her money into some investment where its purchasing power will be better protected and where she'll still get a good return on her money. And if she's lucky, maybe she'll make a profit on her stocks—a big enough profit so that in five years she will be able to take that trip to Europe which she has always promised herself.

But maybe stocks will go down, her stocks included. That's a risk she has to take, and fortunately it's one she can afford to take. If stocks drop, she can probably wait for them to come back without any serious jeopardy, because her job offers her a good measure of security. Quite apart from her own medical hospital insurance, she knows the firm will help her over any rough spots. And as for protection in her old age—well, the firm has an excellent pension program, and that plus Social Security should take care of her quite handily.

What kind of stocks should Ms. Baxter buy?

Obviously, she wants to be pretty conservative in her selections, but she probably doesn't have to make safety her sole objective. She can afford to take what's called a "businessman's risk," and she can look for stocks that pay relatively liberal dividends.

Ms. Baxter should put her money into three or four

different stocks, each of them a blue chip, each a leader
in its own industry—stocks like Sears, Roebuck &
Company, Eastman Kodak, Exxon, International Paper, plus one good utility.

Alternately, to benefit from more diversified holdings, she might put her money into one of the big mutual funds that have growth as their objective—funds
like Massachusetts Investors Growth Stock Fund, Put-
nam Growth Fund, or Fidelity Capital Fund. None of
these funds fared very well in 1974, but neither did the
entire mutual fund industry—nor the stock market.
Ms. Baxter's primary interest is in growth; she should
be much more interested in their longer range prospects.

To make these investments she will have to sell
$3,000 of her E bonds. She should sell the most re-
cent ones and keep $500 worth of the oldest ones, be-
cause as those bonds get closer to their maturity dates
they pay a proportionately higher rate of interest.

As for the $125 a month she is able to save, Ms.
Baxter might prudently keep half as an emergency fund
until it exceeded $1,000. With the other $62.50 a
month she too might open a Monthly Investment Plan,
or some other accumulation plan account. As a matter
of fact, she might even open two or three such accounts, putting her $62.50 into one stock one month
and into another stock a second month on a regular,
rotating basis.

Mr. and Mrs. Chandler face quite a different problem, despite the fact that Mr. Chandler's income as a
skilled toolmaker in an auto parts manufacturing plant
is about $25,000 a year. To begin with, they live on a
very modest scale in a small Ohio town. Still in their
thirties, they have been able to raise two children, now
eight and ten, buy their own home, and still save a
little bit.

They have only about $2,000 in their bank account,
but from now on that's going to grow fast. Mr. Chandler was made foreman just last month, and that means
$75 a week more in the pay envelope. Furthermore,
in just a couple of months the mortgage will be paid

off, and they will have another $100 a month free and clear.

What it all adds up to is that they've got $2,000 now, and they figure on having $2,500 to $3,000 a year to invest from now on.

What about protection for his family? Mr. Chandler has a $20,000 insurance policy, and he considers that plenty in view of the benefit program which his union sponsors for all members.

He has become sold on stocks; he wants to go ahead right now, buying stocks in order to build a little estate and finance college education for his children.

That's a program that makes sense, provided he handles it right. He hasn't a lot of money to put into the market, and to start with, he wants to be sure that money is well protected. What if one of his children has to be hospitalized for a long time?

Where should he start? His local utility—the Ohio Edison Company—might be as good as any. The dividends will help pay his electric bill. That's an idea that has real appeal for Mr. and Mrs. Chandler.

After that, he might buy ten shares of a natural gas company, a stock that offers assurance of a fairly stable price, plus some possibilities of growth as natural gas consumption continues to grow.

His future investments for some time might be of much the same type—fairly stable stocks but ones that nevertheless offer some prospect of growth over the long pull; nothing as spectacular as computers or electronics, which market analysts might call "aggressive-growth situations," but perhaps something like American Can Company, which stands to grow as our population and food consumption increase, or Federated Department Stores, or General Foods.

Mr. and Mrs. Davenport are much better off financially, but from an investment point of view they're not as well off as the Chandlers. As one of the younger officers in a big advertising agency, Mr. Davenport makes $40,000 a year, but his scale of living is such that after taxes, mortgage payments on his $100,000 house, and premiums on a $50,000 life insurance policy, there's not much left over at the end of the year—nothing more than he might need to pay an unexpected doctor's bill. His equity in the house— the unmortgaged part that he owns—and the cash value of his life insurance policy represents about all his savings.

But Mr. Davenport has struck it rich. He just got a special $20,000 bonus, because he brought a new account into the agency last year. And Mr. Davenport knows exactly what he's going to do with that $20,000. He's going to buy common stocks in two companies he has just read about. One of them is a new small airline serving a growing resort area, and the other is a company that Mr. Davenport believes is going to lick the problem of desalting sea water economically.

When Mr. Davenport announces what he expects to do with his bonus, Mrs. Davenport puts her foot down. It sounds altogether too speculative for her. That money, she contends, should be set safely aside to provide a college education for their two children.

How should Mr. and Mrs. Davenport solve their problem?

Probably $5,000 of their $20,000 ought to go into government bonds in case the family meets a real emergency. As for the balance, the stock of a good growth mutual fund or a closed-end investment trust like Lehmen Corporation or Tri-Continental Corporation might represent a happy compromise between Mrs. Davenport's conservatism and Mr. Davenport's "all-or-nothing" impulse.

Ordinarily it would not be prudent for a man to put all his investment funds in a single security, but a mutual fund or an investment trust is an obvious exception because of its diversified holdings. Furthermore, shares in a closed-end trust can be bought on the exchange without any loading charge and are frequently available at a substantial discount—that is, at a price below net asset value per share.

Then too, Mr. Davenport is still only in his early forties and looks like a comer—the kind of a man who will get a number of bonuses and salary increases. As time goes by, he will probably be buying other stocks, and he might just as well begin buying in good-sized units.

Mr. Edwards is a Nebraska wheat farmer. For fifteen years life has been good to him. He has had good crops and has got good prices for them. He is completely clear of debt on his farm and on his equipment, and all of it is in excellent condition. Insurance is no worry to him, because his boys, both of them in college now, could take over the farm and make a good living out of it if anything should happen to him.

He has $19,000 in extra capital, over and above necessary reserves for upkeep of the farm, and he's beginning to wonder if he's doing the best he can with it. His older son started him thinking about that the last time he was home from college. Mr. Edwards has $4,000 in savings bonds, $4,000 in a building and loan association, $8,000 in a savings account, and about $3,000 in his checking account.

Obviously, he has far more cash than he needs. One thousand dollars in his savings account and another thousand in his checking account should suffice, especially since that $4,000 worth of E bonds is really the equivalent of cash and stands as an adequate backlog in case he has bad luck with his crops this year or has to make unexpected repairs to buildings or equipment.

Hence, he could prudently put $9,000 cash into securities, and he probably ought to sell his $4,000 worth of building and loan shares and invest that money in stocks too—a total of $13,000. The building and loan shares provide a good yield, but he can get an attractive return, plus growth potential, by investing that money in common stocks. Furthermore, his building and loan shares really represent an investment in real estate, and since his principal asset, the farm, is also real estate, it would seem wise for him to diversify his investments.

Here is a man who can really afford to take a fair measure of risk with his money for the sake of getting a better-than-average growth potential, because he already has a substantial measure of protection—far more than most people have. In fact, he can afford to be a bit speculative in his selections.

First, it would be natural for him to invest in a good farm-machinery stock—something like Deere & Company—but he ought not to put too large a share of his $13,000 into such a stock, because if farmers suffer a reverse in their fortunes as they sometimes do, so generally do the machinery manufacturers.

He might also properly invest in a company like General Mills that processes the grain he raises.

But he might be better advised to put his money in the stocks of companies that have no relationship to his own business of farming—perhaps natural resource stocks like the Weyerhaeuser Company, or American Natural Gas, or an automobile company like Ford, or chemical stocks like Union Carbide, Dow, or Monsanto. Other stocks that might suit his situation would be stocks like Minnesota Mining & Manufacturing, or Procter & Gamble, or Eastman Kodak, because all these companies operate in fields that show great future promise.

Mr. and Mrs. Frank are a retired couple, both over sixty-five. Social Security and small benefits accruing from a company pension plan are sufficient to provide an income of about $400 a month. Their only other assets consist of a home, which they own free and clear in a small town in Kansas where taxes and living costs are a lot lower than in urban centers and where they can have a good-sized garden plot that helps reduce food costs. They have $85,000 in savings, most of it realized on annuities and life insurance policies in which Mr. Frank thriftily invested through the years.

On the other hand, if their assets are limited, so are their liabilities. Their two children are both married, and their futures are as secure as those of any people with modest incomes and frugal habits can be.

The natural impulse of Mr. and Mrs. Frank is to conserve what they have—to leave their money in the savings bank or invest it in E bonds. But even with a return of 6% on their money, their income from all sources would amount to only $9,900 a year, or a little more than $190 a week. And in a time of rising prices and increased taxes, $190 a week allows little latitude for luxuries—nothing at all for an occasional trip to visit their children and grandchildren.

Without any appreciable sacrifice of safety, Mr. and Mrs. Frank ought to consider investing at least part of their money—perhaps $25,000—in corporate bonds, especially in a period of tight money such as in 1973–1974 when high-rated bonds could be bought at prices that would yield 9% or 10% on their money.

With the balance of their savings they could afford to take some measure of risk. Two or three good growth mutual funds might seem like a prudent investment for them, but it wouldn't be wholly out of order for them to consider something even more speculative, such as a half-dozen cyclical stocks. Since these are stocks in industries like steel, automobiles, chemicals, paper, metals, and petroleum that usually follow the business cycle pretty closely, they can often be bought at attractive prices in periods when business slows down, such as in 1974.

During a business decline, dividends might be reduced, and that could make things a little hard for them. But what if they did have to sell $1,500 or $2,500 of stock in a bad year in order to make ends meet? At their age they can afford to dip into capital if they have to without putting their lives in peril. And consider the rewards they might reap. Dividends of 8%, 10%, or even 12% were not too remarkable on cyclical stocks in 1974. More important, market price increases of 25% or more were rather commonplace early in 1975 and 1976, and there seems reason to believe that such gains can be had over the years ahead with a careful selection of quality growth stocks.

For rewards like these, Mr. and Mrs. Frank can afford a sizable measure of risk on the bulk of their capital.

Finally, consider the situation of Mrs. Gordon, the fifty-seven-year-old widow of a successful doctor. Her principal assets consist of the family home and

$145,000 worth of life insurance. True, the doctor did leave an assortment of stocks, but they proved to have a cash value of only about $20,000, because, like most medical men who have little contact with business and less time in which to study it, Dr. Gordon had bought only the most speculative of securities—Canadian oil shares, stock in a plastic airplane company, and some preferred stocks that must have looked attractive because of big accumulations of back dividends—dividends that were owed but unfortunately never paid.

Mrs. Gordon doesn't want to see her capital dissipated that way. She wants to live off her investments but leave the principal intact, so that she can pass it along to her three children, all of them now well launched on substantial careers of their own.

Mrs. Gordon begins her calculations where every investor in such a situation must: "How much income do I have to have?" She figures she needs $15,000 a year to maintain her standard of living, and that in turn means that she must get a return of 9% on her $165,000.

Time was when an investor like Mrs. Gordon would have had to put her money into common stocks if she wanted to realize a return of 9%. Thus, in the early 1950s, she could have expected to earn only about 3% on government bonds and 4% or so on corporate bonds and good-grade preferreds. But thanks to the bull market that got under way then she would have experienced little difficulty in finding top-quality stocks that would have given her a return of 9% or even more, counting both the dividends and the capital gains that she could have realized.

Of course, in the early 1970s, the situation had changed, and all Mrs. Gordon would have had to do to realize 9% was put her money into certain top-rated corporate bonds and sit back and collect the interest.

But that wouldn't wholly satisfy someone of Mrs. Gordon's temperament, nor would it protect her against the possible ravages of continued inflation in all the years that might still remain to her. Perhaps, down the road, $15,000 a year wouldn't permit her to continue her present life-style. Perhaps she should have one eye on guaranteed income and the other eye on long-term appreciation in the value of her holdings.

For all those reasons it would only make sense for Mrs. Gordon to divide her $165,000, to put half of it into corporate bonds and the other half into good quality stocks that paid good dividends and offered prospects of long-term growth.

Most of Mrs. Gordon's stock selections would probably be industrials of the blue chip variety—stocks that have paid dividends consistently for a long period of years and thus offer some compensation for any compromise she may be forced to make temporarily in the 9% income return that she feels she needs.

About 150 common stocks listed on the New York Stock Exchange can boast records of consecutive quarterly dividends running back at least 40 years, and most of these can be classified as "the bluest of the blue," because many are also the stocks of companies that have no bonds outstanding, and little or no preferred. Hence, all earnings, or virtually all earnings, are available for dividends on the common stock; and this can be important in a period of bad business. Stocks like J. C. Penney, American Can, Borden, Eastman Kodak, General Electric, American Brands, Scott Paper, Pullman, and Procter & Gamble should suit virtually any investor in Mrs. Gordon's position.

As a general rule, Mrs. Gordon should not put more than 20% of the capital that she has for common-stock investments into any one industry or more than 10% into any one company.

No one of the programs outlined for these seven investors is likely to fit your own situation. But a consideration of their problems and the ways in which they might have been solved can serve to illustrate the kind of sober thinking that every investor must go through before he can hope to decide what stocks or bonds are right for him. Remember, there is no all-purpose security—no stock that fits ideally into every man's portfolio. Each man must work out his own investment salvation for himself.

That's why the best advice that was ever given is "investigate before you invest." And the investigation should properly begin with your own financial situation.

CHAPTER 33

When Is the Time to Sell?

THUS far we have been talking almost exclusively about buying stocks—about investing for the long pull.

But just because a convincing case can be made for the fact that it is a good idea to have extra dollars invested, it doesn't follow that it is a good idea to keep them invested in the same securities.

Change is the common denominator of all life, and change can and does vitally affect the value of investments.

The intelligent investor keeps in mind two broad kinds of changes—changes in his own situation and changes in investment opportunities.

As far as the first classification is concerned, it is perfectly obvious that the kind of investment program which is well suited to a young man with no great responsibilities to anyone except himself is not the kind of program he should pursue when he starts rearing a family. And investments which are geared to that period of life when he is carrying the heaviest load are not the kind he should carry when the kids are through school and he is able—at the peak period of his earning power—to branch out on his own again and try to build something of an estate for himself before he has to start thinking soberly about retirement.

It is, of course, always later than we think, and changes in a man's personal situation, in his financial circumstances, come usually so gradually that he is rarely shocked into an awareness of the fact that it is high time he sat down and took a personal inventory of his situation—where he stands now and where he is headed. Most of us are just too used to drifting with the tide.

This is peculiarly true as far as investments are concerned because of the strange, irrational attachment that most men and women seem to feel for the stocks and bonds they own. It's no overstatement to say that many a man becomes married to his stocks and is apt to talk a good deal more pridefully about them to his associates in the clubhouse or on the commuter train than he does about almost anything else in his life.

Once a man buys stock in a company, he seems to feel some sort of compulsion to talk it up to others—sell it to them. Thus he seeks from others confirmation of his own good judgment. In such circumstances, he regards the sale of his stock as tantamount to treason.

There is another psychological reason why most people are loath to sell securities. Very often, his original investment decision—the selection of Stock A over B, C, or D—was so charged with emotional conflict that the buyer wants to shut the door on the whole episode. Certainly he doesn't relish the idea of fighting the issue out all over again and weighing the comparative values against E, F, and G.

Nevertheless, there is that inexorable fact that investment values do constantly change and what was a good buy last year may be an even better sale this year.

Every investor owes it to himself to take an objective look at his holdings—as objective as possible—at least once a year. And when he tackles that job, he should ask himself at least one simple question about every stock in his list: "If I had the money, would I buy this stock at today's prices?"

If the answer is no, if you own a stock you wouldn't enthusiastically want to buy, you should consider the advisability of selling it, even if you have to take a loss on it—or *especially* if you have to take a loss.

And if you don't want to make the decision yourself, you might at least ask your broker for his opinion. As a matter of fact, if you don't want to review your whole investment program once a year as you should, you should submit the problem with all pertinent data to your broker and ask him for his recommendations and suggestions. Brokers are used to such requests, and in the main they do a remarkably conscientious job on them. They know that suggestions for changes that are advanced simply for the sake of building commissions for themselves are bound to backfire and result in the long run in the loss of customers.

Of course, there are some investors who approach the job of evaluating their securities with the kind of relish that all of us should bring to bear on the job. These are the stockholders who carefully read the annual and quarterly reports that they get from the companies whose stock they own and painstakingly compare performance with results in other years and other companies.

Only a trained analyst can get the real meat out of a corporate report, but there are a few simple points that every investor can check on easily and determine if there are any danger flags which might suggest the desirability of a switch to another stock.

If the dividend is cut, even the least sophisticated investor is apt to be properly concerned, but the dividend is actually of less importance in evaluating a stock than the earnings figure. If a company's earnings drop, the stockholder has a right to know why. Often there are legitimate reasons. The company may have decided to put a substantial sum of money into the development of a new product not yet on the market, or it may have embarked on some new program of plant expansion. Such decisions might cut sharply into earnings for any given year, but they hold a promise of expanded profits in years to come.

Again, there are times when business in general or any given industry in particular may go through a period of stress. Hence, a company's earnings record must always be considered on a comparative basis. A bad earnings record on your stock is in itself no substantial reason for a switch in holdings if other companies are doing no better.

Any cut in dividends or drop in earnings is certain to be fully elaborated in the company's annual report, and although the management will place the most palatable construction possible on such unpleasant facts, its explanations are apt to be pretty trustworthy, for they must pass the scrutiny of trained security analysts in brokerage offices and financial institutions.

The price-earnings ratio of a stock, which is shown in the stock tables published in big city newspapers and can always be computed from the reported figures, is actually a more reliable measure of investment value than straight earnings per share, for it reflects something of how other investors regard your stock. Suppose your stock sold last year at a price fifteen times earnings per share but sells now at only ten times earnings. A drop like that would reflect a serious loss of investor confidence in your company, unless, of course, stocks in general had been under pretty heavy selling pressure and price-earnings ratios had dropped all along the line.

A decline in the price-earnings ratio on your stock is the kind of danger signal that suggests a more intensive study of other figures in the annual report. You might, for instance, look at the *income statement* and see how net sales have fared. Have they fallen off to a disturbing degree? And what about operating costs? Have they risen unduly? Has there consequently been a serious squeeze on profit from operations—net sales less operating costs? How does the margin of profit, obtained by dividing net income by net sales, compare with the figure for earlier years? How does it compare with other companies in the same industry?

Next, you might take a look at some of the key figures shown in the company's *balance sheet*. You will especially want to look at the *current assets* and the *current liabilities*. On the asset side of the ledger you will want to see if there has been any big drop in the company's cash position or its holdings of government bonds. You might similarly be concerned about any undue increase in *accounts receivable*—what people owe your company—or in inventories. Any big increase in inventories of finished goods is apt to prove risky, for a sharp drop in prices could cause heavy losses. Or it might suggest that the company had a lot of unsalable merchandise on its hands. On the other hand, a big increase in the inventory of raw material might be regarded more hopefully. At a time when prices are rising generally, an increase in raw material inventories might suggest that your company had very prudently decided to stock up when prices were low. Certainly it implies that your company anticipates good sales ahead for its finished products.

As far as current liabilities are concerned, the most important item is apt to be *accounts payable,* for this represents the money your company owes for raw materials, supplies, insurance, and the like.

More important than the total figure for current assets or the total figure for current liabilities is the relationship between the two. Most security analysts figure that current assets should be twice as large as current liabilities, but that is only a rough rule of thumb. In industries like railroads where inventories are not a major problem and where accounts receivable can easily be collected, lower ratios of assets to liabilities are acceptable. On the other hand, in industries like chemicals or tobacco, ratios of three-to-one or four-to-one are more commonly expected.

The difference between current assets and current liabilities represents a company's *net working capital* —the money it has to grow on—and this is the life-blood of a business. Any serious shrinkage from year to year in a company's working capital is something that might properly worry an investor and make him think seriously about selling his stock.

For an investor, the payoff figure in the balance sheet is the figure for *stockholders' equity* or *net worth,* usually shown on a per-share basis. This is the figure he wants to see grow because over any period of time it's the figure that will determine not only the book value of his stock but the price he is likely to get for it.

The stockholders' equity is made up of three components: (1) *capital stock,* which is the actual declared value of the company's stock when it was originally issued and which may or may not be identical with its par value; (2) *capital surplus,* which is the amount over and above the declared value that the company might have been able to realize on the original sale of stock; and (3) accumulated retained earnings or *earned surplus,* which is the amount of money that the company has earned over the years, less what it has paid out in dividends.

Of course, even if an investor takes the time and trouble to look at just a few of these key factors in his company's annual report—and there is no question of the fact that he should—he is still not likely to have a substantial basis for deciding to buy or sell, for the figures for any given year take on meaning only as they are compared with the same figures for earlier years and for other companies in the same field which may represent alternative investments.

Finally, the most important question of all—how good is the management?—is one to which the investor can find only an inferential answer in any annual report.

In evaluating a company's reports, an investor has the right to look for help and advice from his broker. Within reason, he can expect detailed and specific answers to his questions, reliable data on the basis of which he can make up his own mind whether to buy, sell, or hold.

While brokers are frequently accused of stimulating customers to switch from one stock to another for the simple sake of building commissions, the blunt fact of the matter is that they don't suggest enough sales to enough of their customers, probably because they are afraid of that very accusation. And the customer, left to his lethargic devices, goes along, year after year, holding on to the same old stocks, blissfully ignoring his own self-interest. A few years ago a New York Stock Exchange survey showed that a third of all people who owned stock had never sold any. They had just bought and held on.

This static attitude toward investments is reflected in figures showing the *"turnover rate"* on the New York Stock Exchange. The turnover rate shows the percentage of all the shares listed on the exchange that are traded in any given year. In 1915 to 1920 it was 117%, and although it dropped to 70% from 1920 to 1925, it rose to a peak of 132% in 1928. From then on the trend was almost steadily downward to a low of 9% in 1942. There has been a revival of trading interest since then, but the average figure for 1950 to 1960 stood at only 15%. It dropped back to 12% in 1962 but revived again to 16% in 1965 and headed straight on up to a modern high of 24% in the boiling market of 1968. Falling stock prices and contracting volume took their toll in 1974, however, and the rate fell back again to 16%. Of course, the number of shares listed on the exchange has increased steadily over the years, so percentage figures are somewhat misleading; as the listed shares increase, trading activity as a percent of the total listings is almost bound to decrease.

As far as actual trading volume is concerned, it was not until 1963 that the volume of shares traded surpassed the 1,124,800,000 shares that changed hands in 1929. In 1975, it reached an all-time high—up to that point—of 4,693,426,508 shares.

But in just one month, January 1976, the turnover soared to 635.85 million shares. This volume for a single month topped the turnover total of all but four full years (1928, 1929, 1930, 1933) from the turn of the century to 1955.

The do-nothing attitude of many stockholders with substantial profits on their holdings is unquestionably explained by their reluctance to pay a capital-gains tax on their profits. This is certainly the least defensible of all reasons for failure to sell.

Because the long-term outlook for American business is a bright and promising one, no one wants to preach a doctrine of "sell . . . sell . . . sell." Nevertheless, if you think you can improve your investment position, it is ridiculous to go along comforted simply by the thought that inflation and an expanding economy will rescue you from your own faulty judgment.

It is a truism of the stock market that there are sell orders to match all buy orders. There have to be. That's something worth remembering. The man who sells a stock—some stock you own—very often has done his homework a little more conscientiously than the buyer. He may have a better reason for selling the stock than anybody has for buying it—or than you have for holding it.

CHAPTER 34

The Folklore of the Market

THE cheapest commodity in the world is investment advice from people not equipped to give it.

Many a man who doesn't own a share of stock still fancies himself as something of an authority on the market, and he's ready and willing to deliver himself of an opinion about it on the slightest provocation. If he actually owns stock himself, chances are you won't have to ask his opinion. He'll tell you what to buy, what to sell, and what's going to happen to the market. And you can't stop him.

The more a man knows about the market, the less he is willing to commit himself about it. The wisest of them all, old J. P. Morgan, when asked his opinion of the market, always used to reply, "It will fluctuate." He wasn't just being canny. He knew that was the only provable statement that could be made about the market.

Nevertheless, over the years a number of generalizations about the market and about investing have come to be accepted as gospel. Actually, those homespun axioms must be accepted as just that—little more than folklore. Like most folklore, each of them has a certain element of truth about it—and a certain element of nontruth.

For instance: *"Buy 'em and put 'em away."*

This would have been a fine piece of advice if you had happened to buy $1,000 worth of General Motors stock in 1923. By the end of 1974 that stock would have been worth $22,242, and you would have collected $64,394 in dividends. Had you been lucky enough to sell your General Motors before the gasoline crisis and before the 1973–1974 recession had taken its toll, you would have realized more than $100,000—for General Motors dropped 50 points in those two years.

Of course, in the early twenties the car everybody was talking about was the Stutz Bearcat—not General Motors—and there was a great deal of speculative interest in Stutz stock. You might very well have decided to put your $1,000 into that. How would you have made out on that purchase? The answer is that you would have lost all your money, and furthermore you would never have collected a penny in dividends.

Of course, there is a measure of sense in the axiom. If you start worrying about fluctuations of a point or two and try to buy and sell on every turn, you can pay out a lot of money in commissions needlessly and maybe end up with less profit than if you'd "bought 'em and put 'em away."

Nevertheless, it's only good sense to remember that securities are perishable. Values do change with the passage of time. Industries die, and new ones are born. Companies rise and fall. The wise investor will take a good look at all his securities at least once a year, and he could do worse than to ask his broker to review them with him then.

"You never go broke taking a profit."

That's obviously true. But you can certainly get hurt badly.

Suppose you had put $50 into Sears, Roebuck in 1906. By 1940, the stock that you had bought would have been worth $1,276 at its high. That would have been a nice profit—and you might have decided to take it.

But look what you would have lost if you had sold. By 1954 your same holdings in that stock would have been worth over $4,300, and by the end of 1974 your $50 investment would have been worth $17,029.

Or consider another classic case. In 1914, you could have bought 100 shares of stock in International Business Machines for $2,750, and in just eleven short years you could have sold out for $6,364. Certainly you can never go broke taking a profit of nearly 250%.

But as far as IBM stock is concerned, you certainly would have taken a licking if you had sold in 1925. For by the end of 1974, your original 100 shares would have grown to 72,798 and they would have had a market value of $12,230,123. A year or so earlier when IBM was selling at $365 a share, you could have sold your IBM for $26,571,270; the government's antitrust action, coupled with the recession, whittled away over half of that value in the next two years.

Of course, a profit is always a nice thing to have— in the pocket, not just on paper. But remember too, that 1973–1974 were unusually bad years in the stock market. Virtually all stocks have recovered quite substantially from where they were selling when the closing bell sounded on December 31, 1974.

"Buy when others are selling. Sell when they buy."
This sounds like a neat trick, if you can do it.

Obviously, you can't make money if you consistently buck the trend of the market. Where, for instance, would you have been if you had been selling stock all through various bull markets since 1950?

So the trick lies in anticipating the action of all the others—in buying just before the crowd decides to buy and selling just ahead of them. This is just exactly the trick that the exponents of various formula plans try to turn by hitching their buying and selling operations to some arbitrary decline or advance in the market.

Others, less scientific, simply try to sell at the top and buy at the bottom. But how do you know when the market hits bottom? How far down is down?

Make no mistake about it. Anyone who tries to practice this fine art is "playing the market" in the purest sense of the phrase. He's speculating; he's not investing.

"Don't sell on strike news."
There's some truth to the old adage. Nowadays, labor troubles in any big company or in any industry are apt to be pretty well publicized. Consequently, the market is likely to have discounted the possibility of a strike during the time it was brewing; the stock will already have gone down in price, and it may even advance when the strike news breaks.

Again, many people think that a strike doesn't really damage a company's long-term profit picture. They contend that while a strike is on, demand for the company's products is only deferred, and as soon as the strike is over, the company will enjoy better business than ever.

But such a theory is often little more than wishful thinking. After all, most strikes end with the company facing a higher labor bill. And many times the demand for its products which a company couldn't fill while its employees were on strike has been happily filled by a competitor.

"Don't overstay the market."

A fine piece of advice, but how do you know when to sell and take your profit—if that's what you're interested in?

Sometimes you can tell by watching those basic business indicators that show what's happening to production, distribution, and consumption of goods. But sometimes you can't, because the market doesn't always pay too close attention to them. Sometimes business looks good and the stock market skids. Sometimes the reverse is true.

Nevertheless, if business appears to be on the skids and the stock market is still boiling merrily upward, sooner or later there's going to be a reckoning.

"Always cut your losses quickly."

Nobody wants to ride all the way downhill with a stock if the company is headed for bankruptcy, as W. T. Grant Co.—a formerly well-regarded stock—was in 1975. However, at the same time you don't want to be stampeded into a sale by a price decline that may have no relationship to the fundamental value of the stock.

Remember, the price of a stock at any time reflects the supply and demand for that stock, the opinions and attitudes of all the buyers and all the sellers. If a stock is closely held, if its *floating supply*—the amount usually available in the market—is limited, the price of that stock can be unduly depressed for quite a period if some large holder sells a sizable block of it, just because he may need the cash, or because some institution decides to take a good profit. That doesn't mean the stock is intrinsically any less valuable.

The market on any given day is made by just a tiny

handful of all those who own stocks. On the exchange, 24 million shares may be traded in one day, but that still represents only ⅙ of 1% of all shares listed on the exchange. The 99.8% who aren't selling have some reason for holding on—or think they do.

Of course, there is much truth in the observation that unsophisticated investors do tend to sell a stock too readily when they have a profit in it and to hang onto a stock in which they have a loss, hoping that it will come back.

"An investor is just a disappointed speculator."

This cynical observation has a measure of truth in it. Every stock buyer hopes for a big fat profit, even if he won't admit it to himself. So when the market drops, he does the best he can to assuage his disappointment by assuring himself and everybody else that of course he never expected to make a killing—he was just investing on the basis of the fundamental stock values.

This is especially true of odd-lot buyers who, all too often, finally decide to buy only when the market is already too high.

So often does this happen that some speculators gauge their own actions by the relation of odd-lot buying to odd-lot selling. When that ratio increases—when the proportion of odd-lot purchases rises—the speculators begin to anticipate a reversal of the upward trend.

But in the long run, the small investor often has the last laugh. After all, the stock market has gone pretty steadily up for 50 years, hasn't it? And since the odd-lot man is principally a heavy buyer of the market leaders—the 100 stocks that usually account for two-thirds of the exchange volume—he has made out pretty well over the long pull.

On the other hand, many a big speculator, like Daniel Drew, has died broke.

"A bull can make money. A bear can make money. But a hog never can."

That's one to remember.

The desire to make money leads most people into the market. Call it ambition or greed, it remains the prime motivating force of our whole business system, including the stock market.

But greed is always dangerous. It's an engine without a governor. So you made a killing once in the market. Good. You were lucky. Don't think you can make one every day.

If you own a good stock, one that's paying you a good return on your money and seems likely to go on doing so, hang on to it. Don't keep looking for greener pastures, bigger profits. And forget about the other fellow and the killing he made—or says he made. Maybe he can afford to speculate better than you can.

In short, if you're an investor, act like one.

CHAPTER 35

Who Owns Stock?

If Wall Street didn't exist, it would be necessary to invent it. In fact, that's just exactly what our forefathers did.

Why must there be a Wall Street?

Because in our economy, capital, like labor, must be free to work where it wants to. If you've got extra dollars, you've got the right in our society to say where you want to put them to work in order to make more dollars.

And that's a right which would be a pretty empty one if there weren't some means for you to transfer your funds from one enterprise to another when you wanted to, just as you might transfer from one job to another.

Wall Street provides that means. It's a marketplace for money.

And in the past twenty years, it has played an increasingly important role in our economy. It has made it possible for millions of people to put their savings to work in American business. That has been good for them, good for business, and good for the whole country.

Time was when only the wealthy people owned stocks and bonds. That's not true any longer. For one thing, there aren't as many truly wealthy people as there used to be. Death and taxes have taken their toll.

If business is to have the money it needs to go on growing, somebody has to take the rich man's place. That somebody can only be the investor of moderate means—thousands of such small investors, because it takes 1,000 of them with $1,000 each to equal the $1 million in capital that one wealthy man may have supplied yesteiyear. And tomorrow it will take many, many more thousands of them, because business is constantly in need of more and more investment capital to build new plants and replace old equipment. From the turn of the century to the end of World War II, business put $218 billion into plant and equipment, but in the next ten years expansion accelerated so rapidly that $232 billion of capital was needed—more than in all the preceding 46 years. And industry continues to invest in new plants and equipment at an accelerated rate so that by the mid-1970s such expenditures were running at $80 or $90 billion a year, and the forecast was for a level of $100 billion a year by 1980.

Wall Street bears the primary responsibility for recruiting the new investors who must supply this capital, Wall Street and all its counterparts throughout America—La Salle Street in Chicago, Montgomery Street in San Francisco, and Main Street in many a Middletown.

Wall Street takes its responsibilities seriously. Every year it puts millions of dollars into booklets, pamphlets, and letters to explain securities. It uses educational advertising—newspapers, magazines, television, radio, even billboards. It has taken the story of stocks and bonds to country fairs, department stores, labor unions, and women's clubs. It has even put the story into movies that any group can show free of charge.

How well has Wall Street done with all this educational effort in stimulating new investor interest?

Better than you might think—but not nearly so well as it must.

Not until June 1952 did Wall Street know just how it stood on the job. Strange as it may seem, nobody could say how many stockholders there were in the country until the New York Stock Exchange got the Brookings Institution to find out. American Telephone & Telegraph knew it had 1,200,000 stockholders back then. And 30 other big companies knew they had 50,000 or more apiece. But nobody knew just what duplication there was in those stockholder lists. And nobody knew the grand total for all companies.

The Brookings Institution reported in 1952 that the

total was 6,490,000, representing a little more than 4% of all individuals and just about 10% of all the families of the country. Disappointing as that total figure was when it was announced, Wall Street found encouragement in the fact that about one-fifth of the total had become stockholders in the preceding three years.

Four years after the Brookings study, the New York Stock Exchange retained Alfred Politz Research, Incorporated, to make another census of shareholders. Politz reported a total of 8,630,000 stockholders in publicly owned corporations, an increase of 33% in four years.

Since then, the New York Stock Exchange has conducted similar censuses every four or five years, and until the last report, published in December 1975, each census showed a steady increase in share ownership. In 1970, the exchange reported that the total of individual stockholders had passed the 30 million mark; in 1972, estimates placed the number at a record 32.5 million. But the 1975 census showed an 18.3% drop to 25.2 million.

Here are some of the other highlights of that study:

The typical American stockholder is a fifty-three-year-old woman. Male shareholders had outnumbered women in the 1965–1970 census, but the standings were reversed in 1970–1975. In fact, 11.75 million women, representing 50.3% of the total, owned stocks in the latest five-year period, as against 11.63 million men. However, since husbands often buy stocks in their wife's name the statistics may not be significant, according to the exchange.

The census revealed also that the average age of all shareholders had jumped from forty-seven in 1970 to an alarming fifty-three in 1975—the highest average age recorded in any of the seven censuses that the exchange has conducted over almost a quarter of a century. This increase in the average age of stockholders helps explain why women investors now outnumber men; women simply live longer than men.

The 1970–1975 report also showed that the value of the average investor's portfolio increased to $10,050, from $7,100 in the 1965–1970 period. Chicago replaced New York as the city with the most shareholders. Nearly 50% of all stockholders live in a metropolitan area with a population of more than a million, despite the fact that all major cities and all but six states showed a relative decline from 1970 in number of shareholders.

The average investor was a technical or professional worker with a college education of at least four years and had an average household income of $19,000 a year, 61% more than the national average of $11,800. In 1970, the average shareholder's income was $13,500, compared with a national average of $8,400 —almost the same percentage variation.

Finally, the average stockholder emerges as a community leader; 85% voted in 1975, versus a national average of 50% to 60%; 37% made a speech, as against a national average of 3%; 28% wrote a letter to a government agency, compared with a national average of 16%; 37% held public office, versus the national average of 10%.

The decline in share ownership shown by the N.Y.S.E.'s latest study raised a number of disturbing questions. How could one account for this reversal of the growth trend of the preceding two decades? There was, of course, the 1973–1974 bear market and a severe business recession, but there had been other bear markets and other recessions in prior years, and still share ownership had continued to expand.

Something more fundamental had to be involved, and there were many who felt that that "something" was a widespread loss of confidence in our American system. Vietnam and Watergate had bred a cynicism about big government and big business—the so-called military-industrial complex—and about the fundamental values in which America believed. The particularly sharp drop in share ownership among the young adults lent credence to this interpretation, for these were the people most deeply affected by the revolt that swept through American colleges in the sixties.

The recovery of business and the spectacular upsurge of the market in early 1976 made it easy for many to forget their concerns about social revolution in America. Maybe that decline in share ownership from 1970 to 1975 wasn't too significant after all—just a freak thing. Maybe the long-term trend would reassert itself, and stock ownership would resume its growth curve. Maybe even the young would come back into the market.

But even if that proves to be the case, Wall Street will still find itself confronted by the fundamental questions that have been nagging it for a quarter of a century.

Why is it that so many people who can afford to invest don't own any stocks?

Why should shareowners represent only about a quarter of all U.S. families while 64% have savings accounts, 62% own their own homes, and more than three-quarters have life insurance?

In short, why don't more people invest?

There's one clear-cut answer to that. Millions of people still don't understand stocks and bonds, and what people don't understand they are apt to be afraid of.

We may be the richest nation in the world, the very bulwark of a modern and enlightened capitalism, but the blunt fact of the matter is that we are still as a nation not financially enlightened.

As a part of its last census, the New York Stock Exchange asked a sample of shareholders what they would do if they received a $10,000 windfall. Here are the kinds of investments and the proportion of the people who favored putting the whole amount in one place:

savings account	18.8%
real estate	12.9%
common stocks	11.9%
government bonds	10.7%

Of those who favored diversification:

savings account	31.3%
common stocks	30.3%
real estate	25.3%
government bonds	23.9%

According to the survey, 67% of the respondents planned to make no changes in their current portfolio; 25% planned to buy more stock; 8% intended to reduce their holdings.

Those who planned to add to their holdings said they expected stocks to rise. Those who intended to reduce their holdings said they needed the money for various reasons or they had a poor opinion of the market or the economy.

In a survey conducted prior to 1973–1974, when the stock market was strong and the newspapers were deploring the ravages of continued inflation, *Newsweek* found that most people with incomes below $15,000 would put an extra $5,000, if they had it, in the bank or into savings and loan associations or into government bonds. Fewer than half would have put that $5,000 into common stocks or into real estate, which might give them a chance to beat inflation. Only at the $15,000-and-over level did as many as a third of the people show a preference for common stocks and mutual funds over all other forms of investment.

Yes, ignorance is unquestionably the biggest deterrent to investing. But there's another factor in the picture too. Successful investing isn't simple. It means thinking your own investment problem through to a logical conclusion. It means being willing to study the facts about various securities. It means checking up on a stock before you buy it and after you buy it.

That's not easy, admittedly. But it's not beyond the capabilities of any of us. Not if Nicholas J. Harvalis could do it. You're not likely to remember the story in the newspapers about him when he died in 1950, but he was an uneducated immigrant who worked all his life in restaurants for a wage that never exceeded $125 a month but who still managed to leave an estate of $160,000.

Here is how he did it, as related by his counselor, Max D. Fromkin of Omaha:

Fromkin & Fromkin
Keeling Building
Omaha 2, Nebraska

February 13th, 1951

I give you now the story of Nicholas J. Harvalis, late of Omaha, Nebraska, who departed this life on the last day of the month and year of 1950, to wit, December 31, 1950, shortly after the close of the market for the year.

Nicholas was a friend of mine for over 25 years, and during that time I was his attorney and counselor.

Nicholas came to this country from Greece at the age of 15 years. He was without education and money, and he immediately went to work as a waiter in various cafés and restaurants operated by his countrymen in Omaha at wages which provided a bare living for him.

He was unmarried and lived the many years in Omaha alone in a modest room.

He was thrifty to a point of many times denying himself the comforts of life in order to save from his earnings sufficient to make investments for his security and old age. He employed his leisure hours reading and studying financial papers and books. He also spent many hours in the public library poring over history and philosophy.

On May 18, 1927, he became a citizen of the United States by naturalization. He was a firm and optimistic believer in the opportunities offered the common man in the United States, and he believed that the greatest return in investments was in common stocks of well-managed companies.

Thus, beginning about 1937, he started a systematic purchase of common stocks. His early investments were in National Distillers, Laclede Gas, General Motors, S. S. Kresge, Atlantic Refining, International Nickel, J. C. Penney, General Electric. He bought a few shares in each of these companies and added to them from time to time.

He kept meticulous records of all of his transactions, including dividends received. His dividends, which at first were modest, he would save and reinvest in these same stocks.

He subscribed to the *Wall Street Journal* and avidly read the paper from cover to cover. As a matter of fact, at the time of his death the only thing in his room apart from bare furnishings was a neat stack of issues of the *Wall Street Journal* for the last two years.

In 1943, he began selling stocks for long-term profits

when he felt the market was high, and later he began a repurchasing program.

In 1943, his earnings from wages as a waiter and soda jerk in a local drugstore known as the Paxton Pharmacy at 15th & Harney Streets in Omaha were $1,602.00, while his income from dividends of common stocks was $1,825.00.

In 1944, his earnings from wages were $1,525.00, and his dividends from common stocks rose to $2,285.00. In the same year he made from gains in the sale of stocks the sum of $2,600.00.

In 1945, his wages were the same, but dividends from stocks came to $2,785.60. Long-term profits in that year were $7,713.84.

In 1946, he began acquiring Cities Service stock.

In 1946, his dividends from stocks fell to $1,506.24, but his gains on the sale of stocks were very substantial.

In 1947, his dividends rose to $2,191.24.

In 1948, his dividends were $10,562.98.

In 1949, his dividends were $7,081.24.

In 1950, his dividends were $10,095.50.

During all these years he earned from wages as a soda jerk a sum not to exceed $1,600 per year.

When he died on December 31, 1950, he was the owner of the following common stocks:

 1,370 shares Cities Service common
  200 shares Boeing common
  300 shares Rock Island common
  100 shares General Electric common
  200 shares American Bank Note common
   40 shares Hearst Consolidated Publications 7% preferred
  200 shares Great Northern Iron Ore.

The above shares had an approximate value at the time of his death of $160,000.

Nicholas J. Harvalis kept perfect records and had in his room every statement from his broker of every transaction he had ever made. In addition he made accurate reports for income tax purposes and was proud to pay his government every cent of tax for the privilege of his citizenship and the opportunity that his government gave him. In my association with him as his attorney I found him always to be a very polite, mild-mannered, and courteous individual. He was often asked for advice on the market and was always very cautious to mention only highly rated dividend-paying stocks.

Nicholas amassed this huge sum considering his limitations and in his death he leaves to his brother and sisters (11 of them) in Greece a substantial inheritance, which they will no doubt spend more freely and with less good judgment than the man who earned it.

Very truly yours,
MAX FROMKIN

Or, consider the story of Sam Hamilton, a dishwasher in a mission and a janitor at the Pacific Stock Exchange. The methods by which this shy octogenarian amassed a $300,000 estate will never be known exactly, but according to a spokesman for the Life Line Mission mentioned in his will, Mr. Hamilton must have gathered some pretty good information in his many years of sweeping and cleaning around the stock exchange.

Few of us would be willing to pay the price Mr. Harvalis or Mr. Hamilton did for their achievement. But then most of us would be willing to settle for just a small measure of that success—the success that can be achieved not by luck, not by "inside tips," not by speculation, but by prudent and intelligent investing.

Appendix 1

IN any given year about 90% of the 2,122 stocks listed on the New York Stock Exchange can be expected to pay a cash dividend. Of course, it's not always the same 90%, but approximately half of the stocks haven't missed a dividend in at least a quarter of a century.

Stocks with long records of continuous dividends are generally regarded as very stable, even though in a bad year one or more of them may stumble and have to pass a dividend. This happened to many relatively small companies in the 1973–1974 bear market. But the biggest blow of all was when Consolidated Edison passed its dividend—the first lapse in consecutive payments since 1885.

If stability is of primary concern to you in your investment program, you may be particularly interested in the following list, prepared by Standard & Poor's Corporation, of common stocks on the New York Stock Exchange that have paid quarterly dividends for at least forty years through October 1975, when seventy-six of them yielded 6% or more. Significantly, however, nearly twenty stocks that appeared on this list only three and a half years ago are no longer there, and three times that many new stocks have been added.

Stocks Paying Quarterly Dividends for Forty Years or More Through October 1975

	Year Continuous Dividends Began		Year Continuous Dividends Began
Aetna Life & Caslty.	1908	Duquesne Light	1913
Airco, Inc.	1917	Eastman Kodak	1902
Allied Chemical	1921	Equimark Corp.	1910
American Brands	1921	Firestone Tire & Rub.	1924
American Can Co.	1923	First Pennsylvania	1911
Amer. District Teleg.	1903	Fisher Scientific	1907
Amer. Elec. Power	1910	Ft. Howard Paper	1922
Amer. Home Prods.	1926	Garlock, Inc.	1906
Amer. Natural Gas	1904	General Cigar	1909
Amer. Sterilizer	1914	General Electric	1899
Amer. Tel. & Tel.	1882	General Foods	1922
AMF, Inc.	1927	General Mills	1927
Anchor Hocking	1928	General Motors	1923
Atlantic Richfield	1927	Grt. North. Nekoosa	1910
Balt. Gas & Elec.	1911	Heller (W.E.) Intl.	1921
BanCal Tri-State	1910	Hercules, Inc.	1913
Bank of New York	1920	Hobart Corp.	1906
Blue Bell	1923	Household Finance	1926
Borden, Inc.	1924	Houston Ltg. & Pwr.	1922
Boston Edison Co.	1892	Huyck Corp.	1921
Brown Group	1923	Industrial Natl. Corp.	1921
Burroughs Corp.	1906	Ingersoll-Rand Corp.	1919
Carpenter Technol.	1908	Interco, Inc.	1913
Cent. Hudson G. & E.	1903	Int'l Bus. Mach.	1916
Central Illinois Lt.	1921	Int'l Harvester	1910
Charter N.Y. Corp.	1867	Iowa Power & Light	1916
Chase Manh't'n Corp.	1918	Jewell Companies	1928
Chemical N.Y. Corp.	1849	Johnson Controls	1901
Chesebrough-Pond's	1919	Kraftco Corp.	1924
Cinn. Bell, Inc	1879	Kroger Company	1910
C.I.T. Financial	1924	Liggett & Myers	1912
Cleveland Elec. Ill.	1912	Lilly (Eli) & Co.	1904
Coca-Cola Co.	1921	Ludlow Corp.	1886
Combustion Eng'g	1912	Macy (R.H.) Co.	1927
Commonw'l Edison	1890	Mfrs. Hanover Corp.	1913
Continental Can	1923	Marsh & McLennan	1923
Conwood Corp.	1903	May Dept. Stores	1911
Corning Glass Wk's.	1922	Melville Shoe	1917
CPC Int'l	1919	Minn. Mng. & Mfg.	1916
Dentsply Intl.	1923	Morgan (J.P.) & Co.	1900
Detroit Edison Co.	1909	Morton Norwich Pr.	1925
Dome Mines, Ltd.	1920	Mountain States Tel.	1911
Dow Chemical	1912	Nabisco, Inc.	1899
Duke Power	1926	Nat'l Fuel Gas	1903
du Pont (E.I.) Nem.	1905	Nat'l-Standard	1922

	Year Continuous Dividends Began		Year Continuous Dividends Began
Nat'l-Steel	1908	South'n Cal. Ed.	1910
New England T. & T.	1886	Squibb Corp.	1903
N L Industries	1906	Stand. Oil (Calif.)	1912
Norfolk & West'n-Ry.	1910	Stand. Oil (Ind.)	1913
Northeast Utilities	1927	Stanley Works	1895
Olin Corp.	1926	Stauffer Chemical	1915
Orange & Rock. Util.	1914	Sterling Drug	1913
Otis Elevator	1911	Sun Oil Co.	1912
Owens-Illinois, Inc.	1907	Tampa Electric	1911
Pacific Gas & Elec.	1919	Texaco, Inc.	1903
Pacific Lighting	1909	Texas Utilities	1919
Pacific Tel. & Tel.	1925	Texasgulf Inc.	1921
Pennwalt Corp.	1913	TI Corp.	1915
Peter Paul	1921	Timken Co.	1921
Phila. Electric	1913	Toledo Edison	1922
Pillsbury Co.	1927	Trans Union Corp.	1919
PPG Industries	1899	Traveler's Corp.	1892
Procter & Gamble	1898	Union Carbide	1918
Public Serv. E. & G.	1920	Union Electric	1918
Pullman, Inc.	1867	Union Oil Calif.	1916
Quaker Oats	1922	Union Pacific Corp.	1907
Raybestos-Manh't'n	1898	United Illuminating	1900
Retail Credit	1917	U.S. Gypsum	1919
Rexnord Inc.	1922	U.S. Tobacco Co.	1918
Reynolds (R.J.) Ind.	1901	Upjohn Company	1921
Richardson-Merrell	1925	U.S.M. Corp.	1899
Safeway Stores	1927	Washington Gas Lt.	1885
San Diego Gas & El.	1909	Westvaco Corp.	1895
Scott Paper	1926	Woolworth (F.W.)	1912
Sherwin-Williams	1922	Wrigley (Wm.) Jr.	1911

Appendix 2

MANY investors, especially those who are conservatively inclined, are interested in knowing what stocks are most favored by the big institutional investors—pension funds, insurance companies, foundations, investment companies, colleges and the like. They believe with some logic that the professional managers of such large funds are better able to judge long-term investment values than they are.

Below is a list of the Big Board institutional favorites, prepared by Standard & Poor's Corporation for the New York Stock Exchange as of November 1975. Obviously, relative ranking on the list will change from time to time, but once a stock has been bought by several hundred institutions, it is not apt to be dislodged easily from its position of status.

Thus, IBM still clung to its number 1 spot—indeed, the number of institutions favoring it increased 9%—despite the fact that this premier growth stock dropped more than 47% from a high of 299 in May 1970 to a low of 157¼ in 1975, because of reduced earnings, coupled with the government's big antitrust suit against the company.

Similarly, Xerox showed an increase of 18% in the number of institutions holding its stock and moved up from eleventh to seventh on the favorite's list, notwithstanding a price drop of about 46% from its May 1970 high of 86½ to a low of 46⅝ in 1975, a decline occasioned both by a slower rate of earnings growth and the competitive threat posed by IBM's new copier.

Conversely, Polaroid—a previous favorite—vanished completely from the list, while its price plunged from a high of 82⅝ in May 1970 to 15 in 1975, a decline attributed generally not only to the problems and costs it incurred in launching its new instant-color camera, but also to the threat presented by the entrance of Eastman Kodak into this same field.

Favorite Stocks of Institutions

Stock	Number of Institutions Holding Stock	Number of Shares Owned (000 omitted)
Int'l Bus. Mach.	1220	15476
Exxon Corp.	791	18973
Eastman Kodak	744	11928
Amer. Tel. & Tel.	731	21574
General Electric	695	17254
General Motors	671	13807
Xerox Corp.	597	9685
Texaco, Inc.	530	22770
Citicorp	444	17628
Sears, Roebuck	444	6350
Merck & Co.	420	8083
Minn. Mng. & Mfg.	416	7997
Standard Oil (Ind.)	405	12916
Atlantic Richfield	401	6443
Dow Chemical	398	9090
du Pont (E.I.) Nem.	377	17112
Ford Motor	375	8795
Mobil Oil	369	9594
Burroughs Corp.	358	7962
Union Carbide	355	8876
Amer. Home Prods.	353	11767
Phillips Petroleum	351	6847
Gen'l Tel. & Elect.	343	12903
Kresge (S.S.)	318	11744
Gulf Oil	311	9265
Texas Utilities	311	9806
Caterpillar Tractor	310	6139
Procter & Gamble	301	3374
Standard Oil (Calif.)	292	11517
Pfizer, Inc.	279	9655
Monsanto Co.	275	5682
Warner-Lambert	272	11317
Philip Morris	271	11086
Continental Oil	269	6654
Halliburton Co.	266	2771
Goodyear T. & Rub.	263	10096
Johnson & Johnson	261	4105
Penney (J.C.)	255	3463
Schlumberger, Ltd.	255	5692
Weyerhaeuser Co.	255	10923
Int'l Paper	249	7153
Lilly (Eli) & Co.	244	3986
Southern Co.	242	5657
Int'l Tel. & Tel.	236	7367
Avon Products	235	7383
Schering-Plough	234	6390

Stock	Number of Institutions Holding Stock	Number of Shares Owned (000 omitted)
Int'l Nickel Can.	231	8210
Coca-Cola Co.	226	3083
Morgan (J.P.) & Co.	220	4674
Commonwealth Ed.	219	5869
Federated Dept. Str.	219	4654
Bristol-Myers	216	5247
Deere & Co.	216	5209
Westinghouse El.	215	8803
Sperry Rand	213	7950
McDonald's Corp.	212	8704
Reynolds (R.J.) Ind.	212	5328
Florida Pwr. & Lt.	206	6255
Houston Ltg. & Pwr.	206	4316
Texas Instruments	205	4869
Kerr-McGee	201	5748
South'n Cal. Edison	201	5284
Honeywell, Inc.	190	2205
Central & So. West.	187	8334
Tenneco, Inc.	186	6292
General Foods	183	3102
Chase Manhattan	180	2865
Alcan Aluminium Ltd.	177	6321
Alum. Co. of Amer.	177	6252
Amer. Electric Pwr.	174	2074
Sterling Drug	174	6875
Squibb Corp.	172	6091
Aetna Life & Casual.	171	6998
U.S. Steel	171	5673
Gillette Co.	168	4139

INDEX

nadian oil shares, stock in a plastic airplane company, and some preferred stocks that must have looked attractive because of big accumulations of back dividends—dividends that were owed but unfortunately never paid.

Mrs. Gordon doesn't want to see her capital dissipated that way. She wants to live off her income

Index

account, 155–161
  cash, 155, 159
  custodian, 160
  discretionary, 247–256
  joint, 156
  margin, 157–158, 161,
   183–184, 186–189
account executive, 148
accounts payable, 327
accounts receivable, 326
accrued dividends, 21, 22, 192
accumulation plans, 113–118,
  312, 314
acquisition, exchange, 104
adjustment bond, 32–33
A.D.R.'s, 129
advertising, 142, 143, 282, 337
advice, financial, 233–244
Advisory Committee on En-
  forcement Policy and
  Practices, 237
agency basis, 132
Alberta Stock Exchange, 125
Allied Crude Vegetable Oil
  Refining Co., 162
Allstate Enterprises, 285
American Brands, 321
American Can Company, 220,
  315, 321
American Depository Receipt,
  129
American Distilling, 171
American Electric Power Co.,
  28–29
American Farm Bureau Fed-
  eration, 285
American Institute Counsel-
  ors, Inc., 242
American Institute for Eco-
  nomic Research, 241

American Investor, 232
American Investors Service,
  242
American Motors, 101
American Natural Gas, 318
American Standard, 101
American Stock Exchange, 70,
  120–122, 154, 203, 219,
  223–224, 232
American Telephone & Telegraph, 13, 29, 37, 57,
  220, 222, 337
Amex. *See* American Stock
  Exchange
analyst, securities, 250–255
Anheuser Busch, 129, 135
annual meeting, 9–10
annual report, 9
  how to analyze, 324–328
annunciator boards, 79
Anti-reciprocal Rule, 277
Antitrust Division, Justice Department, 71–72, 277
asked price, 13, 137
assets, 11, 326–327
audits, 161
Automatic Stock Investment
  Plan, 116
automation, xii, 83–85, 121–
  122, 133–136, 252–254,
  295, 308
averages, stock, 219–223
"averaging down," 261
"away from the market," 90

Babson's Reports, Inc., 243
Bache & Co., 168
balance sheet, 326–328
balanced funds, 279
bank loans, 7, 15, 183–184

353

ABOUT THE AUTHORS

LOUIS ENGEL joined Merrill Lynch in 1946 as advertising manager after having been managing editor of *Business Week* for ten years. He became a partner of the firm in late 1953 and vice-president when it incorporated. During his career with Merrill Lynch, Engel was widely recognized for his successful efforts in stimulating new investors to come to Wall Street. Since his retirement in 1969, he has been actively engaged in politics and public affairs in his hometown, Ossining, New York.

PETER WYCKOFF has been associated with the Value Line Investment Survey, *Forbes,* and three Wall Street firms, where he served as account executive and fundamental-technical research analyst. His writings on various phases of stock market activity have appeared in *Financial Analyst's Journal, Investor* magazine, *Forbes, Saturday Review,* and many other publications. He is also the author of *The Psychology of Stock Market Timing, The Language of Wall Street,* and other books. He is now a free-lance financial writer based in Bridgewater, Vermont.

Who Owns Stock?

If Wall Street didn't exist, it would be necessary to invent it. In fact, that's just exactly what our forefathers did.